"Everything You Wanted To Know About
Mergers, Acquisitions & Divestitures But Didn't Know Whom To Ask"

Written by a very successful and eminent authority on mergers and acquisitions, this book is extremely practical, concise and comprehensive. It emphasizes how to buy, sell, and value any kind and size of business and how to maximize the value of companies that are for sale.

This book, now in its third printing, is of special interest to:

- Individuals seeking to maximize their wealth through owning their own business;

- Senior executives of corporations, partnerships, and sole proprietorships;

- Lawyers;

- Accountants;

- Business Brokers;

- Investment Bankers and Bankers;

- Consultants and Appraisers.

The highly acclaimed book will provide the reader with an excellent guide on how to find, structure and evaluate any business, whether it be priced at $50,000 or $500,000,000.

Key topics covered include:

- How to buy any company and not over pay;

- How to value any company;

- How a seller can get the highest price for his company and add at least $500,000 to the purchase price;

- How to find a company to buy;

- How to structure the deal so that the buyer and seller get what they want;

- What the little known secrets are for both the buyer and seller to close a deal;

- What the sources are for free public information that can assist any buyer in finding a company;

- What the comprehensive checklist is that every buyer must have to evaluate a seller and how to use it.

Copyright 1986 Roger Kuppinger
Library of Congress
Catalog Card Number: 78-71201
ISBN 0-9605616-0-9
Updated 1986

Testimonials for

"Everything You Always Wanted To Know About
Mergers, Acquisitions & Divestitures But Didn't Know Whom To Ask"
by
Roger P. Kuppinger

"...excellent book...it is great..." - Vice President, Business Development, major car leasing company.

"We thoroughly enjoyed your comments on mergers and acquisitions..." - Vice President, major California bank.

"Your book is met with wide-spread enthusiasm...It appears to be a very much needed delineation of the principal merger and acquisition considerations..." - Corporate Development, New York Stock Exchange company.

"I found your style of writing easy to read...you have mastered the art of making a complex subject easy to read and digest..." - Vice President, New York Stock Exchange company.

"I found your book extremely accurate, informative and well organized." - Partner, law firm.

"I think it is really well done..." - President, executive search company.

"Just finished your book — great — short — concise and to the point." - Partner, law firm.

"I am impressed with its content and style..." - Partner, Big Eight accounting firm.

"You put a significant effort into your product and your years of experience have served you well..." - Senior Vice President, major bank.

"What a fantastic achievement..." - President, New York Stock Exchange company.

"...contains a sizable amount of worthwhile information for anyone involved in mergers, acquisitions, divestitures..." - Officer, major life insurance company.

"...a very useful reference guide..." - Partner, law firm.

"Your book is most impressive. Congratulations on a job well done!" - Executive Vice President, major financial institution.

"...you had to put forth tremendous effort to write the book..." - Partner, Big Eight accounting firm.

"...tremendous value to me. It covers a number of issues that other authors on the subject failed to deal with in specific terms..." - Partner, major law firm.

"...it is brilliant and contains a wealth of information..." - President, motion picture company.

"...highly practical and useful..." - Partner, law firm.

"...very interesting..." - President, New York Stock Exchange company.

"The book is well done and covers more than all the bases in a straight forward and understanding style." - President, corporate valuation and appraisal firm.

"I think you did a terrific job of covering the many facets involved in (mergers and acquisitions)." - President, private corporation.

"...the material is treated in a most competent and easy-to-read style..." - President, public company.

"It is a great book, very informative and helpful..." - President, restaurant chain.

"I found it very informative and easy to understand." - Partner, law firm.

"It looks like a real winner..." - President, real estate development company.

"...a magnificent achievement...an outstanding job..." - Partner, major accounting firm.

"...it is short and precise and gives an excellent review of all criteria connected with this business (mergers and acquisitions) ..." - Senior Vice President, international bank.

Introduction

Because there is never a "right" price, valuing a company cannot be an exact science. However, there are methods of setting a value which, when applied properly, will yield rather accurate and dependable results. The purpose of this book is to provide both buyer and seller with the knowledge of these methods and the tools necessary to determine a fair purchase price for a selling company. We will show step by step how to analyze companies, how to value them fairly, how to structure various methods of handling the purchase, and how to establish alternative financing packages. Equally important, we will outline how individuals as well as large companies can find a business to buy.

Table of Contents

Chapter 1

Factors Influencing the Value of Any Company

Companies, like people, are individuals. Each has a unique history, its own purpose, and a place in the current economic picture. Because companies differ, it is not appropriate to establish rules which can apply to all of them indiscriminately. It is, however, fairly simple to obtain data that provides a good overview of a company and is also fundamental to a more intricate analysis. As an aid to such a preliminary study, we have developed a checklist (Appendix) that summarizes the facts essential to evaluation and price determination. In this chapter, we will cover the general areas we feel are important in valuing a company; however, we recommend that the checklist be used as a guide whenever a preliminary study is undertaken by either a buyer or a seller.

Management

The nature of any company's existing management is of paramount importance in valuing a company. The buyer should know who the key people are, how old they are, why they want to sell, and what kind of relationship they have to the major stockholders of the company.

Who the Key People Are

Generally, companies with a well-rounded management team and a good secondary back-up for the chief executive officer are worth more than comparable companies that are more of a one-man operation. Frequently, companies that have sales below $20,000,000 and net worths below $5,000,000 are operated by the founder/president, who may not have named an adequate second-in-command nor have developed employees to keep pace with the company's growth. In some cases, the buyer could be facing the risk of buying **one person** and possibly losing his investment if this person were to become ill, die, or just decide to take his profits and retire earlier than anticipated.

In addition, there is justifiable concern among buyers that, once the owner of a multimillion-dollar concern converts his ownership into cash or any other liquid asset, his attitude toward the part he plays in the firm's future might change drastically. Quite often, the selling company's founder/president has had a salary as his only income, his major asset being his business. The success of his business and his personal financial success are closely inter-related. Once his relationship to the business changes, it is questionable whether he will continue to expend the same effort on behalf of the new owners. Many executives experienced in acquiring companies believe that the seller/founder probably **won't** expend as much personal effort as he did prior to the sale.

In summary, if there is qualified management in the company who can replace the owner and if there is key staff in other areas, the buyer's investment is better protected. Conversely, a seller might find his company more marketable if he has taken the time to develop management so that the company's operations are not solely dependent upon one individual.

Why the Key People Want to Sell

If the selling company's founder/president is a key management individual, and if his services are required after the merger or sale, it is extremely important for the buyer to understand the seller's reasons for selling. Our experience has been that the majority of sellers want to sell because they have most of their personal net worth in their company and they want to diversify their risk. At the same time, most sellers want to be able to remove themselves from the daily pressures of management while remaining somewhat active in the business. A seller's motivation can also play an important and often complex role in structuring a transaction. We will discuss this in greater detail in later chapters.

Age of Key People

Age alone does not necessarily indicate whether one will want to remain active or retire. We have seen men 30 years old who want to sell their company so they can cash in their chips and take life easier, and we have also seen men in their 60's and 70's who have no real interest in selling because their business is their life and, without this major activity and responsibility, they would be unhappy.

Relationship of Key People to Stockholders

Reasons for selling may differ among owners of a given company. It is therefore important to know who owns the company stock. If there is some outside ownership, it may be possible to structure a deal so that the stock owners who are part of management receive one purchase price package while the outside investors receive another. As an example, the management group may agree to receive less for their stock initially than the outside stockholders, with the understanding that the management stockholders can receive additional monies or stock if they meet predetermined projections. The outside investors could find this arrangement appealing because they are unwilling to take the additional risk of waiting to see if the management group can perform as promised.

Key People—Summary

Determining the importance of existing management to the continuing success of a company, analyzing management's motivation for selling, and predicting management's continuing interest after the sale are very important in the initial analysis of a company. Knowing the owner's story of how the company began, his philosophy of management, and his reasons for choosing to sell is essential to a prospective buyer, especially if the management is solely in that owner's hands. Such information can either cause the buyer to reject the purchase at once, or can serve as the framework for future negotiations.

Products

Proprietary Products

Generally, a company with proprietary products has greater attraction for a potential buyer than a company with non-proprietary products. A product can be marketed in two ways: it can be sold in the marketplace under the brand name of the proprietary company, or it can be manufactured and sold to other companies who affix their own labels in marketing the product. A buyer often prefers a company that markets its products under its own brand name because the process of developing brand identification in the marketplace is expensive and important in both the consumer and industrial markets.

Some buyers and sellers place considerable importance on patents and trademarks. There are no simple rules in evaluating the value of patents. The importance of the patent relates to the ability of someone else to develop a better product without infringing on the existing patent. Such an ability is difficult to predict. A buyer should evaluate competing products already on the market and research the pre-marketing claims of similar products soon to come to market.

Profitability

It is extremely important to determine profitability by product line. Frequently, one or just a few products generate all the profits of a company. The product's life cycle is also important. If a company is deriving a majority of its profits from several products that are at the end of their life cycle either because of new competition or new technology, there exists a negative factor that must be considered in determining the final price to be paid. Whether the company being considered for sale makes skateboards, bottle openers, fruit processing machinery, recreational vehicle equipment, or any other salable item, the product life cycle is crucial in determining the future potential for revenues and profits by product line.

Customers

The buyer must beware of the seller who has a high concentration of business with only a few customers. We know of one seller who had two customers that accounted for 85% of his business, while in another case a seller had one customer who made up 50% of the business and another customer who comprised 25%. Such a concentration is dangerous because the company's success or failure is dependent upon the satisfaction of one or two customers or even individuals. This situation will usually cause an adverse effect on the value placed on the company.

In smaller companies, frequently the founder and/or major stockholders retain customers' business through personal friendships and longstanding business relationships. Usually, when considering smaller companies, the buyer should ascertain the importance of the founder/major stockholder to retaining business. Often, when a buyer suspects the business does depend upon a key person, deferred payments, earn-outs, minimum earnings level guarantees, or some other approach can help assure the buyer that the seller will not walk away with the customers. We will discuss these various approaches in Chapter 3.

Research and Development

The buyer should review the seller's past and current company policies regarding research and development and evaluate the firm's success in this area. First, the buyer should review the expenditures for research and development for the past three years. Then he should determine the origin of the company's new product lines, asking such questions as: Have the products been internally developed through research and development or have the rights to produce the products been acquired from others? How many new products have been introduced over the past years due to the efforts of research and development? The buyer should also investigate the percentage of current year's sales accounted for by products introduced by the company within the past three to five years. Such investigation becomes increasingly important because of accelerating technologies that put new pressures on all manufacturers. Equally important is whether the company has been spending enough for research and development to maintain product competitiveness. If it hasn't, then its past profits may have been overstated—an important factor to consider when trying to establish the company's true earning power.

Industry

Market

Both the seller and buyer should have a good understanding of the market size of the seller's industry. The buyer should ask such questions as: Is the seller participating in a $10,000,000 or a $100,000,000 market? What is the growth rate of the industry? Who have been, who are, and who are likely to be the seller's competition? If the buyer learns that a tough multimillion-dollar international company, known for heavy promotion and advertising expenditures, is entering the seller's industry, the seller might become much less attractive and less valuable. Such knowledge might even dissuade the buyer from making an offer at all.

Capacity

Capacity levels for both the industry and the seller are important to know. Many buyers are not interested in immediately expanding the capacity of a company because of the additional capital required. For this reason, a seller that has good clean facilities and is able to operate profitably at only 65% of capacity is going to be much more attractive than a seller operating at close to 100% capacity.

A buyer should also learn if a seller is nearing capacity. If a seller is operating at 75% capacity, the amount of unused capacity becomes quite important because an annual growth rate of 20% could cause the company to outgrow its facilities in less than two years. If the buyer of such a company stretched his financial resources to make the acquisition, he may have to expand before it can be afforded.

Expansion of facilities often means relocating property, plant, and equipment; problems involved in moving can be very complex and costly. We know of sellers, faced with the necessity of moving facilities and expanding, who were motivated to sell because they wanted someone else to assume the inherent risks. A buyer should be aware of these risks and view them as part of the total purchase package.

Location

Geographic location greatly affects a company's value. A buyer should understand the geographical distribution of the industry and its relation to the seller's business. Because the expansion of many companies is either limited or complicated by the expense of building or acquiring new facilities in new locations, sellers with good local markets are more attractive than sellers without them. Freight costs can easily prevent one company from competing in another's geographical location. For example, a mobile home manufacturer located in Idaho should have a good potential market in the Idaho area. Such a manufacturer probably cannot profitably serve a market more than 500 miles from the plant, and a large national demand for mobile homes may not be of particular concern to the buyer or seller of that plant. Most manufacturers have some logistical limitations based upon geographical location.

For sellers who are suppliers to an industry, however, such as a supplier to the recreational vehicle industry, it **is** important to understand the national market demand for the product distributed or manufactured. But this type of seller must also know in which main geographical area his customers are located. If the seller's plant is in California and the competition and customers are in Indiana, the seller could be at a major disadvantage even though the industry he serves is very large.

In addition, the buyer of a manufacturing concern should be aware of the logical considerations of the seller's suppliers so that the buyer can anticipate the effect of geographical location on the costs of the seller's basic materials, tools, and fuels.

Supplies

A buyer should investigate the seller's supplies and their sources. Some industries rely upon special fuels and other scarce materials for daily operation. As an example, a brick company that was for sale had a demand for natural gas greater than available supply, causing it to limit its operation during three months of the year. A potential buyer would have to make an evaluation of the fuel supply in order to determine the seller's realistic production capability, which directly affects the firm's profitability and therefore its value. The scarcity of raw materials continues to have major effect on the profitability of many companies in different industries.

Financial Data

Among the areas in the checklist in the Appendix are profit and loss trends broken down by product, customers, and markets. Buyers should realize that the owner of a smaller company may not be familiar with this kind of financial information and may be incapable of developing it. The wise buyer will assist the seller in structuring this data so that the buyer may be certain of its validity and its relevance to his specific interests.

Accounting Practices

Both the buyer and seller should be very aware of the seller's accounting practices, and the auditor's capabilities should be ascertained. The auditing firm need not be one of the top eight accounting firms, but it should be able to produce a financial statement that truly reflects the current earnings of the company. In reviewing numerous sellers' financial statements, we have found that assets were frequently either overstated or underestimated. Such items as inadequate reserves for accounts receivable and inventory, unrealistic depreciation practices, etc., can have a positive or negative effect on earnings.

Audited Financial Statements

We strongly recommend that owners of a company contemplating selling within the next five years employ a competent accounting firm that will provide the seller with unqualified audited statements. Frequently, smaller companies are unwilling to pay the extra amount for an audited, rather than an unaudited, statement. We know of many occasions, however, in which a seller was unable to obtain his price from the buyer primarily because the buyer was not provided with audited statements. On some occasions, even when the buyer and seller agreed on price, transactions were not completed and the sale was aborted because of certain accounting limitations that a buyer incurred when acquiring a seller who had only unaudited figures. If the purchase is a material transaction for the buyer, the buyer usually will require audited financial statements. Otherwise, the purchase will not be made.

LIFO and FIFO Accounting

A buyer should know the effect upon income if the seller was to change from what is called FIFO (first in first out) accounting to what is called LIFO (last in first out) accounting when valuing inventories. During a period of rising prices, if a seller uses a FIFO method to value inventory, reported profits will be overstated because they will include inventory profits. A buyer needs to understand the true earning power of the seller and should take into consideration the difference between inventory profits that may not be recurring and actual business operating profits. Because of the past and current rates of inventory price increases in certain industries, it is definitely necessary to evaluate how reported profits have been determined.

Capitalized Assets

Also important to the understanding of true earning potential is a review of the accounting practices involved in handling capitalized expenses, including research and development, marketing, and financing fees. Accounting rules changes have made it more difficult to legitimately capitalize the expenses that should be charged to current earnings. We have seen numerous companies that have shown inflated profits because of expenses that were capitalized instead of being charged to current earnings.

To illustrate this principle, suppose a West Coast based company decided to begin marketing its products on the East Coast. It might set up sales offices this year that required additional staff, with an attendant increase in operating and rental expense. Probably the increase in revenues this year would not offset the increase in expenses, thus reducing the overall profitability for the year. Most owners would write off the entire marketing expense the year it was incurred; however, some owners might decide not to charge off these extra costs that same year because the new sales facilities would benefit future years' revenues. Instead, they would define the expense as an asset, thus "capitalizing" it and increasing profitability for the current year. These different methods of handling certain expenses become significant when the buyer and seller discuss a price/earnings ratio based on reported earnings that may not be truly representative of the company's profitability.

Depreciation Policy

Depreciation charges should be reviewed to determine whether or not the company has been conservative or liberal in its depreciation practices. If a seller uses an accelerated depreciation method which has a negative impact on earnings, it is wise to point this out to a buyer in order to emphasize that the statement of earnings is conservative and possibly understated.

Backlog Information

A buyer needs to review backlog information. When the seller's backlog figures are higher than in previous periods, he will emphasize the importance of the trend. Naturally, when backlog figures are trending down, he will indicate that the figures do not mean as much. These backlog figures are usually important. If they are trending down, it is particularly important to find out why.

An impressive backlog can be very misleading if it represents unprofitable backlog. Therefore, it is necessary to review the estimated costs associated with the backlog to assess the potential profitability correctly. Many a buyer has made an acquisition under the impression he was acquiring a company whose profits would continue to increase because of increasing backlog. In many such cases, as the backlog converted into costs and revenues, multimillion-dollar losses appeared. A buyer should remember that backlog represents costs as well as revenues. To protect himself from buying unprofitable backlog, he should have his own financial analyst and/or an outside accounting firm review the costs associated with the backlog.

Warranties

Usually, it is impossible for either the buyer or seller to anticipate all the possible liabilities that may face the company being sold; therefore, at the time the buyer and seller agree on the purchase price and method of purchase, it is customary for them to agree to certain warranties made by the seller to the buyer. In such a warranty, the seller may agree to reimburse the buyer for any liabilities incurred prior to the sale but discovered after the transaction closes. These warranties cover a specified time period. For example, the seller could agree to reimburse the buyer for any monies lost due to nondisclosed lawsuits for up to three years after the company has been sold. After three years, it would be the responsibility of the buyer to bear the expenses for nondisclosed suits.

As another example, the seller may not have had a tax audit for the last year or for several years prior to the purchase. In this case, a warranty might indicate that the seller will reimburse the buyer for any additional tax liability incurred prior to the closing of the sale. Similarly, a selling company may have potential product liability on product sales made prior to the closing. The seller could agree to reimburse the buyer for any warranty or product liability expense on past sales.

There are various methods for handling all of the situations involving warranties. The most common method is to open an escrow in which part of the sale proceeds are deposited as a reserve to be applied against any reimbursements necessary under the seller's warranties.

Long-Term Obligations

A buyer should review leases and other long-term commitments to determine if there are any unattractive financial obligations that may have to be assumed. Frequently, the stockholders of the business are also the landlords of the company's facilities. We know of a sale involving a $5,000,000 purchase price where the existing 15-year lease had to be renegotiated with a lower lease payment before the transaction could be accomplished. In such a situation, when major stockholders of the company are landlords under a lease in which the company is the lessee, there could be a built-in inducement for such landlords to make some sort of concession in the lease agreement in order to consummate the sale. We have also seen purchases where the buyers were willing to increase the rent in order to add to the total overall compensation that the seller would receive from the sale of his business and lease of the business facilities.

Outstanding Liabilities

The buyer's acceptance of outstanding liabilities of an unknown potential amount is quite common, but the details must be worked out before the transaction is completed. We know of a company whose net worth was about $14,000,000; the agreed-upon purchase price was $17,000,000. A $2,000,000 lawsuit was pending against the seller, and it would be at least two years before damages, if any, would be known. Neither buyer nor seller wanted to wait any longer than necessary to complete the transaction. Based upon the estimates of all parties, it appeared that, even though the suit was for $2,000,000, the potential liability of the seller was somewhere between $0 and $400,000. The situation was resolved by the buyer agreeing to accept the first $250,000 of liability and the stockholders of the selling company guaranteeing to pay any amount over $250,000.

Pension Fund Liability

Because there has been in recent years increasing emphasis on fringe benefits for employees, a buyer must determine the difference in the amount set aside for pension funding versus the actuarial pension fund liability. Some companies have not set aside sufficient monies each year to meet their pension fund commitments. Where this is the case, the fund will contain a deficiency to be made up at some future date. The pension fund is a true financial obligation of the seller, and if the buyer acquires the company, it becomes the buyer's obligation. We have knowledge of a relatively large merger that was not consummated primarily because of a large deficiency in the pension fund reserves. The buyer justifiably felt this was an additional cost that should be included when calculating the total purchase price.

Summary

In this chapter, several important areas have been identified and examined: Management, Products, Customers, Research and Development, Industry, Financial Data, Accounting Practices, Backlog Information, Warranties, and Long-Term Obligations. These areas, as well as others which are identified in the Appendix, are important for both the seller and buyer to analyze carefully. A seller must understand clearly why his company might or might not be attractive to a buyer, and he should be able to determine a fair market value. The buyer should be able to investigate a potential purchase thoroughly in order to understand its strengths and weaknesses.

Chapter 2

The Earnings Approach

Three basic methods may be used to value companies. These are (1) the Earnings Approach, (2) the Net Worth-Liquidation Approach, and (3) the Comparative Value Analysis Approach. Both buyer and seller should understand these methods and be able to assemble the data necessary to employ them. We discuss these methods in Chapters 2, 3, and 4, beginning with the Earnings Approach.

The Earnings Approach emphasizes the past, present, and future earnings capability of the seller. The value placed on the company results from conclusions drawn from the various interpretations of these earnings.

Earning Power

By earning power, we mean the company's true earnings after taking into consideration all the income or expenses that will have to be adjusted or eliminated after the purchase. That is, after depreciation, fringe benefits, capitalized expenses, and salaries are reviewed, the income statement will probably have to be revised. It is in the best interests of both buyer and seller to establish the undistorted, true earning power of the selling company.

In determining earning power, it is necessary first to review the past earnings of the company, and then to discern the current trends. If the seller's earnings have been increasing on a yearly basis, a buyer usually will suggest that an average of the last two, three, or five years be used as a basis to compute earnings. The seller may try to suggest that the current year's earnings be used as the base, since these earnings will prove higher than a several-year average. In addition, the seller will want to emphasize **next** year's earnings, which certainly should be considered.

Earning power can also be affected by salaries. For example, if the seller/owner's personal salary is unusually high, and this individual is willing to continue at a reduced salary after the acquisition, both buyer and seller should understand that with the salary reduction, the company's profits increase. Similarly, when other benefits the seller has enjoyed from owning his own company are added back to earnings, earning power increases. Both buyer and seller should be aware that in most cases, extra benefits such as insurance, large salaries, profit sharing, cars, and reimbursement for entertainment and trips are usually not of great significance when considering the seller's total earning power. But because profits are underestimated to the degree that such expenses are not added back to earnings, all sellers should specifically itemize these extras irrespective of the amount.

Projections

Reviewing projections can sometimes help a buyer anticipate unexpected but important factors. For example, a set of projections for one selling company, when broken down by product line, indicated a decreasing trend in revenue for one specific product after the second year. This problem area had not been indicated previously by the seller. We know that estimating earnings is difficult for some businesses; and, in our judgment, any projections made for more than a year should be suspect. Despite the uncertainty of projections, however, we feel that they are valuable in determining future trends and that a buyer should ask the seller for three- to five-year projections of revenues and earnings.

When asked to do projections, the seller is placed in a difficult position. If the seller projects only moderate growth in earnings, the buyer may show less interest in the acquisition. However, if the projections are extremely attractive but unrealistic, and if the buyer provides the seller with an incentive based upon these projections, both buyer and seller could wind up unhappy. An unrealistic incentive package could cause the seller to become discouraged and disinterested and leave the buyer earlier than planned.

Price/Earnings Ratios

After establishing the company's true earning power, the company's worth can be established by applying a price/earnings ratio or rate-of-return figure to the earnings. The worth of a company can vary by millions of dollars depending on the price/earnings ratio used. For example, earnings of $1,000,000 annually after tax would yield the company values, based on different price/earnings ratios, shown in Table 1.

TABLE 1
Price/Earnings Ratio and Value

Earnings	Price/Earnings Ratio	Value
$1,000,000	3	$ 3,000,000
$1,000,000	7	$ 7,000,000
$1,000,000	10	$10,000,000
$1,000,000	12	$12,000,000
$1,000,000	15	$15,000,000
$1,000,000	20	$20,000,000
$1,000,000	30	$30,000,000

To determine an appropriate price/earnings ratio, thereby focusing on a realistic range of potential values, the following method can be applied. A buyer must first determine the specific rate-of-return he may legitimately expect to earn on his investment. If he expects to earn at least 10% on his money, and the seller earns $1,000,000 per year after tax, the buyer can pay no more than $10,000,000 to earn his 10% return. This amounts to a price/earnings ratio of 10. If a buyer requires a 20% return on his investment and the seller's earnings are $1,000,000, the buyer cannot pay more than $5,000,000, equivalent to a price/earnings ratio of 5.

The rate-of-return percentage can be converted to a price/earnings ratio by dividing 1 by the specific rate-of-return the buyer is looking for, as shown in Table 2.

TABLE 2
Price/Earnings Ratio and Rate-of-Return

Desired Rate-of-Return on Investment	Calculation	Price/Earnings Ratio
5%	1/.05	20
10%	1/.10	10
15%	1/.15	6.67
20%	1/.20	5
25%	1/.25	4
30%	1/.30	3.33

When using the price/earnings ratio or rate-of-return basis in analyzing the value of a company, it is important to realize that the price/earnings ratios for most profitable, publicly owned companies can fluctuate greatly over relatively short periods of time. For instance, within the last several years, companies in the oil tool industry have ranged from a low price/earnings ratio of 3 to a high of 25 to 30 and then back to a lower range.

If a buyer intends to pay cash based upon a price/earnings ratio of 15, his initial investment will earn 6.67% (1/15). It will be difficult for many buyers to justify cash acquisitions at ratios in their teens when they consider today's cost of money and the minimal rates of return these high ratios bring.

Discounted Cash Flow Approach

Another way to estimate the value of a business on the basis of earnings is the discounted cash flow method. This method takes into consideration not only the initial return on a buyer's investment, but also the seller's future profitability in cash flow over a period of time. By applying the discounted cash flow method, published tables, and a predetermined rate-of-return, one can determine the current value of monies to be received in the future. For instance, if one were content to earn 7% per year, and someone agreed that ten years from now they would pay out $40,000, a discounted cash flow table would show that today's discounted value of the $40,000 cash to be paid out in ten years would be approximately $20,000. Another way of saying this is that, if one had $20,000 today, and it compounded at 7% yearly disregarding taxes, it would be worth $40,000 in ten years.

When valuing a company by means of the discounted cash flow approach, certain information is required: a projection of cash flow (earnings plus non-cash charges) over a given number of years, and an estimation of the residual value of the assets of the company being acquired. In other words, one must determine what the acquired company will be worth in, say, ten years. Table 3 illustrates an application of the discounted cash flow approach.

TABLE 3
Discounted Cash Flow Approach

Year	Net Income	Add Non-Cash Charges, Depreciation, Amortization	Subtract Uses of Money: New Equipment, Reduction of Loans, etc.	Cash Flow	Disc. Factor at 10%	Present Worth at 10%	Present Worth at 20%
1	$1,000,000	$200,000	$ 720,000	$ 480,000	.909	$436,320	$399,840
2	1,150,000	230,000	828,000	552,000	.826	502,519	383,088
3	1,320,000	264,000	950,400	633,600	.751	475,834	366,854
4	1,520,000	304,000	1,094,400	729,600	.683	498,317	351,667
5	1,750,000	350,000	1,260,000	840,000	.620	520,800	337,680
6	2,010,000	402,000	1,447,200	964,800	.564	544,147	323,208
7	2,310,000	462,000	1,663,200	1,108,800	.513	568,814	309,355
8	2,660,000	532,000	1,915,200	1,276,800	.468	597,542	297,494
9	3,060,000	612,000	2,203,200	1,468,800	.424	622,771	284,947
10	3,520,000	704,000	2,534,400	1,689,600	.385	650,496	237,715
TOTAL						$5,415,560	$3,327,848
Value of Company							
After Ten Years $3,520,000 × 10 = $35,200,000					.385	$13,552,000	$5,702,400
Total Present Worth						$18,967,560	$9,030,248

Table 3 is a hypothetical example based on a period of ten years. It includes estimates for both net income and depreciation. Assuming an arbitrary discount factor of 10%, the present worth for each year is determined and then totaled. In this example, it was assumed that, at the end of ten years, the company's residual fair value would be $13,552,000. Taking all this information into consideration, the current value for this cash flow stream would be $18,967,560. This is the sum of the discounted yearly cash flow plus the discounted value of the company in ten years. This means that, in theory, if a buyer were willing to accept a 10% rate of return on his investment, he could afford to pay a total of $18,967,560 for the company.

When developing a cash flow schedule as was done in Table 3, one must also make a judgment as to the annual amount of non-cash charges (depreciation, etc.). Equally important, a judgment must be made as to the amount of capital expenditures necessary to finance the anticipated growth over the period of time used in the schedule.

Although some sophisticated buyers use this approach in analyzing sellers, we believe it has some major weaknesses. As previously mentioned, it is difficult to project three years in advance. Ten-year projections are largely guesses. In addition, the discount factor to be applied to the earnings stream is all-important in determining the current value of the income flow, and there is no easy way to determine what the proper discount factor should be. When one buys a company, it is difficult enough to place a

current value on it. Using the discounted cash flow approach, it is also necessary to place a residual value on the company at the end of an arbitrary period of years, which is an even greater task. Assuming that in ten years the company continues to earn money, probably more than it earns currently, some multiple of earnings, rate-of-return, or evaluation approach should be used to estimate the value of the company at the end of the ten-year period. Obviously, that is not easy to do.

It is a good idea to understand some of the principles, as well as the limitations, of the discounted cash flow method. It is a particularly useful tool for comparing the advantages of acquiring one company over another.

Discounted Cash Flow for Natural Resources, Patents, and Equipment

The discounted cash flow approach is an excellent method for placing a value on such assets as natural resources, patents, and equipment. Again, it is necessary to estimate both the cash inflow and cash expenditures over a period of years. Table 4 is an example of the discounted cash flow approach as it applies to the acquisition of natural resources.

TABLE 4
Natural Resources - Discounted Cash Flow Example

Year	Cash Received	Cash Expended	Cash Flow	10% Discounted Factor	20% Discounted Factor
1	$100,000	$ 50,000	$ 50,000	$45,450	$41,650
2	115,000	60,000	55,000	45,430	38,170
3	132,000	70,000	62,000	46,562	35,898
4	152,000	80,000	72,000	49,176	34,704
5	175,000	90,000	85,000	52,785	34,170
6	201,000	100,000	101,000	56,964	33,835
7	231,000	110,000	121,000	62,073	33,759
8	266,000	120,000	146,000	68,182	34,018
9	306,000	130,000	176,000	74,624	34,144
10	352,000	140,000	212,000	81,832	34,344
Total	$2,030,000	$950,000	$1,080,000	$583,078	$354,692
Residual Value		$500,000		193,000	81,000
				$776,078	$435,692

Based upon this example, the actual cash to be received from the sale of the natural resource is estimated for the next ten years. The costs associated with developing and/or extracting the natural resources are also estimated; the resultant figure is the net cash flow. Then the buyer determines an appropriate discount factor to be applied to the cash flow depending upon the buyer's internal rate-of-return requirements. Assuming that the natural resource will not be used up within ten years, then a residual or remaining value should be estimated for the unused reserves.

The same approach may be used for valuing a patent or equipment. It is necessary to estimate total yearly revenues to be realized from the sale of the product relating to the patent, the costs associated with the sale, and the resultant cash flow. Frequently, the cash flow approach will help to illustrate that, if the buyer must wait many years before achieving a large cash flow, the present value of that future cash flow is not sufficient to justify a high price for the natural resource, equipment, and/or patent to be acquired.

Capital Structure and Earnings

When using the Earnings Approach to valuing companies, it is essential to consider the capital structure of the seller. Capital structure means the amount of debt the company has incurred in relation to the company's net worth. Businesses can show fairly similar earning powers, yet vary widely in terms of total net worth and debt. In Table 5, both Company A and Company B have after-tax earnings of $3,000,000. Assuming the companies are equal in regard to management, industry, product, and potential, it is obvious that the dollar values affixed to these companies must reflect the difference in their net worth.

TABLE 5
Examples of Capital Structure

Company A

Current Assets	$20,000,000	Current Liabilities	$10,000,000
Fixed Assets	$10,000,000	Net Worth	$20,000,000
		Total Liabilities	
Total Assets	$30,000,000	and Net Worth	$30,000,000

Company B

Current Assets	$20,000,000	Current Liabilities	$10,000,000
Fixed Assets	$10,000,000	Long-Term Debt	$10,000,000
		Net Worth	$10,000,000
		Total Liabilities	
Total Assets	$30,000,000	and Net Worth	$30,000,000

Let us assume that each of the companies has after-tax earnings of $3,000,000 and a fair price earnings multiple is 10. One method for taking into consideration both the earnings and capital structure is as follows: First, assume that all long-term debt, in this case $10,000,000 for Company B, is in the form of equity. Next, add back the actual pre-tax interest charge on the $10,000,000 long-term debt to pre-tax profits. Table 6 shows these calculations.

TABLE 6
Comparison of Valuations
Showing Capital Structure

Company A
Restated Earnings

Pre-Tax Earnings	$6,000,000	After-Tax Earnings	$3,000,000
50% Tax	$3,000,000		× 10 P/E Ratio
After-Tax Earnings	$3,000,000	Valuation	$30,000,000

Company B
Restated Earnings

Pre-Tax Earnings	$6,000,000	After-Tax Earnings	$3,500,000
Add Back Interest	$1,000,000		× 10 P/E Ratio
Pre-Tax Earnings	$7,000,000		$35,000,000
50% Tax	$3,500,000	Less LTD	$10,000,000
After-Tax Earnings	$3,500,000	Valuation	$25,000,000

In Table 6, we arbitrarily assumed that both companies are on a 50% tax basis and that Company B was paying 10% interest on its money. Actual tax and interest rates should be used when available. On a restructured basis, Company A earns $3,000,000 after tax while Company B earns $3,500,000 after tax. Assuming a price/earnings ratio of 10, Company B's value would be $35,000,000 ($3,500,000 x 10). The $3,500,000 is the true earning power of Company B, using the assumption that the $10,000,000 long-term loan is equity. Therefore, the purchase price to be paid for Company B would be $25,000,000, in addition to assuming the outstanding long-term $10,000,000 note. Company A, without any long-term debt, commands a $30,000,000 purchase price.

The adjustment to Company B's earnings makes the two company's earnings more comparable. These restructured earnings can be used when reviewing each company's profit margin and return on total assets. Restructuring the earnings eliminates the effects of interest charges on long-term debt, making it possible to interpret more accurately each company's operating profit.

We strongly recommend this kind of analysis of the seller's capitalization, including long-term debt as equity, in order to analyze a company's earning power properly in relation to its capital structure.

Summary

When placing a value on a company, the earning power of the company must be considered and analyzed. There is a specific interrelationship between a multiple of earnings and rate-of-return, and both of these factors should be evaluated in conjunction with the earning power of the seller. The discounted cash flow technique has been described as a possible tool in using projected cash flow to arrive at a current value of a seller. When evaluating a company's earnings, it is imperative that the capital structure also be analyzed. The earnings approach to valuing companies is extremely useful; however, it is only one of the three approaches that should be considered when attempting to place a value on a company. The next approach we discuss for valuing companies is the Net Worth-Liquidation Approach.

Chapter 3

Net Worth-Liquidation Approach

Reviewing earnings is only one sound approach for valuing a company. A different basis for valuation uses the seller's net worth, or book value. There are several ways to value a company's assets, including use of the replacement or liquidation value.

Replacement Value

There are two ways of looking at replacement value. One is to determine the current replacement cost of all assets without reference to depreciation. The other is to calculate cost of replacing or rebuilding the existing assets, taking into consideration their depreciation factor.

Liquidation Value

Liquidation value can mean either a forced liquidation value where assets are sold at auction, or it can mean a liquidation in which the company goes out of business on a gradual basis, permitting more time to obtain reasonable prices for its assets.

It is our experience that a forced liquidation value is applied only in rare instances, such as when a seller is under extreme financial pressure, or when there is a major difference of opinion as to the value of certain assets. Buyers sometimes use forced liquidation value for certain of the seller's assets while giving the seller a right to share in proceeds if those assets are later sold for a higher price. Often, estimates of liquidation value based on the gradual sale of assets comprise the minimum price that a seller will accept for his company.

Reported Net Worth/Book Value

The reported book value of the business is the amount shown on the company's financial statements. This book value can be adjusted to reflect unusual depreciation methods or other accounting practices that have affected past earnings and have had an impact on the value placed on assets. Sometimes, the reported tangible book net worth of a company (assets minus all liabilities and goodwill) is the basis for determining purchase price. Only major and apparent discrepancies are taken into account in adjusting the net worth up or down. Such things as undervalued real estate or equipment that has been owned by the seller for many years may have a direct effect on increasing reported book value.

Omitting Assets in Purchases

Buyers and sellers often differ on the value of some of the assets. After buyer and seller carefully review the situation, one or more of the assets may be omitted from the transaction, either because a value cannot be agreed upon, or because the buyer does not have any interest in acquiring the asset. In one case of this kind, the buyer was impressed by the consistent earning power of the seller but was unable to justify the asking price based on those earnings. Part of the seller's net worth consisted of a large trust deed note that was not an operating asset. The seller agreed to eliminate the note from the sale as the note was valuable to the seller. The buyer had no use for the note, so even though he was not obtaining a true asset in the form of a trust deed, he was satisfied because he was able to purchase, at a lower price, the company's earning power. Similarly, real estate on a seller's books is not always included in the purchase price. Instead, the purchaser may sign a long-term lease that reduces the purchase price and provides the seller with additional income in the form of lease payments over a period of years.

Another way to lower the purchase price and possibly benefit both buyer and seller is for the seller to lease the equipment to the buyer rather than including it in the sale. Under the lease, the seller would be provided with additional long-term income, and might in this way gain a deferment of taxes that would otherwise have to be paid immediately upon the sale of the equipment. The buyer, by financing the equipment through a lease from the seller, can reduce the buyer's immediate cash outlay on the sale.

Summary

The Net Worth-Liquidation Approach for valuing companies places emphasis on the value of the seller's assets. There are several methods for valuing assets, including replacement, liquidation, and book value. These approaches should always be considered when valuing a company because they usually establish the lowest price the seller will accept for the company.

Chapter 4

Comparative Value Analysis Approach

The third approach for valuing companies compares a seller with similar companies. If possible, the selling company, whether private or public, is compared with public companies, although it is sometimes difficult to locate public companies sufficiently similar to the seller to make a valid comparison. Usually there are differences in size, and it is not entirely realistic to compare a company with annual revenues of $5,000,000 with one that has annual revenues of $50,000,000. The other major problem is finding comparable public companies that are in the same field as the seller or that have most of their business in an equivalent industry.

Table 7 shows how Company A was compared with six other companies.

TABLE 7
Company Comparative Statistical Analysis
($000, except per share data)

	Acme General	Virco Mfg. Corp.	Elixir Industries	Kroehler Mfg.	U.S. Industries	Company X	Company A	S&P 425 Industrial index
Sales Current Year*	$15,727	$41,620	$72,847	$139,317	$1,566,679	$7,406	$18,561	N/A
Four Year Sales Growth	6.5%/yr.	14.0%/yr.	9.6%/yr.	6.7%/yr.	6.3%/yr.	15.0%/yr.	16.3%	N/A
Current Pre Tax Profit Margin	13.3%	3.2%	1.1%	0.5%	1.8%	(2.9%)	11.8%	N/A
Four Year Pre Tax Average	18.7%	5.4%	7.7%	3.3%	7.5%	15.3%	12.3%	N/A
Net Income - Current*	$ 1,076	$ 688	$ 404	$ 800	$ 18,171	$ (103)	$ 1,103	N/A
Four-Year Net Income Growth (Decline)	5.1%/yr.	(7.1%)/yr.	(36%)/yr.	(19.4%)/yr.	(27.5%)/yr.	—	18.6%/yr	N/A
Current Earnings per Share	$ 0.75	$ 0.55	$ 0.09	$ 0.61	$ 0.44	$ (0.16)	$ 3.32	$ 9.95
Next Year's Earnings per Share (Est.)	$ 0.50	$ 0.75	$ 0.40	nil	$ 0.50	N/A	$ 1.98	$ 7.75
Percentage Change in Earnings per Share - Next Year vs. Current	-33%	+36%	+344%	-100%	+14%	—	-40%	-22%
Per Share Book Value - Current	$ 6.14	$ 7.10	$ 5.77	$ 41.25	$ 15.39	$11.15	$ 21.24	N/A
Indicated Annual Dividend	$ 0.30	(stock)	nil	nil	$ 0.20	nil	nil	$ 3.80
Return on Equity - Current	12.2%	7.7%	1.6%	1.5%	3.5%	(2.5%)	13.5%	N/A
Four Year Average Return on Equity	21.2%	10.2%	14.9%	4.5%	12.8%	14.9%	14.5%	N/A
P/E Multiple Comparison								
Current Year Price Range (Bid)	7¼-2½	2½-1	7⅝-2⅜	13¼-8⅛	5⅞-2½	7⅛-2	N/A	107.4-77.71
Recent Price (Bid)	5½	2	4⅞	11⅛	4⅞	3½	13	97.75
P/E Current Earnings per Share	7.3×	3.6 ×	54.2×	5.5×	11.1×	—	3.9x	9.8x
P/E Next Year Earnings per Share (Est.)	11.0×	2.7×	12.2×	—	9.8×	—	6.6x	12.6x
Price/Book Value	$ .90	$ .28	$ .84	$ .27	$ .32	$ .31	$ .61	—
Yield	5.5%	—	—	—	4.1%	—	—	3.8%

* Year of Analysis

In making this comparative value analysis, we combined the Earnings Approach with the Net Worth-Liquidation Value Approach. Company A manufactures plastic components sold to the furniture, recreation vehicle, and home building industries. Comparing Company A to other public companies was difficult because the only company that was directly comparable was Company X. All the other companies used in the comparative analysis had some similarities, but also major differences. For example, both Virco Mfg. and Kroehler are major furniture manufacturers that buy Company A's products, while Elixir Industries manufactures primarily recreational vehicle products. A particular subsidiary of U. S. Industries is directly comparable with Company A. However, U. S. Industries as a company is much larger and more diversified than Company A.

The following are some of the financial factors that can be analyzed in a comparative value analysis:

1. Sales growth and net pre-tax and after-tax income growth for a period of 3 to 5 years.
2. Sales growth and net income changes between the current year and last year.
3. Pre-tax profit and gross profit margin comparison.
4. Per share book values.
5. Ratios of book value to market price.
6. Long-term debt to net worth.
7. Indicated dividends.
8. Average return on equity and on total assets.

9. Price/earnings ratios.
10. Estimated earnings per share.

Basically, the Comparative Value Approach may be used in combination with the earnings and net worth/liquidation methods for comparing and valuing companies. This approach will assist both the buyer and the seller in arriving at a reasonable price/earnings ratio range by enabling them to compare the selling company's financial performance, both past, present, and future, with that of similar companies.

Chapter 5

Understanding the Seller

In addition to determining an acceptable value
for the selling company, there are other matters
that the buyer and the seller must consider when
developing the "purchase package," a term used
to describe how, when, and under what conditions the seller will receive his money.

The Seller's Friend Who Got a Great Deal

When a buyer is trying to prepare a package
acceptable to the seller, it is advantageous to
understand the seller's reasons for his asking
price. Frequently, the reasons have nothing to do
with economic reality. Sellers commonly reason
in several ways when arriving at an asking price.
First, many of today's sellers have friends who
were owners of companies sold during the active
merger era of 1968 through 1971. During that
period, sellers got prices that were inflated,
judged by today's standards. However, sellers
usually were paid in stock with similarly inflated values. Some of today's sellers, remember-
ing the selling prices of their friends' companies,
establish their prices on past years' unrealistic
bases. But today's sellers often forget, or perhaps
never knew, many crucial facts about their
friends' companies, and about the purchase packages involved in their friends' sales. In order to

compare two different transactions, one needs to know for both situations the method of payment (stock versus cash) and the terms, conditions, restrictions, and warranties placed on both buyer and seller. For example, if the seller receives stock that is not registered and cannot be sold at the time of the merger, the date on which the stock becomes salable is very important to the seller. Assuming the seller must wait several years before selling—not an unusual condition in such cases—the value of the seller's stock may well have changed considerably. There are numerous instances of sellers who received stock that declined 50% to 80% in the marketplace before the restrictions on selling expired. Today's seller may be totally unaware of circumstances such as these that may have affected the ultimate value of a friend's sale back in 1968 to 1971.

The Magic $1,000,000

Sometimes a seller will want to receive the "magic number" of $1,000,000. If this seller owns two-thirds of the stock in the selling company, the sales price would be $1,500,000. If the seller owns a 25% interest, the price would be $4,000,000. Such figures may be totally unrealistic compared to a value established by sound economic analysis.

Other unrealistic sellers base asking prices on the **net** amount desired. Thus, in order to net $1,000,000 after paying all capital gains taxes, a seller will set the purchase price much higher. With patience and persistence, the buyer may be able to persuade the seller that his desires are unrealistic.

Combining Book Value and a Price/Earnings Ratio

Another line of reasoning erroneously combines the Earnings Approach and the Net Worth Approach. As an example, a seller will review his net worth and state that his company's book value is $1,000,000. He will then add to this book value another value based on a price/earnings ratio. Assuming that a fair ratio for the selling company is ten and it earns $250,000 after tax, the seller arrives at a second value of $2,500,000. This, added to the seller's net worth value of $1,000,000 yields a purchase price of $3,500,000 for a multiple of 14 times earnings ($3,500,000/$250,000). The seller fails to understand that even though it is reasonable to **review** both approaches when arriving at a value, it is not realistic to **total** the results of these approaches.

Structuring Purchase Price to Meet Seller's Goals

Once the buyer has determined the motivation behind the seller's asking price, it may be possible to structure a deal so that the seller gets his **psychological** price within a price range satisfactory to the buyer.

A good example of this is a selling company that had three stockholders, all active in the business.

They wanted $2,200,000 for the company. Each had been receiving $75,000 yearly in salaries, which they were willing to have considerably reduced. The buyer was not willing to pay $2,200,000 for this company but was amenable to paying the three principals their current salaries for three years. The selling stockholders were pleased at the prospect of continuing at the salary level to which they were accustomed. The final deal was negotiated with a total purchase package of $2,200,000—the buyer paying $1,525,000 for the company, a price the buyer considered reasonable, and $675,000 for salaries over the next three years. The salaries were a deductible expense that reduced the cash outlay necessary to acquire the business.

This concept of deductibility is an important one to understand. If the buying company is taxed at a 50% rate, the total of $675,000 in salaries may be shown as an expense. Profits are reduced by that amount, with a consequent reduction of taxes to be paid—50% of $675,000 or $337,500. The buyer is reducing his total cash outlay by the $337,500 tax saving, as well as reducing his immediate cash outlay by $675,000.

Even though in this arrangement the selling stockholders were required to work for the company for three more years and were required to pay ordinary income tax rather than capital gains tax on part of the purchase price, they were happy with the deal. They were able to continue working at current salary rates in a business that had become a part of their lives. This was a **psychological** advantage for them that offset a minor financial disadvantage in the form of taxes. Conversely, the buyer was able to save money on taxes while at the same time maintain the seller's expertise in the operation of the business during the following three years.

Another factor in the transaction discussed above was that the seller's book value was only $1,300,000. By structuring the deal as outlined, the amount of goodwill incurred by the buyer was the difference between the purchase price of $1,525,000 and $1,300,000. Thus, by structuring part of the acquisition costs in the form of salaries, the buyer was able to minimize the amount paid for goodwill.

Deductibility can also be acquired through an Agreement Not to Compete. This is a contract whereby an individual, usually the founder/president, agrees not to enter into a business similar to the one he is selling for a given period of time—usually between three and ten years. The buyer pays the seller a reasonable amount for making this agreement. The money thus paid is a deductible expense for the buyer; however, unlike personal salaries, monies received from this kind of agreement do not qualify under the 50% maximum tax rate for individuals. Depending on the seller's income tax bracket, therefore, such income could be taxed at a rate in excess of 50%.

In another example of a similar but smaller acquisition, the asking price was $600,000. Based upon the Earnings Approach, the Net Worth Approach, and the Comparative Value Analysis

Approach, a fair value would have been $400,000. Usually, the only way a transaction like this can be completed is for the seller to agree to take $200,000 of the total purchase package in the form of salary and/or an Agreement Not to Compete. If the seller is willing to allow liberal terms on the $200,000, the buyer may be able to justify the total price because of the tax deductibility on the $200,000.

Sellers should be aware that they can help themselves get more money by being flexible and by understanding these various methods of payment. If a deal can be structured to assist the buyer in making the purchase, chances are the seller can get a higher price, or more important, sell a business that would not otherwise be salable. We have seen many examples of companies sold primarily because of liberal payment terms afforded the buyers.

The Value of Psychological Factors

In our experience, the purchase price and method of payment are of paramount importance in structuring a deal between buyer and seller. But other factors can also prove important to the completion of a transaction. In many cases, the seller is an entrepreneur who wants a buyer that will build and strengthen "the founder's" company and insure that the company continues to grow. A founder tends to retain some identification with the company long after it passes from his management. Assurances from a buyer, especially one with a prestigious name, may have some influence on a founder's willingness to sell.

Certainly, the rapport that is established between the representatives of a buyer and a seller prior to the completion of a deal can be significant to the outcome.

Summary

A buyer should recognize the importance of understanding the seller's psychological viewpoint. The structure of the total purchase price should take into account the seller's reasons for selling and for deciding on a specific selling price. The point is not to outmaneuver the seller using psychological means, but to negotiate a final agreement that satisfies the subtle needs of the seller as well as the more apparent ones. Similarly, the seller must consider the psychology of the buyer and be willing to make some concessions in order to negotiate a purchase package that is acceptable to both the buyer and seller.

Chapter 6

Alternative Methods of Paying a Seller

An important element of the purchase package is the method of payment. Serious attention to the method of payment is essential in analyzing the true value of a purchase package. The following are some of the more common considerations used in a merger or acquisition.

Cash

In the late 1960's, many sellers passed up the opportunity to sell out for cash, instead taking stock in order to ride the anticipated rise in the buyer's common stock price after the acquisition. Some sellers were successful in this attempt; many others were not. The advantage of cash is that one gets it immediately and knows its present value; there are some people who believe no medium talks louder than cash. The disadvantage of cash is the immediate tax obligation incurred on receipt of the cash payment, and there are many sellers who are extremely concerned about taxes. Because taking stock is the only way to defer taxes other than an installment sale, many sellers will risk accepting relatively low-quality stock in preference to an equivalent amount in cash.

Installment Sales

Prior to 1980, as long as a seller received less than 30% of the purchase price as a down payment, he would be able to pay taxes on only that amount of money he received during that taxable year. Therefore, the down payment on most installment sales was for less than 30%. However, the installment sale was changed in 1980 so that sellers could now receive more than 30% as a down payment and still have the transaction considered an installment sale. The seller will pay tax only on the amount he receives during the taxable year, irrespective of whether the amount is over or under 30%.

As an example, let us consider a transaction with a purchase price of $100,000,000 with the Seller receiving 45% down or $45,000,000, the balance to be paid on an installment note bearing 8% interest payable annually in equal installments over a five-year period. The first year, the seller would receive 8% interest on the unpaid balance of $55,000,000, or $4,400,000, plus a principal installment payment at the end of each year of $11,000,000. The selling stockholder would pay a capital gains tax rate on the installment payments received, assuming the purchase was properly structured, plus an ordinary tax rate on the interest.

Some sellers prefer an installment transaction over an all-cash purchase price because deferring taxes over a period of time is to their advantage. In many instances, however, an installment transaction occurs because the buyer refuses to pay all cash; in order to complete the transaction, the seller must assist the buyer by providing more attractive terms. The major consideration for the seller in agreeing to an installment contract is whether the payor on the note can and will make the payments. This is a concern that requires serious reflection on the part of both buyer and seller. At times, there are some risks involved on the seller's part when he takes back an installment note, but usually the risks are not as great as those imagined. In time, some sellers realize that, in order to consummate a sale, they may have to take back an installment note or accept a major discount for cash.

Collateral for Installment Notes

Collateral for an installment note usually becomes another issue for discussion and negotiation. Many times no collateral is used. On other occasions, the installment note is collateralized by either the assets of the seller's business, the the stock of the seller's business, or both. A seller usually prefers to have the seller's company's assets rather than the company's stock as collateral. The reason for this is that, even though the stock may be in escrow serving as collateral for the loan, the buyer has use of the assets and can pledge them as collateral for another loan for his own immediate benefit. If the assets are mismanaged, the stock may become worthless. The buyer, of course, prefers to pledge no collateral and at most wants to pledge only the stock of the selling company.

It is not uncommon for the buyer and seller to arrive at a mutual understanding whereby part of the seller's assets are used as collateral by the buyer to pledge at a bank in order to obtain the necessary funds to make the down payment or majority of the purchase price.

There are numerous alternatives in structuring acceptable collateral for a seller. For example, the buyer may agree to maintain a minimum net worth level in the selling company after the acquisition in relation to the amount of the outstanding installment note, say 120% of the note, or the buyer may agree to retain a specific percentage of future earnings within the company until the loan is paid in full.

Common Stock

If the selling shareholders are to be paid in part or in full using the buyer's common stock, it is important for the sellers to compare the value they are receiving for their company in relationship to the value and/or marketability of the common stock of the buyer. If the seller is provided registration rights so that the stock can be sold immediately, assuming there is a market for it, the issue loses some importance because the seller has the opportunity to cash in the stock whenever he wants. However, in most cases, there are restrictions placed on the seller with respect to how much stock can be sold and when it can be sold. There is also a practical problem that trading in the buying company's stock could be relatively inactive, thus prohibiting the seller from placing a large block of stock for sale in the open market without taking a major discount from the market price. In addition, there are accounting and legal restrictions as to how much stock can be sold at any given time.

Because a seller may be required to hold the stock for a period of time, an evaluation should be made of the buyer's company just as the buyer is making an evaluation of the seller's company. What usually happens, however, is that the seller arrives at an absolute price desired for the business and then accepts a buyer who has a high enough price/earnings ratio in order to meet the sale price. This type of stock transaction was common in the late 1960's when sellers would ask and receive unrealistic prices, but would be paid in overpriced stock. A seller should consider many factors when comparing competing offers. If a "fair value" for a seller's company is $10,000,000, the seller may be better off with $9,000,000 in Company A's stock than with $12,000,000 in Company B's stock, depending upon future price activity of the respective stocks. Buyers with high price/earnings ratios usually can make acquisitions more easily because it is simpler for them to reach the seller's price objectives. But a seller should be alert to the rapidity with which a buyer's price/earnings ratio can change.

Registration Rights

Some buyers are willing to grant registration rights. This means that, at some specific time in the future, stock that formed part of the purchase price will be registered with the Securities and Exchange Commission so that the seller can sell it in the open market. If registration rights are not granted, the seller must usually wait two years before he begins to sell stock in the open market, and then he is limited in the amount he can sell. Providing registration rights is usually a costly procedure for the buyer, and therefore, there is reluctance on the part of some buyers to do so. Buyers are concerned not only with the immediate costs of registration statements and accounting costs associated therewith, but also with the possibility that issuing a large block of salable stock could depress stock prices over a prolonged period if the stock were placed on the market immediately. In connection with an acquisition, marketability of the buyer's stock is a very important consideration for all sellers. Even some large companies traded on the New York Stock Exchange have limited trading in their stock, thus curtailing the salability of a block of stock.

Preferred Stock

There are several kinds of preferred stock. One type of preferred stock pays a higher dividend than the outstanding common stock and is not convertible into common stock. This type of preferred can prove advantageous to the seller who is looking for higher income and a non-taxable transaction.

Another type of preferred stock is an issue convertible into common stock at a price higher than the current market price of the common stock. Thus, if the current price of common were $20 per share, the preferred might be convertible into common at the equivalent of $24 per share. By using this kind of convertible preferred stock rather than issuing more common stock, there will be, upon conversion, fewer net shares of common stock outstanding. This will benefit the buyer because he has less potential dilution since fewer common shares will be issued if a convertible preferred is originally offered.

Marketability of preferred stock is nearly as important as the marketability of common stock. We know of a large buyer whose common and preferred stocks are both listed on the New York Stock Exchange. Under this buyer's proposal, the seller was to receive in excess of $15,000,000 worth of the preferred stock, which was paying a very attractive dividend. However, even though the buyer was a large company and its stock was listed on the New York Stock Exchange, the seller refused the deal. The seller agreed on the price and liked the buyer, but because the preferred traded only a few hundred shares a day, the seller did not believe it could sell the preferred stock in large quantities on the open market even though it was granted registration rights.

One problem with preferred stock is that many buyers do not want to issue it. Companies that already have preferred stock issues usually do not want to create a new issue of preferred stock unless it will total at least $20,000,000. In making a sizeable acquisition, however, they may find a new issue feasible. For the buyer, a disadvantage of preferred stock is that dividends are not deductible as a pretax expense, as is interest on a loan or note.

Warrants—Convertible Securities

A warrant is an option giving the holder the right to acquire stock, usually common stock, at a specific price for a predetermined period of time. Convertible securities, such as convertible bonds, are usually convertible into common stock. Although these are available alternatives in negotiations between buyers and sellers, neither of these vehicles is used frequently in making acquisitions.

Summary

We have discussed five methods of exchange: cash, installment notes, common stock, preferred stock, and warrants or convertible securities. The considerations used most commonly are cash, installment notes, and common stock. When the stock market is depressed and price/earnings are at the low end of their cycle, more transactions are completed with cash or installment notes than with common stock. As stock prices increase and price/earnings ratios rise, more mergers, acquisitions, and purchases are completed because common stock becomes an attractive medium of exchange. As everyone becomes more optimistic about common stock and buyers have price/earnings ratios that make their stock more attractive to sellers, they pursue acquisitions more industriously.

Chapter 7

Dealing with Goodwill

We have previously discussed several accounting aspects that are important when a buyer reviews the seller's financial statements. Another accounting consideration that has a major impact on the total purchase package is goodwill. It is important for both buyer and seller to understand the effects of goodwill and the methods of dealing with it.

The Problem of Goodwill

The difference between the purchase price and the fair value of the acquired assets is considered goodwill. One of the major problems of goodwill is that each year it must be written off against earnings, but it is not a deductible item for tax purposes. For this reason, most buyers do not want to show goodwill on their balance sheet. In addition, because goodwill restricts the options a buyer has in acquiring a company, it directly affects the price the seller will receive. In many cases, if there is substantial goodwill involved, the buyer will not go forward with the purchase.

Table 8 shows how goodwill can affect the price/earnings ratio.

TABLE 8
Effect of Goodwill

Example:

1. Company's Earnings $ 500,000 after tax
2. Company's Net Worth $2,500,000
3. Purchase Price $5,000,000
4. Goodwill $2,500,000
5. Price/Earnings Ratio   10

Goodwill written off over 40 years: $2,500,000/40 years = $ 62,500 per year

Goodwill written off over 20 years: $2,500,000/20 years = $125,000 per year

Restated Earnings: $500,000 − $ 62,500 = $437,500 per year
                   $500,000 − $125,000 = $375,000 per year

Restated Price/Earnings Ratio $5,000,000/$437,500 = 11.43
                              $5,000,000/$375,000 = 13.33

In this example, the selling company earns $500,000 after tax. Its net worth is $2,500,000; a price/earnings ratio of 10 makes the purchase price $5,000,000. The difference between the purchase price of $5,000,000 and net worth of $2,500,000 is considered goodwill. Accounting rules state that goodwill must be written off over a period of 40 years or less. If the goodwill were written off over a 40-year period, earnings would be reduced each year by $62,500; if it were written off over 20 years, annual earnings would decrease $125,000. Thus, the $500,000 after-tax earnings in our example would be restated as $437,500 or $375,000, depending upon which write-off basis was used. If the buyer can report only $437,500 in earnings, instead of paying 10 times earnings, he has actually paid 11.43 times earnings. If reported earnings are only $375,000, the price/earnings ratio increases to 13.33. Obviously, goodwill can become extremely important to the outcome of the negotiations. One way of dealing with goodwill is to treat the merger transaction as a pooling of interest.

Pooling of Interest

Pooling of interest accounting carries forward the assets and liabilities of both buyer and seller, at values recorded before the acquisition, to the new, combined corporation. In addition, the reported income of the buyer and seller is combined for prior and current years. In order to have a pooling of interest, the acquiring company must tender only **common shares,** with rights identical to those of the majority of its outstanding voting common stock, in exchange for substantially all the voting common stock of the acquired company, at the date of the consummation of the plan. One major advantage of pooling of interest is that no goodwill is recorded on a buyer's books after the transaction.

During the early 1970's there were major changes in the laws regarding pooling of interest and goodwill. Prior to those changes, it was easier to structure an acquisition to avoid goodwill, so there were more transactions at higher acquisition prices than there are today. Now, however, if a buyer pays more for a seller than the fair market value of the assets, the only way to avoid goodwill is to have the entire transaction completed using common stock. For many reasons, either the buyer or the seller may not want to use stock. For example, if the buyer believes his stock is undervalued, he will probably not want to issue more common shares, thus automatically precluding a pooling of interests. Understandably, if the transaction cannot be completed on a pooling-of-interest basis, the buyer may attempt to reduce the purchase price.

Write-Up of Assets

Another way of reducing goodwill is to write up all assets to fair market value upon purchase. That is, if the purchase price were $5,000,000 with $2,000,000 in goodwill, writing up assets by $1,000,000 would reduce goodwill by $1,000,000. For example, if real estate valued on the seller's books at $1,000,000 were reappraised by a reputable appraisal firm and showed a current market value of $3,000,000, that asset could be written up to the current appraised value, thus reducing goodwill by $2,000,000. Similarly, equipment depreciated to $1,000,000 on the seller's books could be written up if a current appraisal indicated it was worth more.

Writing up the seller's assets to fair market value both increases depreciation charges, which are a deductible expense, and reduces non-deductible goodwill costs. In accounting, cash flow is a company's earnings plus non-cash charges, including depreciation. Therefore, the buyer can increase cash flow by writing up the seller's assets.

Chapter 8

Earnouts

An earnout gives a seller the right to receive additional monies if certain earnings goals are reached. Thus, earnouts can act as an incentive for the seller to continue as part of the management team after the sale and to work hard for the buyer.

Following is an example of an earnout:
1. Company A's current earnings are $500,000 after tax.
2. An agreement is made to pay the seller ten times current earnings of $500,000, or $5,000,000. In addition, an amount equaling seven times earnings will be paid on incremental increases in earnings over each previous year during a five-year period.
3. Company A's net worth is $2,500,000.
4. Actual earnings for the following five years appear in Table 9.

TABLE 9
Example of Earnout

Year	Earnings	Excess over Previous Period	Times 7	Additional Payment Cumulative
1	$ 575,000	$ 75,000	$525,000	$ 525,000
2	661,000	86,000	602,000	1,127,000
3	760,000	99,000	693,000	1,820,000
4	874,000	114,000	798,000	2,618,000
5	1,005,000	131,000	917,000	3,535,000

The total payment would be the initial $5,000,000 plus an earnout of $3,535,000, which equals $8,535,000. The price/earnings ratio paid for the total company, based upon initial earnings of $500,000, is 17 ($8,535,000/$500,000).

Before the changes of accounting laws in the early 1970's, earnouts could be used with pooling of interest, and numerous mergers were completed with earnouts that frequently proved extremely advantageous to the seller. Even though the purchase price was substantially higher than the seller's net worth, no goodwill was shown on the buyer's balance sheet. Fewer earnouts are done today because accounting laws now preclude use of pooling of interest and earnouts in the same transaction. Although earnouts can still be used without pooling to reward the seller for increasing earnings, goodwill becomes a much greater problem. If the transaction shown in our example were completed today, the difference between the net worth of $2,500,000 and the total price paid of $8,535,000 would be considered goodwill. We seriously doubt that any buyer would be willing to accept this amount of goodwill.

Chapter 9

Dilution

Dilution occurs when the price paid for a seller reflects a price/earnings ratio greater than the buyer's own ratio. In such a case, the buyer receives in exchange for his stock a value less than the actual worth of the stock, in earnings per share. Table 10 shows an example of the negative effect dilution has on the buyer's earnings.

TABLE 10
Example of Dilution

	Buyer's Statistics	Seller's Statistics
After-Tax Earnings	$1,200,000	$ 300,000
Number of Shares	1,000,000	150,000
Earnings per Share	$2.00	$2.00
Assume Buyer Has		
Price/Earnings Ratio of 7	$14.00 per share	—
Assume Seller is Purchased for		
Price/Earnings Ratio of 10	—	$20.00 per share, or a purchase price of $3,000,000
Number of Buyer's Shares Issued		
to Seller—$3,000,000/$14 =	—	214,286
Post-Acquisition Total Shares	1,214,286	—
Total Combined Earnings	$1,500,000	—
Earnings per Share after		
Acquisition	$1.24	—

In this example, the buyer's earnings were $2.00 per share before the acquisition and $1.89 per share afterward. Buyers are reluctant to suffer dilution, and in most cases they prefer to buy a company using a multiple lower than their own in order to increase their earnings per share. A buyer may be willing to suffer dilution, however, if he believes the seller will grow at a substantially faster rate than his own company, or because he wants to acquire a seller in a market, product, or business area that is new and promising.

Chapter 10

Leveraged Buy Out

A leveraged buy out structures a purchase so that a seller's own management group, or another buyer, can raise most, if not all, of the money necessary to acquire the seller by pledging the assets of the seller as collateral for loans. Frequently, leveraged buy outs are used by private investors to make acquisitions.

As an example, Table 11 is one company's balance sheet showing an ideal situation for a leveraged buy out.

TABLE 11

Example of Leveraged Buy Out

Assets

Cash	$ 1,000,000
Accounts Receivable	$12,000,000
Inventory	$ 8,000,000
Current Assets	$21,000,000
Fixed Assets	5,000,000
Total Assets	$26,000,000

Liabilities

Current Liabilities	$10,000,000
Net Worth	16,000,000
Total Net Worth & Liabilities	$26,000,000

Source of Funds

80% Accounts Receivable Financing	$ 9,600,000
50% Inventory Financing	4,000,000
Seller's Cash	500,000
	14,100,000
Equity Money	1,900,000
Total Purchase Price	$16,000,000

Assuming that net income is $2,000,000, the company earns 12.5% on its equity. The purchase price is $16,000,000 cash, which represents a price/earnings ratio of 8. The company has no long-term debt.

In this acquisition, the debt is raised by using the seller's assets. It is not unreasonable to assume that a buyer could get 80% accounts receivable financing ($9,600,000), plus 50% inventory financing ($4,000,000), and use $500,000 of the seller's cash. These funds total $14,100,000, which means that $1,900,000 in equity money would be needed to reach the $16,000,000 necessary to acquire the company.

Assuming the acquisition could be handled on this basis, it is interesting to review the adjusted earnings of the seller after the acquisition, taking into consideration all new debt. Table 12 shows the adjusted earnings.

TABLE 12
Adjusted Earnings after Acquisition

Pre-Tax Earnings	$4,000,000
Interest Cost on Borrowed	
Money of $13,600,000 at 12%	1,632,000
	$2,368,000
50% Tax Rate	$1,184,000
After-Tax Earnings	$1,184,000 '
Price/Earnings Ratio	
Equity/Earnings	$1,900,000/$1,184,000 = 1.6

If one assumes an average interest rate of 12% on the borrowed money, interest amounts to $1,632,000. After-tax profits would amount to $1,184,000. Most interesting, the price/earnings ratio paid for the company based on the amount of equity raised would only be 1.6 ($1,900,000/$1,184,000). In other words, the ratio is determined by dividing buyer's equity in the transaction by the adjusted after-tax profit.

This type of transaction can best be accomplished when the seller is a well-established firm with little debt and when the purchase price is comparable to book value.

Summary—Valuing a Company

As we have shown throughout these chapters, valuing companies is not an exact science. However, if the reader uses the information provided in this book, he will have the tools necessary to value and to set a fair price range for both a buyer and a seller. In addition, the checklist in the Appendix will be helpful in outlining the major factors to be investigated in considering the purchase of any company. By using the checklist in addition to the information in the text covering the earnings, liquidation, and comparative value approaches, a buyer or a seller can do a good job of analyzing a company and setting its value.

Various methods of structuring the "purchase package" have been suggested, including different methods of exchange, adjustments to salaries, non-competition agreements, and earnouts. The problems of goodwill and dilution have been considered. The methods discussed will be of assistance in understanding many of the factors important to both buyers and sellers in determining a realistic value for a selling company. This information can also be valuable in structuring a mutually beneficial purchase package in a merger or acquisition.

Chapter 11

Developing Specific Acquisition Criteria

The following two chapters outline procedures by which a buyer may organize an acquisition program to find a seller. There are two major steps: first, develop specific acquisition criteria; second, find a seller that meets these criteria.

There are at least two types of prospective buyers. The first type is a corporation large enough to be public. It may have stock that is publicly traded, or it may have chosen not to go public. In either case, it has a financial base strong enough to make acquisitions requiring large capital outlays. This type of buyer will be able to make acquisitions valued from $3,000,000 to $1 billion.

The second kind of buyer is an individual acting alone or with others. Such individuals may have achieved success as executives in larger businesses and now want to own or manage their own business. This type of buyer or buying group ordinarily has between $100,000 and $1,000,000 in cash to apply towards a purchase.

There appears to be no written material concerning how individuals may go about finding a business to buy. These two chapters will attempt to remedy this deficiency by specifying how either type of buyer may locate potential sellers, select the most appropriate one, and complete the acquisition.

Buyer's Goals

Whether a large company or an individual, the buyer should first review his own strengths and weaknesses. He should evaluate his marketing, production, and financial capabilities and then identify the business direction of the firm he now manages or intends to establish. He should analyze the exact nature of the business or businesses he wants to be in and come to some conclusion about the probable future of each of these businesses. He should determine his future goals, evaluating such areas as product lines, management structure, distribution capabilities, potential markets, sales and profitability. If a buyer makes a comprehensive review of himself using the check list in the Appendix as a basis, he will develop an excellent understanding of his own strengths and weaknesses and his potentials for growth.

After a buyer makes a careful review of himself, he is then in a better position to identify how and where he wants to grow. There is no simple right answer. Some large companies develop acquisition programs to strengthen their weak areas, while other buyers, using the same analysis, mirror their strengths in the companies they acquire. The key is first to have the buyer evaluate himself, and then use this analysis as a basis on which to plan an acquisition program.

We recommend that, after his initial self-evaluation, a buyer develop a profile of the type of company he is looking for, being as specific as possible. The following are suggested areas to consider when preparing a profile of the acceptable acquisition candidate.

Size of Company to Be Acquired

Size is usually broken down into ranges of revenues and profitability before and after tax. For example, if a large company looking for an operating business to purchase has made an internal decision not to acquire a firm with sales of less than $20,000,000, this information should be included as a specific part of the buyer's criteria.

At the same time, a realistic maximum size should be established based on volume and/or profitability so that time is not wasted looking at companies too big to be affordable. We always ask the inexperienced buyer how much of his own money he feels comfortable paying out in cash for an acquisition. We recognize that the initial cash outlay can be leveraged in order to buy a company by using terms or by arranging for some type of debt financing to meet the full purchase price. The important key factor here, however, is to identify the specific amount of money that the buyer feels comfortable in spending.

Financial Criteria

In addition to establishing minimum and maximum net profit guidelines for acquisition candidates, criteria can be established regarding return on assets, net worth, and sales. For instance, if a buying company currently is making in excess of 8% after tax and 20% on its equity, it may choose to establish similar profitability goals for the acquisition candidates. Of course, the more exacting the profitability criteria, the more companies that are eliminated because they cannot meet the buyer's initial requirements. Realistically, profitability criteria are established only as a guideline. For example, some buying companies establish minimum earnings criteria that are lower than they really prefer, with the idea that they will seriously investigate marginal companies to determine whether the introduction of management, marketing, or some other asset of the buyer's can increase the profitability of the acquisition candidate to meet the buyer's true desires.

A buyer may also establish criteria based upon minimum growth in profits, units sold, and/or revenues as demonstrated over the previous three years. In addition, he can establish minimum criteria for future growth in revenues, profits, and returns on assets and net worth. Some companies establish guidelines on the amount of debt an acquired company may have in relation to the seller's equity.

Type of Business

A good profile should clearly identify the acquisition candidate's type of business, including a description of the product line or service desired. For one buyer, for example, a possible acquisition candidate may be a company manufacturing plumbing fittings and supplies sold to the recreation vehicle and housing market. Or it may be a company distributing electrical machinery to industrial accounts throughout the United States, or a pet food company manufacturing dog food with a proprietary label sold through pet stores.

The more specific the criteria, the more helpful they will be in pinpointing a proper candidate. In the preceding example of the plumbing supply manufacturer, it might be useful to make a further breakdown of the kind of plumbing fittings and supplies desired, since there are hundreds of different kinds of parts sold to the recreation vehicle and housing market. For example, a buyer might look for a candidate manufacturing primarily faucets, or define more specifically how the parts are to be produced. In the pet food example, the buyer may choose to identify the price range of the dog food to be sold or specifically the type of dog food. Similarly, if the buyer is interested in a company distributing electrical machinery, he should probably describe exactly what he means by "electrical machinery," for such machinery includes many different items. The buyer may also want to specify the average price of the electrical machinery sold and the type of industrial client to whom it is sold.

Distribution Methods

It is important to identify the type of marketing and distribution methods that an acquisition candidate may use. If a buyer is a company with an excellent marketing force, for example, its emphasis is likely to be on acquiring a good product line rather than a strong marketing organization. In most cases, a buyer should consider and specify the candidate's ideal ultimate customer. For instance, if a buyer wants to acquire certain product lines in the computer peripheral field, he should state in his list of criteria whether the products are to be sold to original equipment manufacturers or to end users.

A buyer interested in acquiring a manufactured industrial product may wish to determine whether it is best for that product to be distributed through distributors, representatives, agents, or a direct sales force. If the manner of distribution is important to the buyer, this should be included among the criteria in the acquisition profile.

Location

Buyers frequently have a preference for location, which should be included in the criteria from the outset. We have seen some companies waste considerable time because they neglected to consider location before they started looking. As a result, corporate development officers, given the job of finding a particular kind of company to acquire, spent considerable effort discussing a possible acquisition only to have management finally conclude that the candidate was located "too far away." A buyer should determine, and then list, the most favorable locations. The buyer may not find a company meeting all its criteria, but he will save much time by eliminating from consideration candidates that are simply out of physical range.

Management

The buyer must determine whether he has management personnel in-house to replace some of the key management of an acquisition candidate, should that prove necessary. If a buyer concludes that he wants the management of the acquired company to continue for at least three years, he should state this in his acquisition criteria.

Labor Relations

If a buyer has strong beliefs concerning organized labor's activities in a selling company, these feelings ought to be delineated among the criteria.

Summary

Establishing specific acquisition criteria is an important initial step in developing an organized acquisition program. After a buyer reviews his goals and objectives and his strengths and weaknesses, he should record his criteria with respect to the following areas: size of company to be acquired (sales and net worth), profitability requirements, type of business, distribution methods, location, management, and labor relations. Thorough preplanning can save much time during the search for an acquisition and, in the end, result in a more satisfactory merger.

Chapter 12

Finding a Company

There are two approaches to locating a company to buy once acquisition criteria are established. A buyer can set up a search himself, or he can use an intermediary. This chapter advises the buyer who wants to carry on his own search; Chapter 13 discusses the use of intermediaries. Buyers generally do well to use both outside sources and internal facilities.

The objective of an internally prepared acquisition search is to identify as many companies as possible that meet the acquisition criteria. The following references are excellent sources for locating companies that may meet a buyer's acquisition criteria.

References

Thomas Register. This source identifies companies by product categories. It lists more than 90,000 manufacturers, alphabetically arranged, including company name, addresses, names of chief officers, capital ratings, telephone numbers, zip codes, branch office warehouses, distributors, local representatives, and sales offices. It also lists product categories organized by cities, and thus can be used on a geographical basis.

Dun & Bradstreet Directories. The *Dun & Bradstreet Million Dollar and Middle Market Directories* identify companies by sales, number of employees, geographical location, management, and most important by SIC numbers. SIC numbers are used to identify the type of business for most companies. If someone wished to acquire a shoe manufacturer in Milwaukee, Wisconsin, for example, this source would prove an excellent guide. Additionally, on a fee basis, D & B can usually provide a comprehensive listing of all companies within a particular SIC grouping, showing the size, location, president, and company telephone number.

Guide to Trade Associations. Many industries have trade associations. The reference guide called *National Trade and Professional Associations of the United States and Canada and Labor Unions* gives the name, address, and person to write regarding a particular association. The contact person at an association may be willing to provide a listing of the association's membership and send literature showing facts and figures concerning both the industry and individual members. The association can also provide information about trade journals for an industry. Most large public libraries maintain a variety of trade journals, and librarians can provide trade journal directories.

Sweet's Catalogs. Sweet's catalogs are product catalogs of companies in the construction industry. This publisher also has collections of product catalogs for companies selling machine tools, metal welding equipment, and other products used in manufacturing plants. Sweet's catalogs are a means of identifying companies manufacturing particular products.

MacRae's Blue Book. This directory provides a listing of manufacturers by company name, including a capital rating denoting approximate size, and telephone numbers of branch or sales offices. Its listings are alphabetical, both by trade name and by product classification, and it provides catalogs for most companies.

Electronics Buyers' Guide. This is an alphabetical listing of over 5,000 manufacturers of electronic equipment, components, related materials, and service organization companies. It lists alphabetically by name of company and shows the address, phone number, and contact individual for each company. It also includes the number of employees, the number of engineers, and the dollar volume of sales.

Electronic Design's Gold Book. This is a master catalog and directory of suppliers to electronic manufacturers.

In addition to the sources listed above, the following lesser-used sources can provide helpful information: *AEO Western Catalog & Reference File*, which provides information on building materials and products; *CEC: The Process Industries Catalog*, which catalogs equipment and materials used in chemical and related industries; and *Composite Catalog of Oil Field Equipment and Services*, which provides catalogs on companies manufacturing and servicing oil field equipment.

Suppliers, Customers, Competitors

Some of the best acquisition leads come from suppliers within the industry of the acquisition candidate. If a buyer is trying to acquire a company within his own industry, his own suppliers are an excellent potential source of information as to which companies may be available for purchase. A buyer attempting to acquire a company outside his industry should contact suppliers in that field, indicating his interest in entering the field and asking the suppliers to advise when they find a company that may want to sell.

A buyer's existing customer base can prove a good source of information on companies available for sale. The point is that the buyer must make his desires known so that customers will be aware of the buyer's interest and be alert to possibilities.

Competitors can be a source of information, but it may be difficult to share information with them. The competition may be trying to accomplish the same thing as the buyer—gain intelligence on which companies are available for sale. Suppliers and customers are often the best source of information about what competitors are doing.

Summary

The several methods suggested in this chapter, used aggressively, will develop leads on companies that may meet acquisition criteria. A constant effort is necessary to find sources for leads.

Chapter 13

Using Intermediaries

Intermediaries are frequently in a better position than the buyer himself to carry on an effective acquisition search. For arranging a successful merger, acquisition, or purchase, they usually charge a fee, frequently a percentage of the purchase price. The following are some of the types of intermediaries who can be helpful in an acquisition search.

Banks

A few of the larger banks in cities such as New York, Chicago, San Francisco, and Los Angeles have established special merger and acquisition (M&A) departments. We would encourage all buyers to contact banks with M&A departments, whether the buyer is a corporation seeking a $300,000,000 acquisition, or an individual with $100,000 to spend for his first acquisition. An individual is well-advised to contact as many banks as possible, irrespective of their M&A functions, if he is looking for a small business to acquire. Banks with branch systems have branch managers who are in daily contact with local business people. Although bankers in general are not the most productive sources of leads, branch managers will often know when a customer is considering selling his business and may be able to provide excellent information to a buyer interested in making a small acquisition.

Banks with organized M&A departments charge fees that are comparable to those of other lead sources. Bankers not in the M&A department may be prohibited from taking fees. If they are branch managers, their motivation will be to develop new business for their branch.

Accounting Firms

Some of the larger accounting firms have small M&A departments. Frequently, however, the person in charge of M&A is responsible as well for developing new accounting business and servicing existing clients. Consequently, the time he has to devote to M&A work may be limited. When using the M&A services of an accounting firm, a buyer should try to meet personally with the head of the M&A department. Casual contact by phone is not likely to produce useful leads.

Smaller accounting firms are often excellent sources of leads to locate smaller sellers. These leads may be generated by contacting a number of different accountants, and it is best to contact as many different people within the same firm as one's time permits. One accountant may be privy to information he does not discuss with other accountants in the same firm.

Most accounting firms provide M&A services free-of-charge with the expectation that they will be able to retain a selling client by virtue of its merger with one of their buying clients. The accountant will have a stronger motivation to work with a buyer if he knows that he will be retained after the acquisition.

Investment Bankers

Investment bankers have proven to be excellent sources of leads for larger merger and acquisition candidates. Most large investment banking firms have M&A departments, usually located at their national headquarters. Regional brokerage firms, which specialize in operations in a particular part of the country, can also be an excellent source of leads. A buyer using a brokerage or investment banking firm should contact the persons primarily responsible for M&A in the corporate finance department of the firm. A potential buyer should determine first whether the brokerage firm has an organized corporate finance department handling M&A.

A buyer looking for an acquisition in the $3,000,000 to $1 billion range should work with the large national and regional firms. The smaller regional brokerage and investment banking firms may also be helpful to the individual attempting to find a smaller seller.

Brokers, Finders

There are thousands of individuals who call themselves business brokers. Abilities vary considerably from person to person. Some of them work only part time, while others are full-time brokers. Some states require an individual to be licensed if he calls himself a business broker. Where licenses are required, the functions of an unlicensed person are severely limited by law. This frequently means that the broker is able only to introduce the buyer and seller and is not able to assist in exchanging information or to help in negotiating the acquisition.

A finder can provide a valuable service by meeting with the potential seller and then alerting a buyer as to the availability of the seller. The broker-finder, however, should have developed a sufficient rapport with the seller so that he can provide preliminary information to the buyer and make possible a productive first meeting.

A buyer must beware of the broker-finder who is unable to provide past years' financial statements and a reasonably detailed business description of the seller. Such a finder may not have sufficient knowledge about the seller to be helpful. Perhaps the best way to locate capable finders is to ask bankers, investment bankers, and accountants who are involved in mergers and acquisitions. We recommend that individuals who are buyers looking for smaller sellers try to develop contacts with responsible brokers and finders because this group can be one of their best sources for leads.

Fees

Merger and acquisition departments of banks and investment bankers, as well as brokers and finders, usually charge a fee. Any fee can be negotiated, but assuming the intermediary is capable and has sufficient contact with the seller to develop preliminary information, a fee will probably be based upon the total consideration received by the seller on the following schedule:

5% of the first million dollars

4% of the second million dollars
3% of the third million dollars
2% of the fourth million dollars
1% of the fifth and all succeeding millions of dollars

If an intermediary does nothing more than introduce a qualified buyer to a qualified seller, a lesser fee may be charged. The seller usually pays the fee, but in certain instances the buyer pays and in some cases the fee is split between buyer and seller.

Regardless of who pays the fee, it is good practice for all parties involved to have a written understanding as to the amount and manner of payment of the fee prior to the first meeting of the buyer with the seller.

When the total consideration received by the seller is in excess of $10,000,000, the fee often is negotiated to a specific amount, eliminating the sliding scale.

Manner of Fee Payment

The fee can be paid in several ways. It can be paid "in kind," which means that, if the seller receives stock, the fee is paid in stock; if the seller receives cash, the fee is paid in cash. Or the fee agreement could specify a cash fee irrespective of the way the purchase price is paid.

A fee agreement should specify the timing of the fee payment as well as the amount. Most intermediaries would prefer to receive their entire fee from the first proceeds received by the seller rather than receiving small increments over a period of years as the seller might be receiving his payment. A seller may decide that, for tax or other reasons, he prefers to accept an installment note rather than all cash. In this case, for obvious reasons, the intermediary will want his entire fee at closing.

Who Pays the Fee

Generally, the seller agrees to pay the intermediary a fee. However, there are many buyers willing to pay a fee to encourage intermediaries to work on their behalf in locating sellers. Some buyers have a policy specifically prohibiting fee payments to intermediaries. A seller should realize that an intermediary who is paid by the buyer should be doing his best for the buyer, and not necessarily for the seller. A seller may believe he is saving money when the buyer pays the fee, but the seller may find that he would have received better representation and possibly a higher purchase price with better terms if he had paid the fee.

When the seller agrees to pay a fee, there are at least two ways for the agreement to be drafted. The first is where the shareholders of the seller agree to pay the fee personally. That is, if the purchase price for a seller's company were $5,000,000 and the fee were $150,000, the selling stockholders would receive $5,000,000 and then pay the intermediary $150,000, retaining a net of $4,850,000. The second method is for the seller to agree to have the selling company pay the fee. With the purchase price of $5,000,000, the shareholders of the seller would receive the $5,000,000, but the fee would be paid from the cash account of the seller's company. Technically, the shareholders would net $5,000,000 versus the $4,850,000 previously described. This difference might be illusory, however, as the buyer might pay less for the company knowing that the seller's cash would be depleted in this arrangement.

Length of Time to Complete Merger

Our experience has shown that a successful merger takes from 6 to 18 months to complete. Mergers do not move quickly. Therefore, anyone seriously considering selling or merging with another company should proceed expeditiously. Even after serious negotiations have begun, sale proceeds may not be available for another 12 to 18 months.

For potential buyers interested in acquisitions, the process of locating properly qualified sellers can also be long and costly. We know of individuals who left their jobs and searched for an entire year for a seller that would meet the buyer's exact requirements. In large companies, several high-salaried executives may spend many months attempting to locate suitable sellers, arranging meetings with them, and evaluating their true worth.

Summary

During the period of negotiation between buyer and seller, there are many problems to be resolved, price negotiations to be completed, and factors to be analyzed, as outlined in this book. It is easy to see that there must be compromises along the way if there is to be a successful closing.

During negotiations, then, the professionalism of the intermediary is of crucial concern. The intermediary is responsible for maintaining rapport between a buyer and seller through the long, arduous, and often frustrating process of negotiating a merger. There often are major differences in points of view to be reconciled. The seller generally is an entrepreneur, while the buyer is usually a major corporation. The entrepreneur may have only himself and one or two others to satisfy, while the large company may have to satisfy the corporate development officer, a divisional general manager to whom the seller will later report, the president, and the board of directors.

Resolving all problem points and convincing all parties involved to make a "go" decision frequently is a delicate, difficult, yet essential task. An intermediary must gain the confidence of both buyer and seller and understand their needs, anticipate problem areas, and work out difficulties when the principals are deadlocked. Such tasks point up the need for an experienced, sensitive, professional intermediary.

Summary—Acquiring a Company

In Chapters 11 and 12, we outlined the steps necessary to develop an organized acquisition program and to locate a seller. A buyer should develop definite acquisition criteria, which include defining the minimum and maximum size of a potential acquisition candidate, establishing financial criteria, describing the type of business desired, defining marketing methods, suggesting locations, and stating management policies including those regarding labor relations. We have also shown how, after the criteria have been established, a buyer may develop a list of ideal acquisition candidates, both through internal research and through the use of professional intermediaries.

Finding sellers that meet a buyer's acquisition criteria is usually a difficult, frustrating, and time-consuming experience. The more organized and professional the buyer's approach, whether as an individual or a large corporation, the greater are his chances of success, and the less expensive the process. The professional intermediary may reduce the time required to find a satisfactory acquisition candidate and can materially assist in the completion of complex negotiations between buyer and seller. The intermediary may save both the buyer and seller money by saving them time.

Appendix

General Business Description Checklist

Company Data

History of Company - Provide history of company, outlining major events of the business's life:
1. Date incorporated
2. Place incorporated
3. Material changes in customers, products, finances, stock ownership, facilities, and management.

Description of Product (or Services) - Describe major product categories:
1. Product markets
2. Product uses
3. Competition
4. Patent coverage by product
5. Potential for obsolescence
6. Need for product improvement
7. Profitability by product line
8. Sales brochures and other descriptive information

Major Customers
1. Breakdown of sales by customers for past 3 years
2. Special arrangements given to any customer
3. Names and addresses of all customers

4. Customers serviced by major stockholders vs. in-house salesmen, outside distributors, or outside representatives.

Supplies
1. Top suppliers
2. Trend for past 3 years
3. "Special" buying arrangements
4. Non-arm's-length transactions
5. Raw materials or products supplied

Division/Subsidiary Breakdown
1. Activities of subsidiary
2. Product or service sold
3. Location
4. Past and present profitability
5. Corporate overhead charges
6. Names and positions of key officers
7. Number of employees
8. Labor contracts
9. Any companies in which officers, directors, or major stockholders have interest that are doing business with the seller

Facilities
1. Addresses
2. Sizes
3. Availability for expansion
4. Terms of lease or mortgage
5. Age of location
6. Options for renewal
7. Description of facilities; e.g., refrigeration, special electrical capabilities, zoning variances
8. Capacity per plant and existing usage

Marketing
1. Methods of distribution
2. Number of sales people and compensation
3. Names and addresses of distributors
4. Amount of business done by each distributor
5. Company and industry pricing policies
6. Advertising expenditures for past 3 years

Research and Development
1. Expenditures
2. Results for past 3 years
3. Estimates for next 3 years
4. Qualifications of personnel involved
5. Facilities utilized
6. Number of patents issued
7. Number of patents pending due to research and development
8. Estimated percentage of current year's sales accounted for by products introduced by the company within the past 5 years

Expansion Plans
1. Projected expenditures for new facilities, equipment, products, and people
2. Amount and timing of expenditures

New Products
1. New products recently developed
2. New products in developmental stage
3. Prototype and full stage production schedules
4. 3-year projections of sales and profit potential
5. Projected competition
6. Capital expenditures and patent coverage for new products

Financial Data

Past and Current Operating Statements
1. Financial statements for past 5 years
2. Current interim profit-and-loss and balance sheet information
3. Abnormal non-recurring income and expense figures
4. Officers' salaries and fringe benefits
5. Source and application statements for past years

Projected Profit-and-Loss Statements
1. Projections by product line and/or service
2. Expenses by product line and/or service
3. Explanation of all non-recurring items
4. Cash flow with capital expenditures for growth on quarterly basis for first year and yearly thereafter

Backlog Data
1. Current backlog data itemized by customer and product
2. Major variances

Inventory Schedule
1. Current inventory compared with year ago figures broken down by raw materials, work in process, finished goods
2. Inventory by product line
3. Length of time finished products have been in inventory

Leases
1. Location
2. Square feet
3. Lease expiration

4. Renewal options
5. Costs, including cost of living increases
6. Minimum annual lease rentals for next 6 years

Outstanding Debts
1. Creditors
2. Amount of note
3. Costs
4. Late payments and pre-payment penalties
5. Contingent liabilities
6. Outstanding warranties and guarantees
7. Bank credit lines—conditions and covenants

Tax Information
1. Federal audits
2. Penalties or assessments—why?
3. Application of Government Renegotiation Act
4. Last federal and state audits

Insurance Coverage
1. Names of insurance companies
2. Description of coverage
3. Premiums
4. Deductibles
5. Expiration of coverage
6. Potential renewal problems
7. Review claims for last 3 years

Management, Employees, Stock Ownership

Management Facts
1. Names of president, vice president, general managers, plant managers, and department heads
2. Ages
3. Length of time with company
4. Compensation agreements, including bonus, car, etc.
5. Resumes of key people, including education and work experience
6. Directors, dates elected, shares owned, employment
7. Organization chart

Employee Relations
1. Labor contracts
2. Employee work contracts
3. Fringe benefits
4. Pension fund costs
5. Profit-sharing contributions
6. Strike history
7. Comparative wage scales and fringe benefits
8. Number of employees by categories; e.g., clerical, production, marketing, administrative, and sales

Stock Ownership
1. Stockholders
2. Class of stock
3. Amount of stock owned
4. History of stock ownership
5. Relationship of stockholder to company, its officers, and/or directors

6. Holders of other equity issues
7. Holders of senior and junior securities
8. Stock option holders—price and expiration date

Industry Data

Information on Major Competitors
1. Names
2. Addresses
3. Ownership
4. Size
5. Nature of products
6. Comparative prices and description of quality
7. Method of distribution
8. Advantages of seller's products/services
9. Market value information where publicly owned
10. Potential competition on short-term or long-term basis
11. Geographical breakdown of competition

Industry Trends and Developments
1. Relationship of foreign competition to domestic competition
2. Current advantage of foreign competition
3. Potential advantage of foreign competition
4. Pricing structure of industry
5. Methods of distribution
6. Pricing policies
7. Industry capacity and usage
8. Availability of raw materials
9. Studies and analyses of industry completed during past 3 years

10. Government activity in industry—regulations, assistance subsidies, and research sponsored programs

Other Liabilities or Obligations

Contingent Liabilities
1. Guarantees
2. Commitments and understandings—written and oral
3. Equipment and other off-balance-sheet financing
4. Terms
5. Amounts
6. Penalties
7. Conditions

Litigation
1. Existing litigation
2. Plaintiff/defendant
3. Amount
4. Date suit filed
5. Progress of suit
6. Estimated date for conclusion
7. Resolution of past litigation for past 5 years
8. Pending or threatened lawsuits

Significant Contracts
1. Contracts with officers
2. Contracts with suppliers
3. Contracts with financial institutions
4. Contracts with employees
5. Contracts with outside consultants
6. Termination dates
7. Amounts
8. Terms

Family Therapy
in Pastoral Ministry

J. C. WYNN

Harper & Row, Publishers, San Francisco
Cambridge, Hagerstown, New York, Philadelphia
London, Mexico City, São Paulo, Sydney

1817

For Barbara, Bob, and Chuck,
through whom our joy is made full

A portion of Chapter 1 was first published with the title "In the Light of the Caboose" in the February 9, 1981, issue of *The Presbyterian Outlook,* 512 E. Main St., Richmond, Virginia 23219, and is reprinted by permission.

FAMILY THERAPY IN PASTORAL MINISTRY. Copyright © 1982 by John Charles Wynn. All rights reserved. Printed in the United States of America. No part of this book may be used or reproduced in any manner whatsoever without written permission except in the case of brief quotations embodied in critical articles and reviews. For information address Harper & Row, Publishers, Inc., 10 East 53rd Street, New York, NY 10022. Published simultaneously in Canada by Fitzhenry & Whiteside, Limited, Toronto.

FIRST EDITION

Designer: Jim Mennick

Library of Congress Cataloging in Publication Data
Wynn, John Charles
  FAMILY THERAPY IN PASTORAL MINISTRY.

  Bibliography: p. 166
  Includes index.
  1. Pastoral counseling. 2. Family psychotherapy. I. Title.
BV4012.2.W89 1982   616.89'156'0242   81-47840
ISBN 0-06-069703-2   AACR2

82 83 84 85 86 10 9 8 7 6 5 4 3 2 1

Contents

7053143

Preface

A BOOK is to read. And you, the reader, should begin this book at whatever point you choose. If the first thing you want to investigate is how an interview with a married couple is conducted, you can turn to Chapter 4. If you are more curious to know about the fabled techniques of Virginia Satir in family therapy, you can open to Chapter 3. If your priority is to integrate your pastoral theology with family therapy, you may as well begin at the end.

Nevertheless, the book is laid out in a deliberate sequence. I first examine what is happening to families in our culture during these latter years of the twentieth century. Then, in Chapter 2, I look into family system theory and the games that families play with each other through their transactions. In Chapter 3 some of the outstanding specialists in family therapy are introduced, and their methods are examined for selective usefulness in the parish. In Chapters 4, 5, and 6 you'll find an array of specifics about procedures and techniques. Chapter 7 closes the text with a statement on theology.

I define family therapy as the practice of treating a family in a collective unit, taking into account the system through which the family members interact. I delimit other forms of therapy, including individual therapy, from this writing not because I am opposed to other modalities, but because the book is meant only to discuss family therapy, and even that selectively. These chapters have been written for generalists in ministry, those clergy—and they are in the majority by far—who have multitudinous duties and long work weeks, those for whom the practice of family therapy can be but one of a number of tasks.

Today's ministers, priests, and rabbis have become accustomed to grappling with family problems, often in the parish and sometimes in parishioners' homes. Not only in office appointments, but also at the church door, in the parking lot, or even over a shopping cart at the supermarket, questions concerning family difficulties are broached by perplexed and pained parishioners. The purpose of this study is to consider what it is that family therapists are doing that those in the ministry can adapt for their own vocation. Pastors have much in common with psychotherapists of every sort; but they also have some advantages peculiarly their own. They are frequently familiar with the history, the context, and the crises of the people who seek them out for help. All clergy, whether they know it or not, are already practicing some form of family therapy, if it be only meeting with people around the common ventures of family life: marriage, birth, and death. However, there is a deeper level of family treatment about which family psychotherapists can teach us.

These pages grew out of the Program in Family Ministries in the curriculum at Colgate Rochester Divinity School/Bexley Hall/Crozer Theological Seminary. They are presented here with the hope that this experience may be of use to courses in other theological schools and ministers' workshops. Such guidance as is to be found in these pages includes examples, techniques, modalities, and extracts from case histories from our training program. Our Master of Divinity students and Doctor of Ministry candidates are involved in year-long classroom, workshop, and field placement experiences, through which they learn family therapy for family ministries. To them, and to their responses over the years, I owe a lot of my own learning about this field.

In that work we introduce students to each of the major "schools" of family therapy, and encourage them to evaluate for themselves the usefulness of those examples through their own study and experience. There are several avenues of technique to approach any problem. It is helpful to examine them, know them, and, as Jerry M. Lewis writes, "put them all together in your own way. . . . As these processes come to feel like a part of you, you are becoming a therapist" (Lewis, 1978, p. 9). The objective is to comprehend something of the theory and technique of each, and then to appropriate the most usable aspects into a combination suitable to one's style and preference. Students are encouraged to learn to use themselves; and this same goal is commended to the reader.

In writing this book, it was necessary to make several decisions regarding terminology. First, I have used the term *therapy* for what may be understood by others as counseling, guidance, or care. My major reason for this choice, as set forth in Chapter 1, is its derivation from the Greek *therapeia,* for which one translation is "service." "Service" is also the translation of the Latin *ministrare,* from which we derive "ministry." Both the Greek and the Latin forms highlight the minister as "one among you who serves" (Luke 22:6). The minister in this respect, as in others, is a therapist.

Second, I have taken the position that a married couple is a family, regardless of the presence of children. For this reason I have replaced the familiar but redundant term "marriage and family therapy" with the simpler "family therapy."

Finally, the term used to identify the person seeking help is simply *counselee,* not patient, client, sinner, parishioner, or—worst of all, I believe—helpee, a term that has gained some usage in recent years.

The names of people cited in cases are fictitiously assigned, and each case is actually a composite of several situations.

Acknowledgments

WRITERS, I learned long ago, require and receive a great deal of help from a variety of sources. I warmly acknowledge the influence of a number of people by whom I have been taught and inspired, without whose guidance my work in family therapy would not have been feasible. First of all, I am grateful to my students of the past two decades, who have taught me even while I was supposed to be teaching them. I am equally grateful to my counselees in private practice, from whom I have learned much. To a group of therapists with whom I have had informative conversations, I am deeply indebted: Ben Ard, John E. Bell, Salvador Minuchin, Virginia Satir, Paul Watzlawick, and John Weakland. I am especially indebted to Roy W. Fairchild and to Lyman C. Wynne for reading the typescript and advising me on interpretation.

For their patient supervision of my clinical training in marriage counseling at the Marriage Council of Philadelphia (a.k.a. The Division of Family Study, Department of Psychiatry at The University of Pennsylvania School of Medicine), Emily Hartshore Mudd and Hilda Goodwin are to be especially thanked. In the intervening years I have also gained much from the tutelage of a number of expert teachers at workshops in family therapy. I would be remiss were I not to name Ivan Boszormenyi-Nagy, Albert Ellis, Thomas Fogarty, Philip Guerin, James Framo, Jay Haley, Cloe Madanes, Rodney Shapiro, Lawrence Woodward, and Carl Whitaker.

My special gratitude is extended to the Association of Theological Schools, whose grant made possible research and travel for this task. In addition, I was favored with a fellowship from the

Institute for Ecumenical and Cultural Research at St. John's Abbey, Collegeville, Minnesota. I shall always remember the hospitality of the Benedictine monks at the Abbey, and the encouragement of the director of the Institute, Robert S. Bilheimer.

Not least, I cite with appreciation the sabbatical policy of Colgate Rochester Divinity School, which granted me a semester free of other duties so that I could engage in research and writing.

Some of the material in the chapters that follow was presented as lectures on several campuses. Audience response helped shape the message at the College of William and Mary, Pittsburgh Theological Seminary, Hanover College, and St. John's University. By their invitation to lecture I was honored; through their hospitable reception I was heartened.

Acknowledgments of gratitude in this book about families would be incomplete without mention of my own family. After decades in a career of pastoral theology, but after even more years as a family man, I can testify that I now know more about the grace of God through my home-life than I could possibly have learned about it in tomes and discussions of theology. Love has been communicated through my parents, my wife, and my children. Forgiveness has been practiced (and there was need for it) in the whole family. Reconciliation has been experienced, again and again, through these relationships.

To all these: students, therapists, family, and friends, and to two compassionate typists, Dori Troicke-Green and Debra Watkins, I feel what an ancient prayer calls "humble and hearty thanks."

1. Today's Families Confront the Pastor

Families aren't dying. They won't go away until the whole human race does. What they are doing, in flamboyant and dumbfounding ways, is changing their size and their shape and their purpose.

—JANE HOWARD, *Families*

FAMILY studies are inextricably connected to human pain. We cannot examine the statistics of divorce without realizing that there are wives and husbands in agony. We cannot discuss parent-child conflict without hearing the question, "Where did we go wrong?" We cannot study the problems of the aged without knowing that someone is asking, "Whatever shall we do with Grandpa?"

Today's clergy hardly need reminding that many families are experiencing pain, are in trouble, and are undergoing frightening change. No strangers to these conditions, pastors are confronted by family problems week in and week out. Not a few even experience the upheaval of our times in their own homes.

Families, caught up in the course of inevitable change, have been confronted by what Alvin Toffler labeled "overchoice" in his book *Future Shock*. Vast forces bid fair to alter family living and sexual values through scientific innovations. We have almost become accustomed to reports of test tube babies, of DNA wonders and gene splicing, of duplication through cloning instead of reproduction by sexual intercourse, of the morning-after pill, of artificial insemination from a donor's frozen sperm, and of sex transformation operations.

We have almost become accustomed—but not quite. We cannot avoid an uneasy feeling that measures so extreme, and changes so contrary to our once settled way of life, just might tumble all our values. Modern people are not frightened of scientific advancement; with that they have learned long since, and sometimes happily, to live. What they fear are the adjustments they are called upon to make when the scientists have done their work and leave the public to accept the sweeping changes of nuclear energy, or genetic experimentation, or a sexual revolution.

Change in family life has rushed upon us with such hurtling speed that we pant breathlessly in our efforts to keep up with . rumors, reports, statistics, and innovations. I am indebted to John Hadsell for his review of how massive changes of the past 25 years have affected us: twenty-five years ago we had no heart transplants, no contraceptive pills, no moon landings, no test tube babies, no encounter groups, and no OPEC, TA, TM, SST, or ICBM. But in that same period of time we have been involved in a major war, a revolution of sexual freedom, and a critical breakdown of the environment. We have seen two presidents hounded out of office and another assassinated.

In this stimulating, upsetting time of changes, we search for clues to meaning in a rumble of what Barbara Tuchman (1981) has called "collapsing assumptions." Christopher Lasch (1977) titled it "an age of diminishing expectations." When we try to evaluate it all we run into Marshall McLuhan's "information overload" (1968) and even Paul Ricoeur's "surplus of meaning" (1976). Yet there is no let-up.

Family life has become an immensely popular subject in the media. Newspaper features, magazine articles, television programs, and radio forums center attention upon families. Family studies have become a new intellectual growth industry, comparable to the topic of urban problems only a few years ago. In this chapter we will examine some of the facts and figures concerning American families.

THE DEMOGRAPHIC STORY

Sociologists mount vast arguments over not only what statistics are true, but also over what they mean and how to define terms.

Take, for example, the concept of the nuclear family. Percentage estimates on how many there are in the U.S. vary widely, according to the definition favored by the statistician.

If we define nuclear families in the old, nostalgic fashion pictured in Norman Rockwell paintings—father as the sole breadwinner, mother as homemaker not gainfully employed, and two children selling lemonade on the corner—then nuclear families may add up to only 17 percent of the nation's households. This makes them a minority of all families, and in decline at that.

If, however, we were to define nuclear families as married-couple households (regardless of whether or not they have children living with them), a substantial majority of 59 percent would be so designated. It makes statistical, sociological, and programmatic sense to adopt this latter view. To label families nuclear if they are married-couple households, quite regardless of whether they have borne children or are now older and child-free, provides a continuity in our assessment of family development with most of the nation's homes. Moreover, most scholars are willing to come to some measure of agreement that this type of nuclear family will prevail as the nation's norm from generation to generation. For that church leaders can be grateful; much of the churches' organizational and programming work depends upon just such family units.

Nevertheless, another family configuration is growing in prominence in American life: the single-parent family, an adult living with a child or children. These adults, most of them women, have reached this status as the result of two dramatic trends in recent times. The first of these is divorce; we are witnessing 1.2 million divorces per year now, and the number has been advancing gradually each census. The second is births to unwed parents—significantly to teenagers—at a rate that has tripled since 1950.

A major increase has occurred in the category of never-married women heading families, their number having tripled since 1960. Although we usually think of these women as heading households with children, they are also to be found as caring for grandchildren, parents, siblings, or nieces and nephews.

The total number of families maintained by women of any

marital or nonmarital status nearly doubled between 1960 and 1980, an impressive increase from 4.5 million to more than 8 million. Of the 31 million families with children, almost one-fifth are now maintained by single parents.

Nearly 20 million children are living in single-parent households as this book goes to press; and the figures show no signs of abatement. In fact, this cohort (as the United States Census Bureau dubs such an identified class) now represents 16 percent of all households—and it is growing. By 1990, it is estimated that one-half of all American children will have lived in a single-parent household for some period of time.

The U.S. birthrate has been declining rather sharply for the past decade, a fact attested by the thousands of empty school buildings, the drop in production of baby food, and the shrunken cradle rolls in our churches. In point of fact, demographers remind us, the birth rate has been declining since colonial times. Currently, we are witnessing a slight upturn in the raw number of births because of a temporary phenomenon, namely that contemporary adults of child-bearing years were themselves born during the baby boom that began in the years following World War II. Just now there are more potential parents than we shall see in the population for years to come, if ever.

Meanwhile, the average number of children in households is in decline. At the onset of 1970, families with any children under the age of eighteen had an average of 2.40 such children. Ten years later, however, the corresponding average was 1.96 children.

Approximately 3.5 million children are born annually in this country. The annual natural increase in population (the excess of births over deaths) amounts to about 1.5 million. Currently, our temporary increment in births is also accompanied by a decrease in the death rate; so the population is growing.

Meanwhile, the number of marriages inches upward year by year; but the divorce rate advances more. In recent years our nation has recorded approximately 2.3 million marriages each year and 1.2 million divorces. Thus each year we are confronted by the specter of one divorce decree to every two marriage licenses. The divorce *rate* to the casual eye appears low; it hovers around 5.2 per 1,000 population. The real impact, however, comes from the divorce/marriage *ratio,* which has been one to three but now may be approaching one to two as it continues its gradual advance.

Remarriage has increased. Of those who divorce, 75 percent of the women and 83 percent of the men remarry within three years. The divorce rate for these remarriages remains high; 44 percent of those who remarry tend to divorce again—and of this group half will marry once more. From these statistics, we can also infer 18 million stepchildren.

As Carol Cassell has pointed out, it is important not to depict the family only in terms of the "traditional" model: nuclear, self-sufficient, independent, and economically comfortable, living in its own home. It is a deep-rooted myth that all families fit this picture. Industrialization, urbanization, improved public health, and shifting population trends, not to mention available safe contraceptives, have contributed to the various family life constellations. Dr. Cassell (1980) has said, "There exist parents who are foster, biological, adoptive, step, absent, present, strict, easygoing, single, married, unmarried, widowed, divorced and separated, part-time, full-time, employed, not employed, et cetera. All but one of these characteristics are subject to change, and do change."

From the trends, we can predict that the nation will have smaller families in the future, that the number of births will continue to decline, that sexual freedom will be locked into our social structure, that family life will sometimes be under attack, and that we can expect continually changing family values. It is predictable that the vast majority of persons will marry, but that many will marry later in life than formerly and that a substantial minority will marry more than once.

Ours is a growing nation. The number of households has grown by a whopping 70 percent since 1950. While 75 percent are dwelling in married-couple or single-parent households, another 21 percent of all ages are singles living quite alone; and some 3 to 4 percent are dwelling in "living together arrangements" or in communes.

These trends have influenced the United States Census Bureau to adopt new terms. Its demographer, Paul Glick (1976), reports that the Bureau has moved away from the historic practice of designating the husband as head of household and to the term "married-couple households" rather than "husband-wife households."

Table 1. Composition of American Households 1980*

Type of Household		Percentage
Nuclear or married-couple households		59%
Single-parent households		16
Singles living alone		21
Living together arrangements and communes		04
	Total	100%

* Percentages are estimates, and will vary from year to year.

MARRIAGE AND ITS POPULAR ALTERNATIVE

For all the buffeting it receives at the hands of critics, marriage remains immensely popular. Most people in our culture marry sooner or later. Even though marriage has been dubbed a disaster area, and even though Ann Landers once discovered that a majority of her readers wished they had not married, our marriage rate remains strong and is even modestly increasing.

Some observers have been playing a requiem for marriage and the family. Marriage has been labeled by some a mutual suicide pact, by others a dying institution. Lawrence Casler wrote a book with the startling title, *Is Marriage Necessary?* His answer was a resounding *no*. He advocated marital cohabitation for a mere two weeks each year, then fifty weeks vacation from marriage.

Marriage has been undergoing internal change, too. It has been moving not only from "institution to companionship," as Ernest Burgess (1945) phrased it, and from "structural-functional to intimacy" patterns, as Talcott Parsons (1955) put it; but marriage has been moving into new forms and expectations. Women and men both are expecting more out of marriage now and they are unwilling to settle for less. They are able to leave an unsatisfactory relationship; and, as we have seen, more than one million people in any one year do so. Some marriages of low satisfaction remain intact, while others of high quality end in divorce. According to mental health professionals, the reasons may be found in two factors that influence the relationship: external factors that exert pressure for stability (e.g., religious conservatism, stricter divorce laws, social stigma); and attractive alternatives to marriage (e.g., single life, new romance) and a low tolerance for tension and conflict.

The most obvious impact on conventional marriage in recent years has been the advent of couples (both younger and older) living together "without benefit of clergy," as traditional phraseology would have it. It came upon us so suddenly that we had no consensus about what to name the pattern. Only recently have the writers and journals appeared to be in agreement on nomenclature: general usage dubs the relationship the "living together arrangement," or LTA for short (an alternative, widely used in the Midwest, is the POSSLQ, or "persons of opposite sex sharing living quarters"). Numerous families, in church and out, have been affected by it; and it will continue to present an option for couples of all ages, although its rate of increase appears to be slowing.

It can be expected that the law will seek to regularize the LTA through licensing, a result that may be attributable to fallout from the Lee Marvin case, which set a legal precedent. His long-term LTA relationship with Michele Triola Marvin landed in court precisely because property rights were in question, a problem that has plagued many another couple in this type of household, and which has been extra-legal until now.

Property rights and property inheritance pose problems that confound informal living arrangements and alternative family life styles. Whether we can also look for the licensing of homosexual unions, as some believe, remains a riddle. It seems unlikely that group marriages will come to be licensed (as advocated by Robert Rimmer in *The Harrad Experiment*). We may even come to the licensing of parenthood, as the late Margaret Mead predicted. Certainly parenthood shows signs of getting out of hand.

The clergy, in recent years, have had to meet more questions about LTAs than almost any family problem. College-age sons and daughters of church members, officers, and of the clergy themselves have opted for this alternative style with dismaying frequency. Although a minor trend, it is conspicuous. And its proportion of the total number of households is holding steady. Before 1990 we should have enough data from longitudinal research to understand whether those unmarrieds who lived together eventually made steady marriage partners, whether those marriages lasted, and whether their premarital LTA served them well. To date we do know that their divorce rate is comparable to that of the general population.

Certainly this arrangement is not about to die out. Jane Howard (1978) is altogether accurate in her observation: "There are ways of achieving kinship of which birth and marriage are only the most obvious."

ADOLESCENT SEXUALITY AND ADULT SEXISM

Of the 21 million teenagers between the ages of fifteen and nineteen, more than half are sexually active. For a number of years Johns Hopkins University researchers Melvin Zelnik and John F. Kantner (1980) have been keeping track of adolescent sexual statistics. They have learned that the incidence of sexual activity for this age range has nearly doubled in the past decade. For some years, also, more than one-half million births have been registered each year for teenage women. Indeed, more than twelve thousand births are registered annually to girls fourteen years of age and younger.

One can only agree with the report that now children are having children. And within one year of giving birth, one in four teenage mothers is again pregnant. There are now more than one million teenage pregnancies per year.

Such are the statistics. But we also know that the younger a mother is, the more likely she is to wind up in poverty, that the majority of high school girls who conceive babies never graduate, and that teenage mothers attempt suicide at seven times the rate for all women in their age group.

Candor compels us to admit that adolescents in our society are caught in a dilemma. As Talcott Parsons (1955) observed, the youngsters grow up in small families where their dependent needs must be satisfied in relation to a very few people. On the other hand, youngsters are expected to become adults with characteristics of self-reliance and independence. It should not astonish us that many teenagers try to solve this dilemma by means of sexual expression. It is one area of choice where they have some power.

It is not only sexuality, but also sexism that has presented new challenges to traditional family values. Sexism, to which our consciousness has been sharply raised by the world's women, has impinged upon family life with force. Feminism, inextricably connected with family life, has been taking a new turn. Since the mid-60s, when Betty Friedan's manifesto *The Feminine Mystique* was published, any emphasis on women's liberation has been correlated in the public mind with a de-emphasis on family life. And for good reason—many women who had known oppression identified their families as the oppressors. The cliché "Mom and apple pie" suddenly felt not so loving, tasted not so sweet. Some women, angered by the too oft-quoted dictum from Sigmund Freud that anatomy is destiny, reacted with vehemence about society's expectations in general. They declared that women were no more destined to assume child care than they were foreordained to cook spaghetti.

Some feminists found family life to be restricting and oppressing; and some militants in the liberation movement advanced the cause by selecting family life to be the prime target for their campaigns. For some time feminists and families seemed to be at odds.

With the 1980s, we came into a new day. Betty Friedan herself wrote of the turning point in a *New York Times Magazine* article. She declared the feminist movement now to be in sympathy with family advancement, and that to be liberated need not mean being disconnected from family life. The challenge of today is to create new patterns of equality for the sexes, both in marriage and in family life.

In regard to business obligations that interfere with family duties, we can now expect to see the same kind of autonomy expressed by women as by men. Both sexes are represented among those independent thinkers who reject business promotions that threaten to upset family life, and object to long distance moves and fractious travel schedules that could harm family relations. Even for men, from whom we are not accustomed to hearing such reports, we now learn that family life is a greater source of both involvement and satisfaction than work is. Increasingly, we hear parents say that if they achieve professional success but experience failure at home, their achievements amount to little.

Now we can expect that fewer couples will implicitly expect ownership of their spouses as a condition of closed marriage. They are more likely to see their roles as marital equals. It may no longer be necessary for women to emphasize their careers so strenuously as a prime goal in self-actualization. Although that battle is still a long way from victory, there are signs that make us hopeful. Women are gaining wider opportunities in the marketplace, and as time goes on they will need to spend somewhat less energy in contending for those opportunities.

THE POLITICAL STATE AND ITS CONSTRAINTS

The United States has never yet articulated a national family policy. We offer no family allowances, as Canada does for its families; except for deductions allowed on federal income tax, no concessions are made. We have no national policy of maternity leaves from employment; and young mothers occasionally still sue in court for the right to keep their jobs when they give birth. We have no federal standards for flexible hours or shared shifts for working mothers, although these innovations are increasing in certain local situations. Alone among the advanced nations of the world, the U.S. appears to expect families to shift for themselves in some grim application of social Darwinism. Although 43 percent of all mothers with children under the age of six are now employed in the marketplace, we have only local, uneven arrangements available for their children's care.

Certainly it is not that our national government lacks policies that affect families. We have a gaggle of plans, from aid for dependent children to food stamps, but these are not coordinated for the common good. Former vice-president Walter Mondale has noted that we have housing policies that destroy family life, welfare regulations that force families apart, and tax policies that penalize the poor!

Moreover, the political state has made deep inroads into family life. As Walter Lippman once observed, the state has the power to tax families to penury, draft sons into combat in distant lands, jail the breadwinners, and even execute family members in capital punishment.

Historians of family life catalog a spate of functions that have been transferred from families to other institutions—to the police, the courts, social agencies, hospitals, and others. Complicated social conditions, often beyond parents' control and family members' ability to cope, contribute to family breakdown and open the way for governments to take over family welfare for the sake of social stability.

The harsh truth is that despite national programs of the New Deal and the Great Society, we have not yet found a way to protect families against the intrusion of the political state. Jacques Donzelot, in his book *The Policing of Families*, depicts the state as taking such an active role in the formation of families of France (and by implication other nations as well) that the families' internal structure may not be strong enough to withstand the massive force laid upon them. With that observation, Christopher Lasch agrees; in *Haven in a Heartless World,* he decries the mindless invasion of nuclear families both by bureaucracies and do-gooders of the helping professions.

Our problem may well be that, when we at last gain a national family policy (and make no mistake about it, we shall inevitably forge one), it could be terribly restrictive. The script for the future may limit severely what families can realize. Arnold Toynbee (1971) foresaw this; he forecast our material decline, as resources we once supposed to be unlimited run out altogether. But Toynbee, characteristically, correlated the expectation that our spiritual strengths would grow in that crisis. Less sanguine, Linus Pauling (1962) prophesied that the end of our civilization will come with human starvation, air pollution, destruction of our vegetation, and accompanying disasters. Disappearing resources must inevitably bring new constraints. We may be moving far faster than we realize into controls, limitations on choices, restrictions on mobility, and a lowered standard of living.

Families could be catapulted from the condition that Alvin Toffler has called overchoice to a new condition of underchoice. He foresees a new "prosumer" era (that is, a combination of producer and consumer within the same person), a less child-centered culture, and indeed a system of electronic cottage industries that will involve the reintroduction of child labor, with the children and their parents working side by side (Toffler, 1980). With the advent of a new national policy for families we can hope that it will aid families through the predicted era of adversity; for we need help all the more if our world faces yet harder choices in a time of gathering storm.

It is of no small significance that it was at the beginning of the decade of the 1980s the first White House Conference on Families was called into being by President Jimmy Carter. It had been a process, rather than a single event; for its history and residuals stretch into years to come. Despite its early political problems, it bids fair to influence policy-making to the benefit of American households. With six major concerns, the conferees began their work: the diversity of families, the impact of institutions upon families, special needs of families, strength and support for families, changing realities in society, and the impact of discrimination. More than four thousand people participated in the sometimes unbridled sessions of the conference. They let the federal government know their opinions about the weight of economic conditions upon families, the need for family life education, for sex education, and for marriage and parenting preparation. That new legislation and needed programs to aid families will result is certain; what is far from certain is the quality of such measures and their results. Yet out of this process grew the Office for Families in the federal government; and that was a first.

The Church *qua* Family

Today's pastor is not without a sober understanding of the significance of these demographic statistics for the parish church. The lower birthrates mean fewer infant baptisms and dedications. The delay of marriage means fewer young adults in church life; for if they return to church after the too-traditional moratorium so many take in their college years and early twenties, it is after marriage. The lowered death rate means that women and men are living longer, thus raising the median average age of congregations. Therefore contemporary churches have a larger proportion of older persons, smaller Sunday church schools, fewer youth groups, more widows, and tighter budgets.

Nevertheless, the church—and perhaps the church alone—touches people at every possible age. From birth until death, one can be part of the church's mission and ministry. Nearly every other institution (school, employment, club, or neighborhood) proves more temporary. The church is unique as the sole body (outside the family itself) that can be in touch with a person throughout life, a shared distinction that could draw family and church closer together than they now are. For the church is also a family, the household of God (Eph. 2:19). Its intergenerational composition makes possible programs and emphases often overlooked. Its familial structure implies a relationship that few parishes live up to; for we are all brothers and sisters of one another because we are first of all thus related as the brothers and sisters of Christ (Matt. 12:48).

Our churches may as well identify the family of today for what, in truth, it has become: a major *mission field*. Nothing short of proclaiming the gospel in an evangelization of the households of this nation should be our goal. From the neo-familism of the 1950s, when church membership was large and corporate worship was popular, families have slipped dreadfully in relation to their practice of Christianity. Many denominations have since jettisoned their programs and curricula for families. The Roman Catholic Church alone stands out with a worldwide ten year emphasis on family ministry. But all of us have a large assignment to reach today's families with the Christian message in a mission to families.

The church must also renew its concept of *the family of God* as a metaphor for the church itself. Charles Stewart (1979) has argued for the contemporary congregation to become a virtual extended family, gathering in the different generations of the parish to become what they are meant to be: the household of God.

The church as an extended family can reach out to the lonely, support the weak, help the helpless, and love the unlovable. That's what families, when they are at their best, do for their members.

The church, in fact, is a family of families; or, perhaps more accurately, a family of households. Like an extended clan, it draws together those who are related to one another in Christ. Like the clan, some members may not really like other members; for in family life we can be assigned relatives to care for, although we might not have chosen them freely.

The extended family has never been a prominent form in American history, hovering at an estimated 6 percent of all households for more than a century (Bane, 1976). But the nostalgic longing for a larger and richer mixture of family members will not be quelled. The church can fulfill that longing; it can again be what it was for the outcasts of the first century, a welcoming family of God.

Our churches, too, can call families anew to their *vocation.* The Reformers extruded the concept of vocation beyond the medieval church's application of the word, which had been confined primarily to the religious professions set apart from the laity in special, exclusive ways. In the Reformation, the doctrine was applied to everyday life and to the homes of that era. Family life, itself, was seen to be a calling in the order of creation.

It was by the hearthside that children were brought up to understand the priesthood of all believers. It was at a mother's knee that they learned about justification by faith. The home was meant to be an extension of the church; and its very life was a vocation all its own.

We urgently need to renew that theological dogma for our own day. Marriage is a vocation. Family life, in and of itself, is a calling. God has sanctified these relationships, the Christian believes, for the welfare and happiness of humanity; and he has put his blessing upon them. Parents who know their task of bringing up sons and daughters in the "nurture and admonition of the Lord" (Eph. 6:4), and who realize their marital relationship as potentially a means of grace, will also realize that the common tasks and meetings of daily life can be encountered by the spirit of God.

The church must also aid the organization of its families with *power.* An isolated nuclear family of today is all but powerless. Confronted by rapidly changing economic conditions, the vagaries of sexual freedom, the incursions of the political state, and much more, such a family can be virtually defenseless.

The World Council of Churches sponsored a research conference in 1980 on Family Power in Social Change. We who attended that conference did not completely realize, until we experienced that conference in action, how unintentionally ironic was that theme. Research report after report revealed quite artlessly that the family has virtually no power. Families can be ignored by principalities and municipalities, brutalized by corporations and governments, scattered by decrees as well as by natural disasters.

Unless Christian families unite together under the aegis of the churches, unless they form alliances with other groups that can exercise real power, they will not be empowered but will be tossed about by the forces that divide and weaken. For the empowerment of families we must rip pages from the theology of liberation and learn how to replace weakness with strength and fear with courage.

Something harder than mere piousness is demanded for today's education of Christian families. Once we were too easily satisfied by promulgating "family worship" as a fulfillment of what the churches wanted for their families. Now we know better. Worship certainly ought to be done; but other needs ought not be left undone. Those needs involve realities that go well beyond the holy state once described by Dorothy Sayers as "at the name of Jesus, every voice goes plummy and every gesture becomes pontifical" (1949).

PRODUCERS AND CONSUMERS

Families are in the course of inevitable change. Traditional functions have been undergoing vast alteration along with government, church, education, and economics. That shifting functions have greatly altered families cannot be denied. Whether these have left families worse off is arguable. Once families were their own providers, making their own clothes, growing their own food, baking their own bread, and churning their own butter. But that was a long time ago; and one would be hard put to debate that the disappearance of such functions as these had led to what Christopher Lasch (1977) calls "the erosion of the family." Rather, it would appear that family functions have been so altered by global circumstances and by material progress that we have now become consumers rather than producers. A modern family's function is less survival and more the provision of emotional security in a setting Gibson Winter (1958) has called "the last bastion of intimacy." In any case, it would appear that the only families who need a butter churn in these days are antique collectors.

In today's transitions of family functions, the children are no longer "hands" on the farm, but "mouths" in the house; consumers rather than producers. Children are admittedly an economic liability. When the family struggled for physical survival, work was hard and everyone labored. The family was forced by harsh need to become a unit. Individuals were known by the family reputation: "That's Tom Martindale's lad; they're good people"; now individuals are known by their attainments: "That's Jim Martindale; he's playing pro ball now."

Family functions have changed dramatically; and family patterns of relationship and mutuality are altered. Still, the average family is an overloaded institution. More is demanded from the family than it can deliver in our complex society. Expected to provide effective socialization of the young, to be an example of loving togetherness, to act as a shock absorber to the world, and to exhibit responsible and responsive parenting at all times—it is small wonder that at times families are overwhelmed. Too many fathers and mothers feel obligated to maintain parental stability when they, themselves, are unstable. Too many husbands and wives feel the weight of some demand to be each other's best friends when they are insecure within themselves. Too many children are overwhelmed by injunctions from church and society to embody steady maturation when the conflicting signals all about them confuse and discourage.

It should occasion no dismay that these idealistic goals remain unattainable, that generational gaps remain as profound and as traumatic as scripture shows them to have been in ancient times; or that new freedoms are often tried, first of all, against one's own family. The family is a rather unprepossessing group, as Harold Christensen (1964) has pointed out, for an athletic team, or a production unit, or even a training group. Yet the family has assigned to it a monstrous task—to bring the next generation to maturity. It is more to the point that families are doing as well as they are. They represent one of the finest problem-solving units in our culture. Even dysfunctional families go on handling some of their problems every day.

Families, caught up in the throes of massive change, are deeply affected by the macro-influences of inflation, urbanization, politics, and industrialization. Such global forces immediately affect the micro-relations of any family through marital adjustment, parenting, and the household budget. Yet to suppose that such circumstances foreshadow ineluctable decline of families is unjustified. The burden of proof is upon anyone who makes the general assertion that families are "an endangered species."

PASTORS AS FAMILY THERAPISTS

There has never been any question about whether pastors ought to be doing family counseling; in this matter, they have no choice. The problem is how well they do it and to what extent they are prepared. That they will become involved with marriage conflicts and dysfunctional families is inevitable; there is no escape. Parishioners and townspeople alike bring to the clergy their squabbles, their misunderstandings, their desperation with one another.

All too few pastors possess an orderly, knowledgeable way of going about the task of helping families find relief—even though every minister has been engaging in family therapy as an integral part of ministry. The predictable stages of family development all call for therapeutic assistance. Because birth, marriage, and death are among the most naturally anticipated of all family crises, the pastor must be ready for these. Because the church is in contact with families in all ages and stages, we have programs and liturgies that encompass such events. In daily contact with families of the parish, any pastor is aware of at least some of the drama that goes on in the homes of church members.

That drama, of course, includes not only normal stages of the family life cycle, but also those rude interruptions of adversity, such as accidents, unemployment, illness, et al. Into these disasters and disappointments the pastor is called; into them he or she volunteers even when not summoned. To bring comfort, aid, and healing in such emergencies is to participate in family therapy. To go still farther and assist family members in working through their altered relationships as a result of these intrusions is a deeper level of therapy. It is that level to which this book is addressed.

My goal is for pastors to begin to think in a new and holistic way about people *within the family context,* rather than as isolated individuals. Such conceptualization will lead us to treat the entire family at the same time in the therapeutic setting. Intimidating as the notion may be at the outset, we will learn to summon forth not just the principals in a family problem, but the network of the others who are involved. In time, we will see some marital breakdowns that intimately and inextricably implicate the children and will invite the children into counseling sessions. We will have advanced to a more inclusive form of family therapy.

Most clergy still tend to deal with family problems as if they are idiosyncratic, caused by a particular person. When they advance farther and counsel both wife and husband together about a marital situation, they still are tempted to deal with them as two individuals, even within a joint session. Systems theory, now widespread throughout the physical sciences and psychology, may be either unknown or still unconvincing to most clergy. That Johnny can't read and hates school is more often seen as the difficulty of one little boy than the outward expression of a family tension that is otherwise hidden from an outsider's gaze. The tragedy of the "kitchen alcoholic" tends to be diagnosed as the peculiar, isolated behavior of the woman rather than one strand of a complex system of family relationships in which her husband's attitudes and her children's behavior also assume a large role.

It is one thing to minister to the common ventures of family living, bridging the generation gap, resolving marital conflicts, or working through grief. It is quite another to deal in depth with the family system.

Family therapy, in its fullness of meaning, involves more than comforting the bereaved, instructing the engaged, or interpreting baptism. All pastors accomplish these tasks, and more as well. The place to which few of them come in their ministry is working with the whole family as a system. Family therapists are convinced that counseling only one individual about a marriage or family conflict is relatively unproductive, and that treating such problems as if they were personal instead of interpersonal is downright counterproductive.

The traditional approach to these problems was to treat an individual as if family connections were secondary or irrelevant. The family therapist, however, takes an opposite stance and meets the family as the context for any change to take place in an individual.

The pastor as therapist has an obligation to bring more than symptomatic relief to families in distress. Such relief is a first objective; but it is unwise to terminate there just when people begin to feel better. Pastoral therapy also includes a component of growth. Every family crisis has within it the potential to aid people to self-understanding and mutual acceptance. It also has the potential of deepening faith. Both contribute to growth and upbuilding in love (Eph. 4:16).

THE PASTOR AS FAMILY THERAPIST—SOME DEFINITIONS

What Is Therapy?

The ministry has long been accustomed to the traditional terms of "pastoral care" and "pastoral counseling." Gradually, however, the term "therapy" has been advancing into wider use with clergy, as well it ought. Derived from the Greek *therapeia,* meaning "service," it carries the same connotation as *ministry* (from the Latin *ministrare*), also meaning "to serve." When the term therapy is demedicalized, and this sense of service is emphasized, pastors truly are therapists.

This more inclusive term of therapy has been gaining wider

acceptance throughout the helping professions. Only a few years ago, the American Association of Marriage and Family Counselors (which counts a large number of clergy in its membership) changed its title to the American Association for Marriage and Family Therapy. This organization, in common with a growing trend, shortened the term from the longer and formal "family psychotherapy."

The newer designation begins to ease a long-standing misapprehension about the popular term "counseling"; for counseling can be defined severally as advice, prescription, guidance, persuasion, or even enforcement. Therapy, on the other hand, carries a more theological meaning, in that the therapy of persons is tantamount to the long honored phrase "the cure of souls." A therapist is "among you as one who serves" (Luke 22:26).

What Is a Family?

The word "family" no longer possesses as clear and accepted a definition as once it did. Questions crop up about whether a commune can be a family, or a couple in an LTA, or an individual living alone far from home and kin. Nor does the old solution help us much. For years we adopted a definition from the Census Bureau and dubbed a family any two or more people related by blood, marriage, or adoption, and living under the same roof. Yet this definition is unsatisfactory for those who are away for some years in school or hospital or work and who consider themselves members of the family.

For our purposes, *a family in therapy can be any relationship of people in marriage, adoption, or in blood, sharing the same lineage of origin.* This makes it possible to include not only the nuclear but also the extended family. It connects the roots and lines of a family tree so that, in therapy, it becomes feasible to bring together all those who are relevant to the system. Such a definition frees us from the difficulty of subscribing to some normative description of the family that one sees in idealistic literature, or from buying into such cynical definitions as the Charles Manson family, or a Mafia family, or the Jonestown family cult.

What Is Family Therapy?

Family therapy is a term that covers a multitude of methods. Yet they all share in common the conviction that relationships are of greater importance in the experience and behavior of people than unconscious, intrapsychic material. Beyond that, "What unites all family therapists is the view that change, which is significant to the psychotherapeutic endeavor, takes place in the family system. With this unifying thread, they may vary considerably as to the size of the elements of the family they engage, the techniques they employ, and the theory to which they adhere" (Bloch, 1973).

Family therapy is the practice of treating a family as a whole unit and taking into account the system in which the family members interact. The treatment focuses on the family as a relational system.

Pastors are accustomed to dealing with families as a whole; they are also familiar with family and sexual problems. Few, however, meet with the entire family system to help members deal with some disabling problem in their relationship.

That research data can enlighten us about the possibilities and limitations of conventional family therapy is vouchsafed by Charles H. Kramer in *Becoming a Family Therapist.* He has summarized the findings as follows:

- About two-thirds of the studies that compare family therapy with other types have found it to be superior in its results; about one-third have found no differences. But no studies show individual psychotherapy to be clearly superior.
- Couples benefit most from treatment when seen together rather than separately. Individual therapy for marital problems is not especially effective; this treatment strategy yields improvement in less than 48 percent of those treated.
- The personal relationship skills of the therapist have a major impact on the outcome of marriage and family therapy, quite regardless of the therapist's clinical theory or particular methodological loyalties.

What Is the Purpose of Family Therapy?

The purposes of family therapy are fairly simple. Most therapists agree that the treatment should:

- Aid the family to gain some relief from the pain and dysfunction that troubles them, and give them some hope they can improve.
- Aid them in solving their current problems and help them to form a method of solving future problems.
- Aid them in mobilizing their own strengths and their mutual understanding so that they can work together as a peaceful unit and still stand individually as whole persons.
- Aid them in freeing themselves of the helping professions so that they become able to live competently without special restraints and supports.

What Is a Dysfunctional Family?

The dysfunctional or conflicted family is not hard to spot. They may be burdened with any one of a hundred disabilities; but they tend to repeat certain patterns. They may be isolated as a family from the sociocultural environment. They may show a blurring of the generational boundaries, such as a persistent sexual confusion in the relations between parents and children. They may detain their growing children from maturing into emancipation. They may fail to develop their own family life because one or both parents is still dependent upon their own parents (Lidz, et al., 1960).

A troubled family in crisis is likely to pass through predictable stages of mounting intensity. Gerald Caplan (1964) has identified four phases in the anatomy of such a crisis: first, the family will seek to solve the problem in ways that formerly worked for them; second, their tension will increase if these former methods of problem solving prove ineffective; third, the family will move into emergency methods and attempt to revise their definition of the problem; and fourth, if the problem is still unalleviated, the family may experience disruption and disintegration. If some counseling intervention prevails at the earlier stages of this sad progression, it need not advance to a disruptive and final stage.

Pastors have long been aware that family problems fall into several anticipated typologies:

- One whole group is centered around marriage adjustments that may occur in *early months of settling,* with relations to in-laws, with conflicts that grow through the years, with infidelities, or even breakdown and divorce.
- Another set is grouped around tasks of *parenting:* the establishment of generational boundaries and limits, exercise of discipline (self-discipline as well as discipline of sons and daughters), communication needs, or reciprocal development (i.e., getting used to our own changes as well as our children's).
- Yet another grouping is seen in the *ages and stages* through which a family develops: handling the early years with small children, living through adolescent adjustments, coping with our own middle-age crises, launching young people into their lives apart from home, absorbing demands for liberation (not only of women, but of any family member), and meeting the problems of the aging (both of ourselves and of our parents).
- Still another cluster involves the additions and subtractions of family life, crises caused by the *arrival of new births, or persons* moving into the household, or those moving back after they had left; the departure of others to schools, to armed forces, to their own new homes, to hospitalization, prison, or death.
- In addition, there are *special emergencies:* violence, runaways, alcohol and other drug abuse, gambling compulsions, job-related and other economic challenges, and illnesses (emotional, physical, and handicapping).
- *Sexuality* presents a category of difficulties of its own: sexual identification, various dysfunctions (e.g., impotence, under-

standing of homosexuality, pathological behaviors), and much else.

THE PROSPECTS FOR FAMILIES

Anyone who reviews the current plight of families has some reason to ask what has become a somewhat trite question: can families, as we have known them, survive? The data reveal breaking marriages, an increase in single-parent families, vastly altered family functions, and a plethora of problems in the homes of the nation. The data also reveal that most marriages still persist until the death of one partner, an average of forty-four years; that families are surviving through change in functions, challenges, and handicaps; and that agents of help are increasingly available for families in trouble.

The increasing attention to families that has made family studies a new intellectual growth industry has also multiplied the availability of family social agencies, helping professions, and family therapists available to those in pain and need. Among these are the clergy. There are signs on the horizon that the decline in family stability will bottom out and that families will again emerge as the strong and basic unit of our social order. We may well return, as Paul Watzlawick (1978) contends, to "an extremely family-oriented society" within a generation.

In any case, we have seen the question of family survival raised again and again in history; and families are still here. Some families are wounded. Some are downright sick. Fresh hope, however, has been awakened by the new resource of family therapy. To its theory and promise we now turn.

2. Games Families Play

It didn't seem to matter what the complaint was, or the traditional
diagnosis. Troubles, it seemed, came in families. If the problem
was the family, the family should be the focus of therapy. The
family, in fact, should be the patient.
—AUGUSTUS NAPIER AND CARL WHITAKER, *The Family Crucible*

FAMILIES are forever playing games. In a series of moves toward
each other they operate little tricks and snares designed for one-
upmanship, for attracting affection, for influence, or a host of
other ulterior outcomes (see Berne, 1948, p. 48). Even loving and
healthy families engage in game playing, while disturbed families
overlap one grim game upon another.

Adam and Abby were like that. Along with their adolescent
children, they maintained a chronic turmoil. Their neighbors,
weary with the recurrent crises, said that this family would always
stay together because they couldn't live with each other, yet
couldn't live without each other either.

What no one seemed to notice until they came in for marital
therapy was that, whenever their marriage was on the edge of
dissolution, Adam and Abby got hauled back together by some
new emergency. Once it was fifteen-year-old Nora's running
away to Chicago, where she was found by police and sent home.
Another time it was Adam's serious auto accident that laid him
up for three weeks following a drinking bout. Still another time
it was son Nathan's arrest with two buddies for smoking pot in
a public square.

The pattern was clear enough, but not to Abby and Adam, nor
to their teenagers. Each time this marriage was ready to break up,
someone in the family got into sufficiently deep trouble to force
the couple back together to work out the new problem. Foment-
ing crises in order to unite for working out the difficulty is just

one of the games families play. It is a clumsy attempt at self-styled therapy; and the family seldom recognizes it has that purpose.

About such family games we can note three points: (1) they were all caught up into a *system* wherein whatever one person did affected the behavior of the others and that, in turn, doubled back and affected everyone again in a new way; (2) the crises they had learned to initiate invariably brought the family back into their familiar but uneasy balance, a state called *homeostasis;* and (3) unnoticed by these unhappy people, they were playing by a set of *rules* that required one player to make a disastrous move whenever family breakage was theatened. To each of these points we shall return again.

SYSTEMS THEORY

Every family is a system. Interrelationships abound, and each life impinges on the others. It can be predicted that any change (such as engaging in family therapy) will produce changes in the individual lives of family members, and that every change will affect the total system.

If you observe that Ben cannot hold a job for more than a few months, and that Beulah's paycheck from the knitting mill is responsible for keeping food on the table, you're seeing something of their system. If you further observe that just when Beulah begins to feel confident that her Ben is gainfully employed, she then starts to develop some personal interests again in her lodge and women's church school class, and he once more becomes dissatisfied with his job conditions, you're watching a system at work. And if you see that daughter Beth's school grades improve when her father is unemployed and around the house, but worsen when he is working, you are onto a complicated family system indeed.

Systems of interaction can be spotted everywhere—in astronomy, in medicine, in community life, and in church. A friend of mine once stopped to watch an experienced crew moving a large house. The workers stopped for a coffee break and he chatted with them. "I suppose," he said, "that you jack up one corner of the house at a time to get it off the foundation." "Nope," the foreman replied. "We lift the whole house at once; less damage that way." Whether he knew it or not, that foreman was speaking out of systems theory.

Systems theory got its start in World War II through the development of weapons and material that used computers, radar, and new perspectives for armies. In time Ludwig von Bertalanffy (1968) developed a general systems theory; Norbert Wiener (1961) devised the concept of cybernetics; and A. C. Robin Skynner (1976) expanded on family systems theory. Scientific explanations of systems theory can become discouragingly complex; but they do agree that at least it means that a music composition is more than its notes; that the solar system is greater than the sum of stars; and that we all exist within an ecology where plural conditions of the system affect each of us.

Admiral Peary, on his Polar trip, once traveled briskly all day by dogsled toward the north; but at night, when he checked his bearings to ascertain his latitude, he found he was even farther south than when he had set out that morning. All day long he and his dogs had been running as hard as they could, but on an iceflow driven south by the ocean's currents (Minuchin, 1974, p. 2).

A family is something like that iceflow. It provides an environment whose totality is greater than all its individual components. The system in which its members dwell has a mighty impact on them, propelling them in directions they might not choose to go, and might not even understand. Even singles who live alone have been so influenced by their families of origin that the ongoing system leaves its indelible mark on them.

Systems theory represents a radical change from a position wherein we considered individuals to be isolated units, to a new position wherein we view those individuals *in relation* to their functions and to other individuals as a whole. With some of the heat off the individual person, we may be able to view disordered family behavior as an understandable reaction to a dysfunctional social system. As Vincent D. Foley has written, "To view pathology from the point of view of a person and to see it from the point of view of a system is not just to get another picture but to see a new reality" (Foley, 1974, p. 40).

One well-known fictional dysfunctional family is the Willie Loman family in Arthur Miller's *Death of a Salesman*. Willie, the unhappy salesman, is the husband of a depressed Linda. Their sons, Biff and Happy, are slices off the old ham. They duplicate numerous traits of their father: poor employment records, duplicity, a certain callousness, and false heartiness. From their mother they seem to inherit a talent for ineptness and a vascillating tendency between willfulness and resignation. When the dissatisfied Willie seeks a temporary affair with a receptionist, Biff learns about it and reacts with disillusionment and anger. His life is affected by that discovery and by his own inability to come to terms with his father. A circular response of disappointments, breakdowns, failed promises, and decreasing quality of relationships follows in this sick system. By the drama's end, as every playgoer knows, Willie, the salesman, is a suicide.

THE DISCOVERY OF FAMILY THERAPY

In the early 1950s, a large mental hospital stumbled upon some of the truth of family systems when it reviewed the new difficulties they encountered with patients following visiting hours. Schizophrenic patients could be upset for days on end after a compassionate visit by their mother or father. Searching for the connection to this dismaying situation, the staff began to question their long-term assumption that the patients were simply acting out of their own interior, distorted view of the world. They began slowly to bring the patients together with their parents in order to learn more about these disturbed family reunions. They talked with them about their conflicts, asked about family histories, and observed the patients' interactions with their relatives.

What therapists learned in those sessions edged them closer to family therapy because they began to detect differences in the behavior of their patients when the families were together in discussions with them. Gradually, the therapists learned that they could elicit the families as allies in therapy, and that their very relationships could be useful in treatment. This turned out to be one of the sources form which today's family therapy arose. It was the product of systemic action.

It was discovered in those family gatherings, begun so experimentally, that the families had had a history of severe marital conflict. It was noted, moreover, that each of the patients' episodes of emotional disturbance was related closely to the conflictual cycles within the family. The staff had begun to grasp a handle on the background of those unfortunate episodes during visiting hours. Now they could go on to work on another factor: the parents' relationships. To relieve those marital problems would, in some fashion, relieve the patients' symptoms. Next, they also began to discover that many of the fathers in these families were passive, distant men. It was clear that they did not easily relate to their sons and daughters, that they were noticeably less active than their wives. To these parents, Frieda Fromm-Reichmann would endow the name "schizophrenogenic," because their involvement apparently gave rise to schizophrenia in their children.

The family system has power both to damage and to build lives. "By the family you were broken; by the family you will be healed," the familiar adage runs.

Any systems approach must go beyond the family to church and to community. The family is often the victim of the social system in which it is located. The neighborhood, the government, the schools, the work experience of breadwinners: all these are macrosystems that have an impact upon the family. In the long run, family therapists often become social activists. Too often they have seen a family reconciled and reunited only to be thrust back into a housing problem or a disintegrating neighborhood that again takes its toll of the family's well-being. Everyone, indeed, is related to several systems: one's place of employment, the educational system, the market place, or a circle of friends, to name a few; and often these systems rival the family in influence. Family systems exist within other systems, an ecological fact we dare not ignore for long.

THE FAMILY IS THE PATIENT

Therapists began to see the power of the family system in another way; and they were impressed—but hardly happy. Time and again they had brought about improvement with some disturbed patient only to find themselves "totally defeated by the family's power over the patient; or seeing a client 'recover' only to witness all the progress undermined by the family; or treating the scapegoat child 'successfully' only to find another child in the family dragged into the role; or working with an individual patient and feeling the fury of the family's sudden explosion just as the patient improved" (Napier and Whitaker, 1978, p. 48).

In other circumstances, therapists were to discover the power of the system in family collusions. The so-called "well" partner was discerned to have a greater stake in the alcoholic illness of the patient than had been previously noted. The ever loving martyr in a family showed up with a larger responsibility in the behavior of a worthless, cruel spouse than had been admitted before. The new direction was to examine what was happening between people and not simply what their symptoms happened to be. From the conviction that troubles come in families, it proved a short distance to the realization that "the family is the patient."

Systems theory can hardly be a new concept to anyone who is educated by life in the church. The pastor is acutely aware of its implications at times for it can be seen at work in the congregation's daily life.

- A youth travels to a young peoples' conference and there discovers new inspiration and spiritual depth in an experience which for him is a dramatic awakening of the "Aha" sort. But thereafter he returns to parents who ridicule his thrilled reports. He sinks back into the bland and conventional faith he had exhibited before, an imitation of the family's faith. (Gradually, now, we are learning to involve parents along with young people in their church activity and along their faith journey. It's about time.)

- A woman attends a devotional retreat and plumbs what for her are new depths of understanding and self-realization. However, she comes back to her jocular, teasing husband, who all but wipes out her new gains during that first evening at home.
- A man becomes involved in the lay ministry of his local congregation, and through committee service learns a deeper enthusiasm for the church. But his wife fails to share that enthusiasm and her attitude detracts from his satisfaction. At year's end he drops out of leadership responsibilities.

The systems network of these families is altogether too clear to the pastor. What might be just as clear is the systemic solution: to engage both members of the couple in shared responsibility in parish life, so that they have greater opportunity to remain mutually interested. In recent years we have begun to see the importance of couples' retreats and the programmed involvement of married couples in their church experience. Not a few churches now elect married couples as well as individuals to their committees and official boards. This enables husband and wife to grow together and to share at deeper levels those spiritual discoveries and related activities that might enrich their relationship instead of fracturing it (Goldman, 1977).

ORIENTATION TO SYSTEMIC THINKING

In our Divinity School training program it has been necessary to work on the systemic question at some length with each new class; for ministerial students are conditioned to think independently and to consider both themselves and others as separated individuals. To replace that misconception, and also to convince the students of the systems theory, requires reorientation exercises.

We have sometimes used a device from the human potential movement that has come to be called "the rope trick." In order to demonstrate the way a system can work through the relationships of a family group, we fashion a pseudo-family from five members of the class and have them stand in a ring. Stretching a clothesline from one person to others, we connect each person in that circle of five to each of the other four. This gives each a handful of four ropes, making a total of ten intertwining, tangled lines. When one pulls on any part of that rope it will tighten somewhere else. The others are affected at once by the tautness of the connection. No part of that entangled system is immune to tugs when any change is made in its slack or tightness. Despite the spaghetti-like tangle into which the demonstration sometimes collapses, the point becomes clear: everybody is connected.

In another exercise, students use large sheets of newsprint and crayons to draw a picture of their family of origin around the dinner table when they were ten years old. That age is chosen because it has some chance of summoning up memories of a family still intact, and an era before the onset of their own adolescence with its many changes. The exercise awakens old memories and reviews old times as they begin to recognize the interactions that were influenced by a family ritual. Who was assigned to each chair, who it was that performed certain chores, what rituals of liturgy or etiquette, the topics of conversation, the networks of relationships: these and considerably more will be probed in the steeps of memory.

Then, in groups of four, the students tell each other about their drawings. They reminisce about what kind of man father was; how it was that mother got her way; what the sequence of eating, speaking, and understanding had been among family members. The covert and invisible rules of family living begin to emerge.

Close to this same time, two other assignments are scheduled to round out memories of the system in the family of origin. Students are asked to write short biographical essays that emphasize the systemic features of their families, and also to draw a genogram outlining their places in the family tree (for a description of and instruction in genogram design, refer to Chapter 6).

Behind these exercises is a pair of convictions. One is that we shall better see how systems theory applies to a family if we are both familiar with that family and sufficiently removed from it to be somewhat objective. Our own families of procreation prepare us for just such a double task. Most of us can look back on our home lives when we were ten with an objectivity of which we should be incapable if we were examining our present family constellations. Something of this same sort of interior reflection upon personal experience remains important to the minister doing family therapy. The internal dialogue that keeps us critically alert to our memories and their influence, to our sexuality and its impact, to our relationships and their importance can make any of us better counselors.

Our second conviction is that, unless we understand clearly what kind of family we came from and how we interacted with them in those plasticene years of childhood, we may tend unconsciously to veer other families into the direction of our own familial experience. In our counseling we might err in attempting to remake other families over into a new model of the one we enjoyed (or even disliked) during our childhood. Awareness of the systems in that childhood home makes us more alert to what we are doing.

Once we gain the systems perspective, we should no longer regard any person as an isolated individual apart from all others, but as one who belongs to a network of significant interrelationships. Each of us is a part of others in the context of a larger bundle of humankind.

In one course, a student confessed to grave difficulty in understanding the systemic theory as well as to some resistance in adopting the viewpoint. Then one day it dawned suddenly on him. "Why, it's like a wedding rehearsal," he exclaimed. "I have to keep aware of the bride and the bride's mother, the groom, and the best man, the groom's mother, the attendants, the organist, and my own cues too." He had it. The wedding rehearsal is but one of many events where clergy must pay attention to a number of persons and their interactions within a total connection. When we realize we have this ability already, we can begin to apply such learning to other occasions and to other systems by direct transfer. From this point it is only a short step to conceptualizing family therapy within that same context and counseling with an entire family in regard to some disabling relational problem, a topic to which we will return in the following two chapters.

MASTERING THE LANGUAGE OF FAMILY THERAPY

The Berlitz Schools of Languages published a series of advertisements several years ago that caught the eye with the phrase, "You are already speaking German!" (or French or Italian, as that month's emphasis had it). Then, with assurance, the ad listed common words in the language that we already knew—*Gesundheit, Schnapps, Frankfurter.* The point was obvious, the pitch beguiling: it should require very little additional effort to add to our knowledge of the language and to begin speaking it like a native. The parallel in this case is obvious. Clergy are already in the practice of family therapy. Dealing with a grief-stricken family at a time of sudden death; working with a couple in premarital guidance; instructing young parents prior to the baptism of their child; counseling with a husband and wife about their adjustment to each other, or their concerns about an adolescent daughter, their aging parents, or their financial crisis: these are experiences that partake of family therapy.

When clergy realize that they have been operating within a system theory for some time without being aware of it, it makes the next steps easier. They can then move on to a systemic understanding that is at once more conscious and more effective.

FEATURES OF THE SYSTEM

Systems, those complexes of interacting elements, show us three basic characteristics. Nearly all family therapists refer to them, use them for diagnosis, description, and treatment; by them the family's structure and relationships can be described. They are (1) homeostasis, (2) the identified patient, and (3) the double bind.

Homeostasis (Greek for "the same place") suggests the equilibrium the family tries to keep, a balance that may be functional or dysfunctional, but one to which it has become accustomed. Because any family will tend to feel more secure in following its customary patterns of interaction, it may struggle to return to these patterns even if they are painful or awkward.

For example, we may turn to the all-too-familiar experience of an alcoholic man whose neurotic interaction with his wife is so damaging that even if he quits drinking and enters some new life adjustment, she may sabotage that improvement. In some manner, she may induce him to begin drinking again because she has learned how to deal reciprocally with him in that kind of behavior. Thus resisting new patterns of conduct, they both revert to their former balance; that is, they return to the same place.

Another example is our earlier story of Adam and Abby, whose teen age boy acts out his parents' conflict when he smokes pot in the park, thus propelling the family toward homeostasis. When the husband-and-wife conflict reaches the breaking point, the son gets caught. Then Adam and Abby must band together, go down to the police station, bail out their son, and all come home as a family. In shame and in anger they drive home; but they *are* together. That shaky marriage is thus preserved until another crisis. Meanwhile, the adolescent's rather sick choice (be it conscious or unconscious) has brought them back to that homeostatic balance they knew before.

Homeostasis can work positively, too. It may operate in a healthier family which, in time of dispute, calls a family council to struggle through differences and thus returns to its former harmony. Another family may remind each other that "everyone gets a turn" in time of argument. Or a husband and wife who find their marriage slipping into dull doldrums may engage a sitter and leave for a weekend trip by themselves to repair their romance, their sexual relationship, their communication, and their mutual understanding, thus returning these to equilibrium.

This basic concept of family therapists can be employed to understand why families slip back into bad habits. The therapist can intervene to change the balance with "neostasis" (that is, leading them to a *new place*) by jolting the system, altering the communication patterns, or teaching them fresh methods of problem-solving.

Thus, if therapy has been successful, the family emerges with a new level of relationship, a more balanced system, an improved condition of stability. They find themselves standing in a new place—and standing together.

The identified patient (I.P.) is that person in an upset family who is designated as "the problem," or who owns the problem. He or she may be the family scapegoat, bearing the guilt of others. He or she may be the symbol bearer who takes on the shame of less-approved behaviors the others would like to adopt, but are too sophisticated to exhibit: such characteristics as belligerancy, sexiness, rebelliousness, and so on.

Usually, when such a family comes for counseling, it will thrust forward the problem person as the one who must be changed. The family members' agreed understanding is that, if this individual's personality adjustment is altered for the better, the family's problems will disappear. To them it is obvious that their collective difficulties must be the direct result of this one member. They will find it strange and hard to understand that the therapist may wish to meet with the parents and siblings as well. Knowing full well where the trouble is located, they will resist any new input that suggests their system of living has anything to do with the identified patient's problems. After all, the value of having an I.P. in the family is to have that martyr bear the load for all the others. And all too often the designated I.P. falls compliantly into the role.

Elaine is marched into the pastor's office by her mother. This seventeen-year-old has become sexually involved with a male teacher at her high school. The indignant, shocked parents want her to be straightened out (and, indeed, she does need help). What they do not want is to have their own long-standing marital quarrel put in the spotlight for examination. Still and all, the pastor, if mindful of the system, will see connections between the parental problems and their adolescent daughter's problems, and will know that all the system must be examined as a whole. Like the house, the family must be seen together and lifted to some new balance, rather than corner by corner, one person at a time.

Communication psychiatrists discovered long ago that some families are so pathological in their relationships that they need a sick person to help them cope! Families assign one of their number to this position as a way of handling their collective problem; and the wonder is that this measure does accomplish what it is designed for. That there are better problem-solving techniques for a family to utilize is a lesson that the helping professions teach. A schizophrenic child or a dysfunctional adult really may serve such a sick purpose, and take on the task of the identified patient for the entire household. For the therapist to work alone with that individual, as if there were no relatives in the family, is counterproductive. This challenge calls, instead, for work with the entire family system. It was this growing conviction that sped the development of family therapy in our time.

A child's problem can serve the practical purpose of helping conflictual parents to avoid their difficulty in a socially approved way—i.e., to focus on the child. Such children may get the message that the family's emotional survival is somehow dependent on them. Family therapist Don Jackson once worked with a family who had a schizophrenic son. He focused on the question of what they would ever do and how they could cope if their son were to become well. The family naturally resisted the question; but Jackson persisted. Meanwhile, the son was making more sense than he had before, and by the interview's end he told the therapist that he thought his family needed him to be sick so that they could feel well!

A *double bind* message is a compulsorily confusing communication that cuts across two levels in a relatively contradictory style. The person who speaks of a tragic event, but smiles throughout the explanation, is sending a double bind message. A women who demands that her husband kiss her, and then glares at him angrily as he complies, puts him into a double bind. The father who takes his son to the circus grumbling, "You'd better have a good time or I'll never take you to another circus" places the boy in a double bind position. The critic who, after a hostile remark, placates with, "Aw c'mon, I was only kidding," is double binding. These people resemble the legendary English schoolmaster who is said to have taught his students: "I want you to have the love of God in your hearts; if you don't have the love of God in your hearts, I'll flog you!"

"The Palo Alto Group," a famous fellowship of family therapists (Virginia Satir, Jay Haley, Don Jackson, Gregory Bateson, and Paul Watzlawick), refined the double bind theory and found that it is not just the habitual way that many dysfunctional families talk with each other; it is also typical of most families at some time or another. The father who gives his son two shirts for his birthday and then accosts him the first time he wears one with, "What's wrong; didn't you like the other one?" is double binding him. A mother who is apprehensive about intimacy may recoil when her child approaches her. Then, unable to tolerate herself as unloving, she tries to correct her position with a contradictory message of love. But the child is confused—and now in the wrong, caught in a double bind because whichever message he obeys he will be disobeying his mother.

A colleague at the University of Rochester tells of his boyhood problems with a double binding mother. It was she in his male-oriented household who set the table, cooked the dinner, and cleaned up the dishes afterward, while Stanley and his father watched television. Mother would clatter about the kitchen, washing the dishes and calling to her son, "Stanley, would you like some more ice cream?" "No, Mother," Stanley would refuse, "I'm not hungry."

"But, Stanley, it's your favorite—chocolate."

"Thanks, Mother, I've had enough," Stanley would reply.

"Stanley, I'm dishing it up and putting it on the table," the persistent parent would call out.

Then when the wearied son would reluctantly go to the dining room for the proferred ice cream, his mother would exclaim: "See what I mean? My work's never done!"

That's double binding. It is typical of some problem families to keep each other confused and defensive through double binds. They use such messages to score points, to play nasty games, and to foment the conflict in which they have learned to live. This has become their system, part and parcel of their mechanism of homeostasis.

CHARACTERISTICS OF A SYSTEM

Central to systems theory are five basic concepts that flesh out the meaning and clarify our understanding of that theory. They are (1) transcendence, (2) equifinality, (3) relationship, (4) mutability, and (5) feedback.

Transcendence is a term familiar to anyone who has ever studied theology. The concept of a power over and above, and having meaning apart from and beyond ourselves, is not new to the theologian. The term is applied in much the same manner to systems theory. The family system takes on a power of its own. It is more than the sum of its separate parts. As a synergism, it possesses a wholeness that takes account of the interactions within it. It's the feeling that prompts the actor in a TV soap opera to sigh, "This thing is bigger than both of us." It's the realization of the therapist that the family system is more pervasive and potent than any easy intervention can be. If we wish to assist a troubled family to work out of its pain, we shall need to keep in mind that the complexity of transactions adds up to more than the mere number of people involved.

The idea that the same result might be reached by any of a number of avenues in known as *equifinality*. If the marital system has produced a conflict-habituated marriage as Lederer and Jackson (1968) classified one type of union, that result could have been influenced by any number of factors: money disputes, sexual dysfunction, religious differences, in-law battles, and so on. Thus the pastoral therapist would be ill-advised to indulge in a long, detailed history of the family conflict; for how they got to their present situation could be less important than what the present dynamics are. Equifinality can operate in cases regardless of the impetus; the resulting pattern can be much the same. It will be important to note the couple's interaction; it may be less important to probe for the whys and the whats of their background. Family therapy, in common with much of modern psychology, works with the here and the now.

It was that enigmatic, brilliant psychiatrist, Harry Stack Sullivan, who awakened us to the stimulating concept of *interpersonal relationships*. As a result of this realization, we can hardly consider a man in depression as if he is solely depressed from within himself—that is, intrapsychically. He is part of a marriage; perhaps he is also the father of five children. He may have reasons for his depression. In any case, his emotional health is ineluctably connected to his relationships (Sullivan, 1953).

A runaway in Greenwich Village can hardly be treated as if she, herself, is her whole problem. The question must also be asked what she is running away from at home. Who else is bound up in her bundle of relationships, and what is their part in her difficulty?

Clergy counselors have to be alive to the contextual aspects of related people throughout their whole system. To see them in isolation is to distort the picture. To see them in relationship is to utilize Buber's concept of "between," "where 'deep calls unto deep' . . . where *I* and *Thou* meet" (Buber, 1948, p. 204) in immediate mutuality.

Mutability is the fourth of these basic concepts in family systems

theory. Because connections within any system are always changing—whether in biology, physics, astronomy, or society—the
family therapist must also remain aware of constant changes. It
is not enough to take a family history and to assume that relationships stay the way they are reported. People change. It is hardly
necessary to prove this to ministers, who know that people can
be converted, are improvable. Their ingrained habits may make
the process gradual; and they may be resistant. But it is a stupid
maxim, though oft repeated, that human nature never changes.
Human nature, in fact, is ever-changing. Of that truism the therapist can take advantage in counseling a family. We can count on
the change possibility not only in our therapy, but also in education and in evangelism.

There is yet another dimension to family systems called *feedback;* and from it we can learn much. Essentially, the term conveys
the notion that any reaction is a lead to other events in a constant
flow of connectedness. Families, like other organic systems, will
make adjustments in their living based on information gathered
from their environment. Such information is constantly being fed
back to families.

In feedback, the elements of a family system circle around each
other in a constant series of transactions, not in simple cause and
effect so much as a continuous loop. What is known to social
workers as the multiproblem family is a glaring example of feedback. A man who has been laid off from the foundry becomes
depressed and then abusive to his wife and children who, in turn,
break down with a series of respiratory illnesses. The children's
absences from school lead to lower grades and the threat of
failure for the year. Their parents are called into conferences with
school administrators. Hurt by this development, each reacts
differently: the mother with a new illness, and the father with
fresh abusiveness toward his children. He takes to spending more
time in bars. His wife's concurrent illness prevents her from
caring for the children. Their son is arrested with a gang of young
vandals who set an abandoned building afire. The children, now
eating irregularly and then with improper nutrition, suffer new
illnesses and further difficulties. Thus the coiled and ever-mov-

ing feedback within this one family demonstrates the dynamic of the system run to havoc.

That the example could somewhat less easily have turned to *positive* feedback must be noted at once. One can imagine the healthy family in more auspicious circumstances whose inter-actions lead to happier results, but with similar character-istics of multiple causation, circular actions, and reinforced behaviors.

FEATURES OF THE PROCESS

Family process is the total sum of all interactions in the family; and that is a very great deal. A useful and oft-used concept, it offers the answer to a therapist's customary query, "What's going on in this household?" One succinct characterization of process puts it:

> When you are asked to describe a family that lives down the street, you might say something like, "Oh, they don't seem to be too happy. They never do anything together, the kids are all in trouble, there's lots of yelling, the place is a wreck," and so on. You would be talking about their process. (Ogden and Zevin, 1976, p. 6)

Typical of every family process is how they administer their *rules;* for every family has rules. The family, in fact, is a rule-making society. Some believe that the family's main task is to transmit rules to the children. This, of course, is a theory of socialization; and while it may be debatable, there can be little doubt that such transmission is of ultimate importance to every family.

Perhaps the most frequent use of rules is in decision-making. This is an area fraught with disputation; those families who mas-ter their rules about how decisions will be made stand a good chance of living with harmony.

Rules are also utilized in every family to determine how power will be distributed. It may be tacitly understood by all that Cleo exercises decisions over the family budget; but, in a peculiar *quid pro quo,* her husband Caleb always has the privilege of speaking for the family and, what is more, telling humorous stories at her expense at parties. Each is observing a rule.

Typical rules involve a wide variety of issues. It may be that no one is ever allowed to disagree with grandfather because that would be disrespectful and, ultimately, expensive (in the event that he might change his will). Another may involve chores: only the males will do mechanical and exterior work; only the females will do tasks inside the house; that's a rule. Or if Danny, the designated awkward son, makes any remark, others are to laugh about it, and at him, and belittle his remark.

Frequently, rules are established to govern what topics may not be discussed in the family. Some conditions, like Laura's lameness in the play *The Glass Menagerie,* are never to be noticed or to be mentioned. Nor does such a rule stop with the simple prohibition. It often goes farther, as R. D. Laing (1971) has shown, to determine that there are rules never to discuss the rule that certain topics are never to be discussed.

Or just imagine the rule, once described by Jay Haley, that a wife should adopt a pose of helplessness in order to cover an even more helpless husband, who wishes to appear to be a very adequate person. This sham frustrates him and leaves her depressed. It is one of a thousand defeating rules couples employ.

That there are numerous disagreements about rules in families is no surprise. They can, however, be adjudicated rather promptly if it is possible to focus on the rule rather than on the people involved, thus saving dignity for those concerned. Couples can even contract with each other about what rules they need, who is to set them, how they are to be administered, and what their significance is. This kind of open negotiation has the value of making implicit rules explicit, and frankly acknowledging the operating principles of the marriage.

Family process also depends, in large extent, upon the *roles* members play in their relations with each other. One plays the clown, another the fat and jolly personality, still another the mediator. Roles are complex, for "one man in his time plays many parts." The clown may also enact the role of arbitrator another time, or even the martyr with a different set of people. Mature or healthy people are capable of choosing and adjusting to several roles; dysfunctional people may be stuck in one role, incapable of change. They may play the martyr even when the occasion calls for them to be responsible; or they may still be clowning when the opportunity has arrived for serious commitment.

In therapy, it is valuable to discover what roles each member plays in the family process, as that will provide one key to their relationship.

Rituals are also involved in our family process. These are routines of relatively predictable feedback in which our interactions follow a set pattern that has been imposed by long-held expectations. Taking leave from each other is such a ritual. It involves saying goodbye in the programmed, approved manner that the family has customarily followed.

Some rituals are as simple as the grace before meals, for which all heads bow and mother intones the blessing. Others are organized around the routine of seating arrangements, entry into the automobile, or going to bed. In most cases (and this is in contrast to rules) we are barely conscious of the rituals we follow and are amazed at their detail when someone calls attention to what we have been doing.

Rituals can be complex. The pastor's wife who, in protest against her husband's too-busy schedule, falls into a two-week bout with the blues or lapses into an illness that prevents her from any of her customary activities is opening a ritualistic dance to which he responds with contrition and compassion; this allows her to berate him until he feels cleansed and she feels better. It's their ritual—hardly healthy or commendable, but understandable. It remains a feature of their family process.

THREE SPOOKS

In family process there are also three "spooky" influences: secrets, ghosts, and mystification.

Secrets prompt unconscious belief systems that are held by the entire family and, often as not, are based on myths. Like Mary in Eugene O'Neill's *Long Day's Journey into Night,* a person can be chemically dependent on drugs but regarded, in the family myth, as altogether circumspect. The family belief system protects her image and displays her as a respectable, model matron, shielding a family embarrassment. Secrets often inspire a family to withold information, e.g., Uncle Joe's prison sentence. Secrets may make therapy an extremely difficult task at times; but after awhile a child may tip the secret, or an adult may begin to unload the story with relief.

Ghosts are family expectations passed on from generation to generation. Ghosts cause married couples to assume that they will assume the same positions in life as did their own parents. When the ghosts—hardly recognized in the dim past of their family life—are at odds (e.g., in her family father carved the roast; in his, mother sliced it and served the plates from the kitchen), misunderstandings develop. Ghosts can be persistent and insidious. Child abuse is one, as abused child grows up to become a child abuser. The exorcism of family ghosts is a difficult challenge to the therapist, and necessitates delving into the family of origin to begin the process.

Mystification is the masking of one's own interests by representing them as if they were really to the advantage of someone else. It is a dandy method of one-upmanship and an exercise in self-justification as well. "Run along to bed now; you look very tired," may really mean that the adult is fed up with the child's noise and high energy, and hopes that the youngster will quiet down to sleep very soon.

In one of Agatha Christie's murder mysteries, *Appointment With Death,* a nasty dowager uses mystification as her habitual method of operation. When her daughter wants to go on a sight-seeing tour with other young adults one afternoon, this tyrannical woman declaims:

"Jinny had better not go. She'll lie down and have a sleep."
"Mother, I'm not tired. I want to go with the others."
"You *are* tired. You've got a headache! You must be careful of yourself. Go and lie down and sleep. I know what's best for you." (Christie, 1938, p. 126)

The reader is rather gratified when, in the twelfth chapter, the old woman is done in.

But note the mystification in these familiar messages: "I know you'll want to pay your own way." "You'll want to finish the ironing before your father comes home, I'm sure." "You're going to feel much better if you go and apologize to Uncle Dan right now."

The therapist will break into this callow communication system to teach people to use "I-messages" and to say what they really mean, in messages that are clearer, and through arrangements that are more honest. An I-message is a straightforward communication that frankly states an opinion about an issue, takes a position on it, and yet does not blame another: "I become annoyed when I see such a messy bedroom."

BY THE FAMILY BROKEN

These features of family process are not mutually exclusive. They overlap and combine to produce rules about rituals, rituals about secrets, mystification about roles, and so on. A family in motion is as complex as the system of a galaxy. The key to their puzzling behaviors will be found in awareness of their relationships.

To do this work of family therapy, we in the ministry must reorient our thinking toward those relational categories. There is a great difference between viewing the marital problem as if it belonged to two individuals in pain, and viewing the relationship between them as if it were a bridge in need of urgent repair. Much of our work is focused on individuals, and many of our habitual thought patterns are individualistic; our learning has veered us toward such a direction. We are assured that we must bear our own burden (Gal. 6:8) and that we must work out our own salvation with fear and trembling (Phil. 2:12).

Much of emotional disturbance, far from being only a private intrapsychic experience, is patently systemic. Dysfunction, whether in human sexuality or in parent-child relations, is systemic. We do not live or die to ourselves; all of us are part of a web of relationships that affect our mental health, our knowledge, and our customs. The keen observer can look into an individual's problems and see much; but that same observer can examine a troubled family and diagnose far more. The rules, and rituals, and roles of that family will throw bright light on the behavior and reactions of each of the individuals within it.

By the Family Healed

It is the conviction of family-oriented counselors that whatever is therapeutic in the long run will come out of the family itself—not directly from the minister, nor the psychotherapist, nor that family scapegoat, the so-called identified patient. Each of these has a potent part to play in the new balance (the neostasis) of the family, for better or for worse; but the enduring pattern of health will emanate from the very source from which came the dis-ease to begin with. "By the family broken, by the family healed."

The family has far more continuous impact upon its members than any therapist: more than one hundred hours per week as compared to perhaps one hour in the counseling office. The family can bring about major changes on its own—or block any major progress as well. Therapists can aid the families in these changes. They can direct attention to difficulties and their origin and to patterns of interaction. They can intervene to alter rituals, or assign family members to new ways of relating to their family ghosts. But, in the main, therapists do not solve problems for families; they only aid the changes that are brought about. Therapists, whether clergy or lay, are not so wise that they know fully what is best for a family. That which fits a family's patterns is felt most intimately by them; and they are, in the end, the expert judges of that. Even when the therapist might rather see them take a different course of action or make their adjustment on a higher level, it is often wiser to settle for what is realistic in some altered arrangements or compromise. We are advised to remember that only God is omnipotent, that we cannot always know exactly what is best for other persons, but that we can help them discover this for themselves.

With all this emphasis on relational therapy, the reader is entitled to wonder whether our counsel is to ignore the individual. Such is not really the case. Indeed, the therapist must use techniques of individual therapy at times. There will be occasions when one member of the family can be singled out for some special attention because his or her personal pain has become disproportionate to the total task, or because he or she may be obstructing the family therapy to such an extent that a corrective has to be applied. This can be done in the midst of the family group, as when the therapist says to the others, "Please sit back and relax for a while and I'll talk just with Sally about this problem; then we'll all come together again." In the midst of the family, then, the therapist "fishbowls" attention on Sally and deals with her problem as if it is the only one that matters. Other family members, observing this procedure, are not left out; for they often learn things they had not previously known and they see the counselor model behavior that they can emulate.

An even more extended individual concentration can be arranged through an extra appointment for Sally by herself. An hour of her own, with none of the others present, may be necessary in order to give her the freedom to express herself as she needs to—or to give the therapist a chance to work on the case uninterrupted by some of the more disturbing members of the family. Whichever way it is arranged, the individual treatment ought not to be allowed to work against the family therapy and the family's integrity. Careful introduction of the procedure and conscientious summary at its conclusion will obviate some of the expected feelings of jealousy and suspicion. Equal time and attention to others in the family, and eliciting their assistance to help the case, go a long way in keeping the case viable.

FAMILIES BEAR A FAMILY RESEMBLANCE

Long ago, family therapists began to find out that there was less difference between healthy and dysfunctional families than had been supposed. There is no absolute division line between the two. As Murray Bowen writes, "Much of the early family research was done with schizophrenia. Since the clinical observations from those studies had not been previously described in the literature, it was first thought that the relationship patterns were typical of schizophrenia. Then it was discovered that the very same patterns were also present in families with neurotic level problems, and even in normal families" (Bowen, 1976, p. 60).

Therapists know that every family will have double bind messages now and then. Every family engages in mystification at times. We all scapegoat one another on occasion. There is no ready way sharply to divide wholesome from disabled families. Instead, all families would fit somewhere along a continuum between the extremes of the healthiest and the grossly dysfunctional.

Jules Henry, in his landmark study *Pathways to Madness,* relates how he went to live within households of schizophrenics to study their ways of coping. An anthropologist, he immersed himself totally into their lives. He ate, slept, worked, conversed, observed, and played with them. After his experiences, he could only conclude that so-called sick families are much like healthy families, that distinctions between them are relative rather than absolute.

It all seems to confirm the one-genus theory of Harry Stack Sullivan: that we are all much more alike than unlike. Families resemble each other more than they differ from each other. Leo Tolstoy was only partly correct when he said, in the opening lines of *Anna Karenina,* "Happy families are all alike; every unhappy family is unhappy in its own way." The fact is that all families everywhere bear a family resemblance. African or Scandinavian, affluent or impoverished, they still have inner relationships that look alike. They squabble, they rely on one another, they solve problems together—even sick families solve some problems every day. They have a commonality of being human.

3. Family Therapists You Should Know

> When all is said and done, therapy of every sort comes down to people influencing other people in a controlled way, and adding new, learned behavior to their repertoires.
>
> —JOEL KOVEL, *A Complete Guide to Therapy*

HOW IT ALL GOT GOING

Family therapy got off to a rocky start. Psychotherapists opposed the movement as an unjustified innovation, and many out of the psychoanalytic tradition considered family treatment to be invalid—even unethical. Sigmund Freud, of course, had been poignantly aware of the family's impact upon mental health; it was his opinion, in fact, that parents have considerable responsibility for the mental health of their children. But still, for more than fifty years, he treated patients individually. Even in his famous case of Little Hans (Freud, vol. 10, 1955), Freud interviewed only Hans's father, through whom he extruded the treatment toward the little boy. Although he did not overlook the importance of families, he was committed to "the exclusion of the patient's relatives in treatment" (Freud, vol. 16, 1955, p. 459). To have met with intergenerational family groups would have been wholly unacceptable to him.

Most psychoanalysts who followed Freudian theory made no move to enlarge therapeutically on his family insights. The emotionally ill continued to be treated intrapsychically rather than interpersonally. Even J. C. Flügel's *Psycho-analytic Study of the Family*, first published in 1921, supposed that family problems were to be treated with each individual alone. Throughout the nineteenth century and into much of the twentieth, the therapist worked only with the identified patient in sharp contrast with today's widespread conviction that the *family* is the patient.

In time, however, two parallel but scarcely related movements began to move toward various approaches to family treatment. One was the mental health movement, led by those psychiatrists who had been deeply impressed by the impact of interpersonal relationships in their patients' lives. The other was the tradition of marriage counseling and the child guidance movements, with their largely educational methods. Once the practice of family therapy began, it moved forward so resolutely that it is possible to note its growth by decades.

In the 1940s, psychiatry was being moderated in many fashions by the influence of numerous sociocultural factors. Harry Stack Sullivan's interpersonal psychiatry, Karen Horney's social interests, and Kurt Lewin's teachings were laced with social psychology. Thus, when systems theory was developed during World War II, and group therapy was proliferating at the same time that communication theory was expanding, circumstances suddenly were ripe for family therapy. New material from studies of schizophrenia and the social milieu of the patient was now couched more in an interactive model of psychotherapy (Bloch, 1973).

Gradually, the basic principles of family therapy began to emerge in several areas. Courses in social psychology promulgated the teachings of George Herbert Mead, taking account of the social and familial context of patients far beyond clinical interviews and office calls. The Federal Council of Churches, at the urging of Leland Foster Wood, opened training seminars for ministers to help them better understand the counseling process with married couples and parents.

These influences notwithstanding, many psychiatrists tended to view the new therapy as a heresy. The early innovators, a veritable underground movement in hospitals and institutes, sometimes conducted their family therapy as exploratory research in order to disguise their real activity, to avoid the charges against so uncertain an enterprise. The literature describes their careful experimentation in the face of inimical clinical administrations and colleagues, characterizing their struggles as a time of severe testing.

Others, not yet in contact with each other, were working toward the same end. Carl Whitaker in Atlanta was training young medical students in child psychiatry at Emory University and conducting a private practice that set the style for his development of family therapy. Emily Hartshore Mudd established a treatment center known as the Marriage Council of Philadelphia, actually a division of family study for the medical school's psychiatric department at the University of Pennsylvania. John E. Bell began to experiment with the treatment of whole families.

It was during the forties, too, that Nathan Ackerman pioneered in family treatment at several organizations in New York City, and then founded his Family Institute. In his therapeutic work, he had seen that sick children often had disturbed parents. He began to send out his staff social workers and psychiatrists to make home visits. He began writing articles and reading papers at conventions about the importance of family health for individual health, a contribution for which he initially received little gratitude.

Child guidance clinics came alive in working with the parents of troubled children. Mental hospitals, learning that families frequently subverted the progress made in treating patients, began to bring schizophrenics' mothers to treatment sessions. Then someone noticed that "patients have fathers too," and soon the staffs were seeing whole families.

By the late 1950s, family therapy was becoming a movement throughout the country. Spurred on by numerous ancillary developments, the movement now developed openly. Developmental psychologists like Evelyn Duvall, Arnold Gesell, and Erik Erikson had awakened everyone's attention to the ages and stages of family life. Talcott Parsons, with his background in psychoanalytic education, had alerted sociologists to the depths of family theory. Churches of all denominations were alive to a post-war emphasis in family programs. Popular media, like

McCalls' magazine with its slogan of "togetherness," had taken up the enthusiasm.

Meanwhile, at Topeka, Murray Bowen was innovating methods of treatment for problems of mother-daughter symbiosis at the Menninger Clinic. He established special cottages to enable families to stay on the grounds with their hospitalized relatives. Later, when he moved to the National Institute of Mental Health at Washington, D.C., he carried on this unusual (at least for that time) psychiatry. Termed "the Camelot of family research", it was short-lived. Staff politics, professional opposition, and administrative coolness brought about its demise and Bowen's removal to Georgetown University.

Lyman C. Wynne (also at the National Institute of Mental Health), working with mother-son dyads, advanced the research into family therapy, establishing a number of famous concepts and terms (e.g., pseudo-hostility, pseudo-mutuality, and rubber fences) that are now commonly used throughout family therapy.

In California the now-famous Palo Alto group (Gregory Bateson, Jay Haley, Don Jackson, Paul Watzlawick, and John Weakland) were at work on communication theory. They had adopted systems theory from the physical sciences and applied it to the family, had worked out the theory of the double bind, and were exploring the disease of schizophrenia from the standpoint of its "crazy communication" in the family.

Philadelphia, now home for several distinguished training institutes in family therapy, was in that decade to see Ivan Boszormenyi-Nagy and his colleague James Framo arrive at the Eastern Pennsylvania Psychiatric Institute to begin their trail-blazing work.

It was at the Chicago meeting of the American Psychiatric Association in 1956 and the American Orthopsychiatric Association in 1957, however, that family therapy seemed to come of age. It was then that the earliest professional attention was given the new discipline at a convention. Papers were presented, discussions prolonged. The leaders of the burgeoning field were present, and excitement was high.

By the 1960s Virginia Satir had moved from her Chicago home to Palo Alto to join the Mental Research Institute with Don Jackson; from there she went to Esalen, where she was to become program director. Jay Haley was migrating from Palo Alto to Philadelphia to join Salvador Minuchin at the Philadelphia Child Guidance Clinic. Murray Bowen, disappointed by now with the possibility that family therapy might bring about a prompt cure of schizophrenia, was turning to disturbed, but more normal, families. In any case, pharmacology was now in wide use with the mentally ill; and although drugs brought relief, they did not necessarily improve family interaction. It was an age of diagnostic and therapeutic growth in family therapy. The changes that had been so frightening to some were clearly liberating to others.

What had still been a minority movement at the beginning of the 1960s exploded into a mass movement during that decade. The widening influence of family therapy touched not only psychiatric treatment, but also preventive psychiatry, social work practices, public school guidance and counseling, and theological seminary training and the ministry.

The 1970s were a time of consolidation. Prolific publications, production of films and video tapes, workshops, and conferences across the nation marked those years. The public began to become acquainted with family therapy through magazine articles, TV programs, and experiences of friends or relatives.

That the movement will continue to develop in the 1980s seems assured. Already family therapy has been combined with any number of therapeutic modalities: transactional analysis, gestalt therapy, behavior modification, and client-centered therapy, to name but a few. It is adopted widely in family medical practice, and is being introduced into many medical school curricula and divinity school programs as well.

How did so marked a change come about? Murray Bowen credits two factors:

One was a shift in the observing lens from the individual to the family. The other is man's inability to see what is in front of him unless it fits his theoretical frame of reference . . . . Man had stumbled over the bones of prehistoric animals for centuries without seeing them, before Darwin's theory permitted him to begin seeing what had been there all the time. (Bowen, 1976, p. 54)

In its impressive growth period of the past decade, family therapy has developed a number of different branches that distinguish themselves from one another in emphasis, style, and sometimes in open competition. Attempts to form any classification of these branches are thwarted by challenge of using stationary concepts to describe an ever-moving picture. Charles Kramer (1980) believes there are probably several dozen separate, identifiable forms of therapy; and Murray Bowen (1976) is able to describe some sixteen different forms of family therapy. Our classification, for the sampling that follows, will nevertheless be organized under four broad categories: (1) the problem-oriented therapists, (2) the psychodynamic tradition, (3) the intergenerational theorists, and (4) the behavioral therapists.

THE PROBLEM-ORIENTED THERAPISTS

The therapists of the problem-oriented school were doubtless the first in this work who did not trace their origins back to experience in individual therapy. They founded their very theory in family studies traceable to two main sources: social psychology (with a strong input from anthropology) and communication theory. All along, they have been strongly convinced that personality is conceived in terms of personal relationships, that family therapy depends on better communication, and that the intrapsychic model of therapy is inadequate for family theory.

There is something pastoral about this group of family therapists, which may be why they appeal so noticeably to clergy. In the first place, they work with relationships; and that is what ministry is about a considerable portion of the time. In the second, theirs is a clearer theory, and more readily comprehended than some of the other schools. Third, much of what they do and how they conceptualize can be readily transferable into ministry.

The problem-oriented therapists, committed as they are to helping persons solve family problems, are steeped in communication theory. Communication theory, of course, presumes an encounter between persons who are attempting to arrive at some meaning of their encounter. Such communication goes on without ceasing. It is impossible not to communicate; even silence is communication. We communicate with body language only slightly less than with verbal language. Scientists estimate that some six thousand units of information pass between individuals for every minute they chat with each other.

Communication can be exceedingly complex. Mixed messages may make someone's "no" sound very much like "yes." The "no" a boy gets from his father may impel him to continue some delinquency because that inhibited father's "no" may be subverted by a covert wish that his son actually *would* be a rowdy. The communication sent may not be the communication received at all; for much depends upon the mood and the capacity of the receiving person.

Breakdown in communication tends to bring conflict and fracture into relationships. For this reason, the therapist helps families repair their broken communication to the end that their total relationship will also be benefited. Yet communication, for all its power and symbolism, also has limitations. Simply to observe that a couple has a communication problem may be a mere cliché. Their communication barrier is sometimes the cover for a more serious difficulty. Simply to help them talk more freely may not solve that difficulty; it could even increase their arguments. In this case, open communication is exactly the wrong prescription. Communication is used also to wound, to harass, and to dominate. One woman in an interview once avowed: "We have no trouble with communication at our house. . . . I do it all!" Some communication can worsen family relations.

In the main, however, improved communication remains a key to better relationships. To understand how three family therapists act on this conviction, we turn to Jay Haley, Virginia Satir, and Salvador Minuchin.

Jay Haley, director of the Family Institute of Washington, D.C., stands out among family therapists for his clear and lively writing. Working from a base in systems theory, he reflects an impatience with "conventional therapy," its diagnostical and medical approach, and its theoretical basis in psychoanalysis. Sharp in his opinions and in his polemics, Haley has little patience with therapists who make large claims for the benefits of achieving insight and personality change.

Haley is the leading authority in strategic family therapy, a modality that attempts to reshuffle the locus of power within a family. He makes canny use of paradoxical directives and reorganizes family relationships to free them from their unhealthy symptoms. For instance, in this theory, a scapegoat in any household may be symptomatic of the whole family's problem; she is in an inferior relation to the relatives who take care of her. Yet she is in a superior relation insofar as she can subvert their efforts; she's in charge. The therapist challenges that dysfunctional pattern to move the entire family toward a therapeutic change—to solve the presenting problem, to intervene so as to make the presenting problem unnecessary, and to issue a directive that will change the ways these persons relate to each other (Madanes and Haley, 1977).

Haley believes that power tactics must be exercised in confronting a resistant family. With his speciality as a trainer of trainers of family therapists, he has become widely known for his methods of issuing directives, framing paradoxes, and his bon mots. Believing that therapists have no choice but to exert power tactics with families, he teaches how to issue firm, strong directives. These directives may be direct orders, metaphorical and indirect nudges, or paradoxical imperatives. Paradoxes in therapy are ways of impelling the counselees to maintain their continuing behavior until they themselves reverse it. This is "prescribing the symptom," as in encouraging a family to keep their school-phobic child at home because "it would be too upsetting for the family's way of operation if the child began to act like other children."

Haley advises family therapists to invest themselves in full participation with families, and to stay clear from what he has dubbed the five Bs: being passive, being inactive, being reflective, being silent, being wary. It is obvious that he, himself, is none of these. With all this, and despite his leadership in the field, Haley manages not to take himself too seriously. Once asked to define a normal family, he simply replied that it is one in which no one has ever been in prison or in therapy.

Virginia Satir's best-known book, *Conjoint Family Therapy*, bears a title that also defines her method. As her writing and training films demonstrate, she works with couples and with whole families to increase their insight and to improve their communication. Her therapy zeros in on the counselees' need for self-esteem and for growth into emotional maturity. She has no use for the concepts of pathology and emotional illness.

She enjoys a reputation as a trainer of social workers, physicians, and therapists across the country. Once the program director at Esalen, in Big Sur, she has more recently roamed the world to present her popular workshops and seminars. Vivid language and metaphors stud her teaching. Perhaps the best-known is her classification of four troublesome communicators in troubled families. The *blamers*, are scolding, accusing, unpleasant people who feel superior only when they can make another feel inadequate. *Placaters* are the ever-pleasing martyrs who will give in to others in order to be accepted and loved. *Computers* are superlogical and frequently haughty people who attempt to out-think others and to demonstrate one-upmanship in their intellectual analyses. The *distracters* face few issues directly, change the subject if the issue looks as if it may become uncomfortable, and avoid every possible confrontation. Satir would contend that all these people suffer from low self-esteem and communication of poor quality.

Her method of therapy is to come into a family relationship like a concerned aunt. Through her warmth and understanding, she begins to move the family members into better communication among themselves, and into more penetrating insights into their own behavior. Skillful at modeling her message, she uses good communication herself. She translates their messages to each other, checks out meanings, persuades them to review their family history with one another, and encourages them to look and listen in new ways. One method is to "relabel" behaviors in more positive and usable terms. Thus a person accused of being glum may "be showing concern."

It is Satir's belief that warm, specific, straightforward questioning is therapeutic in itself. When she has taught the family something of her own skill, modeled and discussed in the therapy, she considers the treatment concluded. She once said, "I enter the therapeutic situation with the expectation that change is possible and with a clear delineated structure for encouraging change." Those who have watched her work or who have learned from her instruction have little reason to disagree. Of her, psychotherapist Robert Harper once wrote: "Her skill, wisdom, and clear thinking as a theoretician and her skill, wit and charm as a practitioner have set her firmly at the top of the family therapy field" (Harper, 1975, p. 3).

Salvador Minuchin, feisty and energetic in his therapy and teaching, has been called "the Pavarotti of the family therapists" in tribute to his impressive performances and stunning accomplishments. Able to work in front of more than six hundred people at once, he will frequently meet a family he has never seen before, delve precipitously into their problems, and bring them to new resolution within an hour's time.

Minuchin's contribution is known as "structural family therapy." It is aimed at helping the underorganized and dysfunctional family to restructure itself into better organization and more adequate coping. He challenges the family through a dialectical struggle; their old order must be undermined to allow for the formation of the new (Minuchin and Fishman, 1981).

Minuchin is known for his immediate interventions when he enters a family in distress. He operates like the director of a play, instructing people how to act, correcting their lines, and frequently changing the scenery by having them exchange their chairs and positions. With the activity-oriented, emotional families he has often worked with at Philadelphia Child Guidance Clinic, this approach has been effective. But he is also known for a speciality: working with adolescents who have "the starvation disease" of *anorexia nervosa.* The families of these fasting youngsters (far more often girls than boys) become the network through which healing can come.

Bold in his interventions, Minuchin sometimes operates by "escalating the stress," that is, increasing tension in the family until they will move therapeutically toward their problem. In therapy, Minuchin challenges his counselees, mimics their words and actions, and orders people around. He talks easily about himself and his own life and chats with them about theirs, meanwhile constantly "mapping" the family in order to make an evaluation about their dysfunction. In an adroit move he "joins" families so as to accommodate to their style and to their thinking. Being inside their patterns makes him the more able to meet some of their needs.

In his book *Families and Family Therapy* (1974, p. 90), Minuchin wrote of his therapeutic philosophy:

> Change is seen as occurring through the process of the therapist's affiliation with the family and his restructuring the family in a carefully planned way, so as to transform dysfunctional transactional patterns. . . . The family therapist regards himself as an acting and reacting member of a therapeutic system. In order to join the family, he emphasizes the aspects of his personality and experience that are syntonic with the family's. But he also retains the freedom to be spontaneous in his experimental probes.

Problem Orientation in Pastoral Ministry

Pastors have much to learn from the problem-oriented family therapists. The awareness these therapists bring to their practice makes them ever alert to the systems that operate in families, to relationships among family members, and to the means they use to communicate. To be systems-conscious is, for example, to be aware of the interactions in the Samson family—how when the father comes home intoxicated, his wife manipulates the situation and the children hide in terror.

Moreover, the pastor is acutely aware of the ways that people choose to communicate in their relationships. Communications that are affirming, communications that are damaging, communications that remain ambiguous—these are all too familiar in church life. Family therapists, who have found an avenue through the obstacles of communication to the clearer expressions of intention, point the way toward solving communications problems that arise between persons. Here the line between therapy and education is all but invisible. As in other aspects of psychotherapy, much is sheer teaching.

From the family therapists in this group we can learn to model clear communication. By delivering I-messages in our relationships, we can show the way for others to likewise express themselves without giving a secondary impression that the people being addressed are somehow less worthy. For a large number of people it takes an act of courage to present an I-message of candor, so the good example of a pastor can be an encouragement.

The pastor can also model active listening for counselees. This reflective technique demonstrates at once that the listener is patient, attentive, and understanding. To be able to put into words what the counselee is feeling, to aid in its expression, is the genius of active listening. When a woman complains that her husband has again let her down by overlooking their wedding anniversary, the response might be, "It's a real disappointment for you when he fails to celebrate with you; you probably felt deeply angry." Such a reflection offers an opportunity for the wife to agree with, expand, alter, or deny her statement. In any case, it opens the way to understanding and to exploration of relationships.

In addition, the pastor can note and emulate these problem-solving therapists in their frank use of power in relationships. Jay Haley assumes power at the outset and makes obvious that he is in charge. Salvador Minuchin uses his position vis-à-vis the family to direct them toward healthier relations, advising one to be silent and another to speak, rearranging the chairs to alter the alliances in the family, even expelling one or another person for a while. The pastor, appropriately adapting power tactics for the church, will be less aggressive than this, but can nonetheless maintain control of the family group sessions. Without some authority about times of meeting, who is to be present, and how the sessions should be structured, the effectiveness of the work will be limited.

The pastor can take a page from Virginia Satir's book and learn to relabel emotions and events to help people better understand each other. To help parents grasp that the tantrum may show a child who is afraid or that Grandpa's seeming obstinacy may be his way of protecting his energies at this developmental stage in his life could open the way to easier relationships within the family.

THE PSYCHODYNAMIC TRADITION

Family therapists in the psychodynamic tradition follow more closely the pattern of psychoanalytic orientation, and they are mostly Freudian. Most of them have accepted psychoanalytic theory about individuals and translate it into family practice. In the words of Charles Kramer, they try to "come to terms with the unconscious effects of unresolved conflicts by resolving their developmental vicissitudes" (Kramer, 1980, p. 139). By this he means that family problems are attributed to unsuitable behaviors that have arisen out of memories from counselees' past "object relations." If Sharon cannot abide her husband, unconsciously linking his inadequacy with conditioning from her own Super Dad, they're in for trouble.

The therapist in this tradition will maintain a therapeutic distance and utilize interpretation as a key to insight and the correction of such dysfunction. In common with Sigmund Freud, these therapists understand anxiety as traceable to the family of origin. For years, however, this school continued to treat individuals alone while discussing their family problems. Gradually, through marital counseling and through group therapy, the practice of conjoint therapy became more respectable among the psychoanalytically oriented practitioners. They, too, now see marital pairs or families together.

Nathan Ackerman was the earliest and the best known of the psychoanalysts to break away from orthodox Freudian practice and begin working with families, and for his break he was criticized by some of his colleagues. Yet his vision of bridging the tension between the old practice of psychoanalysis and the new emphasis on family groups came to influence a number of contributors to the field, among them Charles Kramer, James Framo, Salvador Minuchin, and Donald A. Bloch.

Ackerman, founder of what is now known in his memory as the Ackerman Family Institute, managed to hold two forces in tension: his accustomed intrapersonal bias, in which he had been trained, and his newer convictions that accounted for personality change from the interactions of people. He is known now as the grandfather of the family therapy movement.

His pioneering work advanced the movement at the cost of his own struggles. As one who began to understand and theorize about family systems, Ackerman met stiff opposition from colleagues who were more conventionally tied to psychoanalytic practice with individuals. Yet his clear conceptualization and his readiness to speak and write about his growing conviction that the action is *Treating the Troubled Family,* as he expressed it in his 1966 title, won numerous converts to his way of thinking and not a few imitators as well.

It was his method to treat the disturbed person within the family context. Always the clinician first and then a theoretician, he plunged immediately into diagnosing the pathology in a person or persons' problems. He was informal in his approach, having long since shed his habits of sitting with notebook in hand at the head of a patient's couch. He was willing to make home visits and interested to learn how his patients lived in the midst of family conditions.

Ackerman saw his work as the re-education of families and the opportunity to teach them a new way of living. He strove to help them reorganize their sick patterns and to turn to healthier methods of living. For him the resolution of pathological conflict was a major goal. But he did not claim too much for such cures. He agreed with Freud that the patient who completes psychoanalysis may be wise, but is also sadder and lonelier.

Like Don Jackson, the pioneer of communications theory, Ackerman learned that the psychoanalytic method did not fit neatly into the family network. In fact, a family sometimes subverted the therapy accomplished with one of its members. The way out of that quagmire was to work with the entire family. To that solution both of these early family therapists turned. It may be fairly put that because they did, thousands of others now have done the same.

Helm Stierlin, a contemporary therapist from the psychodynamic group, practices for the most part in his native Germany, although he has spent some years in the United States, training with Lyman C. Wynne and working in family therapy. To his Freudian orientation he brings fresh insight and a dialectical theory straight from the writings of Hegel. His thinking is close to that of Ivan Boszormenyi-Nagy, with whom he shares not only common concepts but also a long working acquaintance.

Stierlin's system grows out of five main perspectives that partake of both his psychoanalytic background and a family system theory. First, he works with patients toward what he calls "related individuation," a goal in which each member of the family can speak for him- or herself in unambiguous communication and with a sense of personal responsibility. Second, he aims to loosen the bindings that are too tight in a family network, or to facilitate a better binding where there is none. (These two evils he entitles "the transactional modes of binding and expelling.") Third, he aims to help people come to terms with their "delegation" by which they seek to fulfill parents' assignments and missions, a bind into which perfectionistic persons often tumble. Fourth, he seeks to aid people in understanding and redefining their "legacies" (i.e., a set of obligations forwarded by the family, such as the duty to carry on the family business). These are much the same as Boszormenyi-Nagy's "invisible loyalties" (Boszormenyi-Nagy, 1973). Fifth, he aids families to work through their "state of mutuality," a stalemate of relationships that may leave them almost immobilized. Sometimes he will use a tape recorder to play back to family members the record of their own talk to help them hear their own strange ways of relating to one another when they have come into such a clinch.

Stierlin's *First Interview* (1980) is a systematic layout of his theory and practice of family therapy. In it he makes several characteristic comments about the parallels of intrafamily strife and that of nations. Having noticed how the conflicts within Adolph Hitler's family of origin may have misguided him in adulthood, he also writes of the "conduct and results of . . . arms races and power struggles in marital and family relationships" (Stierlin, 1980, p. 29).

Psychodynamic Theory in Pastoral Ministry

When the Rev. Elisabeth Martin visited the home of her parishioners Sam and Sally Omer, she was wary. She knew something of their ongoing tension, having witnessed it at the church. Sam recently had been testy in committee sessions, angry out of all proportion to the issue being discussed. And Sally's unusually devoted attention to her Sam, coupled with her exaggerated dependence on him, added up to a situation that awakened concern.

The pastor's home visit alerted her to yet more of this family's tense relationships. Sally, although almost subservient to her husband in order to placate him, dominated the movements and words of her children to a high degree. Her apparent need to be needed by them led to constant interference with their behavior and their speech: "Sit up in your chair like a lady," "Don't interrupt when your father is talking," etc. The children, meanwhile, registered their resentment of this heavy-handed correction by acting out some of their feelings—hitting each other, glaring at their mother, and pulling tufts of wool out of the carpet.

The power of anxiety operates through such personality conflict to influence human behavior to an extent that interpersonal relationships, especially the more intimate, are profoundly affected. Thus insecure persons, psychodynamic theory contends, exhibit widespread dependency patterns. They make large demands of others; they lean heavily into their "object relations."

The pastor, who carried a tape deck and training casettes in her automobile, excused herself to bring the cassette equipment into the house. Without asking the family's blessing, she hooked up the recording equipment, simply noting, "We may want to save some of this conversation for ourselves." For a short while the family self-consciously watched the turning spool, but then everyone accepted the machine and became unmindful of it. The family reverted to type, arguing again, wheedling, scolding, and competing with one another.

Then the pastor rewound the cassette tape and replayed the family's words. The effect, no surprise to those who have experienced it, astonished Sam, Sally, and their children. They simply did not realize how they sounded. Sally heard her own whining, scolding voice and was reminded at once of the way her own mother had sounded. Appalled by that memory and the growing realization that she was repeating patterns she had detested in her girlhood, she sat silently for the remainder of the short visit as Sam and the children talked more calmly with Pastor Martin. In conclusion, the pastor made a few brief comments about the need for all families to tolerate each other's differentness and departed.

The next morning Sally telephoned her pastor to ask about the possibility of working out some of her feelings and problems of low self-esteem. In time, the entire family began to work on their problems of bickering, misunderstanding, and deficiencies of ego strength.

The psychodynamic therapists' development of ego strength in patients and their guidance toward decision making both have elements of value that pastors can use. To this school of therapy, which represents the oldest continuing tradition of such work, ministers owe much. From them we have learned something about our conduct of ministerial therapy, and we can adapt those techniques that are transferable to the church.

THE INTERGENERATIONAL THEORISTS

That there is some notable overlap in the work of the different schools of family therapists is obvious. It is therefore hardly astonishing to learn that the intergenerational group, as I classify them, have a profound conviction in common with a number of other schools, namely that both family dysfunction and family therapy emerge in part from the same source: the family of origin. Once again we can hear in the background the adage of the therapists: "By the family you were broken; by the family you will be healed." The selection of two masters from this group will exemplify how the intergenerational understanding is brought to bear on cases.

Carl Whitaker, a senior professor of psychiatry at the University of Wisconsin Medical School, operates within an existential framework; but he has gained a reputation for what is sometimes known as "therapy of the absurd." In his self-styled craziness, Whitaker has long since learned that he can use himself in unconventional ways to bring out healthy responses from unhealthy families.

Whitaker and his cotherapists (he habitually works in a team) assemble the largest system of family members they can find for the opening sessions of therapy. Only gradually do they begin to eliminate those who are peripheral to the problem and retain those who are central to it.

They deal with the entire system because they have less concern with its individual components. They will even bring in lodgers and friends of the family to complete the outreach with which this home is linked. Whitaker is known to be so adamant about some of these large family gatherings in therapy that he may tell an applicant patient to bring the entire family or not to come at all; that he will dismiss the family with no interview when they show up for a session with someone missing, and yet charge them for it; or that he will demand that divorcees invite back their ex-mates in order to complete a family group in its former constellation during several sessions of therapy.

Whitaker makes a point of disregarding theory in his therapy. With the same tongue in cheek that he exercises in other subjects, he purports to care nothing for theoretical aspects of therapy and to disregard basic principles. His, he insists, is a therapy aimed at results.

Being as autocratic as this, Whitaker sees therapy as a contest in which the therapist versus the family is "system against system." Unless the therapists get control of the process at the outset, the family will call the shots, and nothing therapeutic will occur. He comes into cases like a burly grandfather, lovable and gruff. His antics are reknowned. He will play with children, wrestle with boys, listen to the stereo player during interviews, or take over as the scapegoat of a family in order to give their own picked-upon member a rest. (See Napier and Whitaker, 1978.)

Long ago in his professional life, Whitaker learned to speak "schizophrenese"; he can talk crazy, he says, with crazy people. On one occasion when a family arrived with a young son who was schizophrenic, he challenged the youth, who replied, "Contac is good for colds." Whitaker responded with, "You find this meeting to be a cold experience." The youth said, "Yes"; and they were at once into their therapy.

Whitaker will promote the despair in a family in order to move them off the place where they are stuck. He sometimes helps them to get worse in order to help them get better. He has been known to tease a woman who had attempted suicide by telling her that, instead of banks of flowers and weeping mourners, her funeral might have been a modest affair, sparsely attended, and that her husband might have immediately turned his attention to finding her "replacement."

Whitaker's lack of convention extends to the sacred cows in therapy, for which he has a fine disregard: he argues against theory, gathers a family history in piecemeal style, and makes a show of being seemingly indifferent to the issues that concern his patients.

One can believe him when he testifies, "I love every minute of my work and that is what I am interested in. I am interested in staying alive." Whitaker's sometimes zany behavior may not be our best example; but his sly wisdom may inspire wisdom in us.

Murray Bowen, also an intergenerational theorist and the author of *The Bowen Theory,* is by contrast a man most serious. He is so convinced that the family of origin is the key to family therapy that he sends alienated husbands and wives back to work out problems with their own parents and siblings. He maintains also that the training of family therapists hinges on their taking a "voyage home" to their families to work through remaining disturbances of relationship.

Bowen is known for his advocacy of the *genogram,* a pictorial device adapted for taking the family history. Through its use and that of a series of related questions, therapy is advanced; the disparate threads of family connection can be untangled and evaluated. But the cornerstone of his theory pertains to the differentiation of oneself, the most frequent outcome of a voyage home. People who had been fused or stuck together with the old family begin to grow up and also to allow their families to become sufficiently disengaged to be individuals and to stand on their own feet.

In his therapy, Bowen searches out the triangles of family relationships, the father-mother-scapegoated child, or the husband-wife-lover, or perhaps the husband-wife-bourbon bottle. His aim is to break down the triangular conflicts into more manageable two-person dialogues. In this he looks into the "nuclear family emotional system," and how it repeats the interplay of elements from previous generations. The time may well have come to intervene and head off the inheritance of family problems out of the past.

Meanwhile, Bowen would be concerned with the "family projection process," an insidious habit of dumping frustration and blame on one scapegoated family member. He believes that people who have been crippled by this process are less able to cope with independent living and have less chance at differentiation for themselves apart from family enmeshment. Their opposites are the persons who have experienced "emotional cutoff," the disowned and the disowning, the isolates, and the runaways. The person who cuts off the family of origin can be as dependent as the person who never leaves home. They both need help.

"The multigenerational transmission process" hands on family traditions, values, and problems alike to the younger generations. The abused child may become a child abuser one short generation later. We all tend to some degree to repeat somehow the treatment that we ourselves received. In teaching people to restudy their family history, Bowen and his associates aid them toward self-understanding and differentiation of self.

Few leaders have exerted as heavy an influence on family therapists in recent years as Murray Bowen. Because of his intricate theory, which we have but sampled here, his writing in *Family Therapy and Clinical Practice,* and his own heralded practice, he has made a noticeable impact on family studies. Continuing research will aid in evaluating some of his theoretical teachings, a number of which have relevance for the pastorate.

Intergenerational Theory in Pastoral Ministry

Pastor Fox was in his study when the telephone call from Martha Peters came. Her marital problems were no secret; the entire community had some knowledge of them. But never before she had asked for help. This time Michael, her husband, had gone too far even for long-suffering Martha. Always hard on the children, he had become especially punitive with young Mike in recent months.

The events that led to the telephone call had begun when Mike left his tricycle standing in the rain. His father, with an anger that Martha sensed was out of proportion to the circumstances, had given Mike a harsh spanking followed by a denouncement that left the boy shaken and deflated. Told that he was irresponsible and obstinate, he had been subjected to what Martha was calling verbal child abuse. "Why, the way Michael talked to his son was more damaging than the physical punishment itself," she exclaimed.

It was not difficult to get Michael to discuss the problem. He himself was appalled by what he had done to his relationship with his son. Over coffee at a local café, Pastor Fox and Michael had their first of several meetings. Michael poured out his grief over the strife in his marriage and the alienation he felt from his children. He was all the more puzzled by these problems when he recalled how his own father, a tough disciplinarian, had been much respected by sons and daughters for his toughness and strength. Pastor Fox said nothing; he only looked down into his nearly empty coffee cup and suggested that they pick up this conversation another day.

When next they returned to their discussion, the pastor asked Michael to tell more about the disciplinary techniques and strong methods of his father. As the story unfolded, Fox asked a few quiet questions, requested some clarification, even repeated some questions when the answers seemed incomplete. After awhile Michael lowered his defenses enough to alter his memories a bit, to admit that mingled with his respect for his father was resentment. It was not long thereafter that he openly admitted having never allowed himself to speak out about his anger at his harsh father.

Pastor Fox pondered how to work with this new material, as well as with the increasing realization that Michael's roughness with his son had been justified upon the rather shaky principle that this was the method of the previous generation. When they next met, the pastor inquired into the current relationship between Michael and his old father. It was no surprise that they had a tenuous contact and infrequent, uneasy meetings.

The pastor then moved toward a suggestion. Michael might go back home and visit his own father, talk with him about the family, share with him stories about life and work and problems. Michael seemed to want to try. On that first visit, father and son visited Uncle Jeb's grave at the family plot and they came away a bit easier with each other.

Pastor Fox commended Michael on this progress and coached him toward a second visit, this time a "drop-in" (eighty miles away) for a long talk over dinner in a nearby restaurant they both liked. There the two of them drew close enough together that they planned a family reunion for the clan the following summer. When they parted, they clasped each other in a brief hug.

After the third voyage home, Michael said to the pastor, "I can't say exactly what the connection is. But now that I'm better friends with my father, things are going better at home with Martha and the kids." Young Mike still annoyed his father; and they had their arguments. But now when the boy was touched by his father it was more often in affection than in punishment. Both generations were on the way to a renewed appreciation of their family ties.

Intergenerational therapists help to make us aware also of the whole network of relationships that make up what is known as a family. Too long prejudiced by a nuclear model, we have been slow to recognize the profound impact that comes from the more remote generations. And in this era of impressive longevity, we are becoming accustomed not only to four-generation families, but even now to five-generation families with living great-great-grandparents. Although one can justifiably worry about a room so full of family members as that vision conjures up, a Carl Whitaker and his cotherapist might gleefully invite all that tribe into a therapy session.

At the very least, we in ministry need to take into serious consideration the "ghosts" of a family's past and the influence of forebears upon a family in treatment. To draw a genogram of the family and its connections, as described in Chapter 6, to reach into the past through the family of origin, is to open a host of questions and possible realizations that may be unavailable through other means. There are different ways for a person or a family to take a "voyage home" as Murray Bowen prescribes it. The search into past relations and their present meaning can involve visits to the homestead, a content analysis of the photograph album, the writing of a family autobiography, or even inviting the grandparents into the therapy sessions for one or two occasions. (The astonishing outcome of such an invitation is that the grandparents are often eager to join, the counselees themselves being the hesitant ones.)

BEHAVIOR THERAPY

The behavioral therapist is convinced that every bit of family behavior is learned. Behaviors in the home become reinforced through a complex, often unnoticed network of encouragements and discouragements over the years. When a family at last applies for family therapy to relieve its problems, the patterns of relationships are so cemented in habit that it will require an entirely new learning process to shape the new behaviors required for daily life and transactions.

The behavioral school teaches that misbehavior is also learned. *Robert Paul Liberman,* research professor of psychiatry at the UCLA School of Medicine, has long been a leader in this approach to family therapy. He traces how misbehavior is unintentionally rewarded by family responses. Even punishment may appear to the deviant family member as positive concern and interest, he contends. The message that is transmitted seems to say, "You will get our special attention as long as you continue to misbehave."

Of course, the vast majority of parents do not believe that they actually want their children to misbehave. Yet when the therapist observes what they do with their children, they cannot avoid the conclusion that misbehavior is, in fact, what they are encouraging. In therapy, then, it will be the parents and not the professional, who are "the key agents" of behavior change in the family (Patterson, 1961, p. 10).

Therefore the behavioral therapist attempts to teach the family to award one another recognition and encouragement for more approved behaviors. Gradually, instead of showing worry and frightened concern at undesirable behavior in some identified patient, the family members will switch over to approval for positive behaviors.

Behavioral therapists consider themselves to be educators, and their philosophical foundation is in learning theory. Their basic assumption is that deviant behavior is subject to the same laws of learning that govern all human behavior. Thus the procedures that are useful in changing any type of behavior are also applied to modifying deviancy. The therapist's goal is to alter those events through which the deviant gets satisfaction via the attention of others. Thus if a child who bumps her head on the floor brings cries of panic from both parents, it will be necessary to change those drives that give rise to all this tumult. That, at least, would be necessary if the goal for the behaviorist is to eliminate the head bumping activity. Elimination of such undesirable behavior, indeed, is a typical goal in this therapy.

Behavior therapy utilizes a variety of methods in treatment. Most common among these are desensitization, implosion, modeling, aversion, and operant conditioning.

Desensitization—the best known of these modalities—is a graded approach. To ease fears and worries, the behavioral therapist proceeds from one item to the next higher until the fear or worry is eliminated. Gradually, relaxation responses are substituted for those of anxiety in this graded approach. If a child is terrified of animals, the therapist might alleviate the fear by offering first a cuddly terry cloth teddy bear, then a larger toy animal, then a small live animal, and so forth until the child responds positively to animals.

Implosion works quite contrary to desensitization. In this modality, the counselee is asked to imagine the feared object or experience (e.g., sexual intercourse in marriage) in its most anxiety-producing way. The objective is to build up to an implosion, a rapid arrival at overwhelming anxiety, and then a sudden deceleration of it. Implosive therapy, at its simplest, offers the anxiety ridden person a vision of the worst possible case so as to move away to a safer and tolerable position. When we have faced the worst, we can be confronted with the more realistic, but less extreme, conditions that are more likely to confront us.

Modeling is a treatment principle "based on observing other people's behavior and its consequences" (Harper, 1975, p. 115). Through observational learning, the person catches on to new and better ways of behavior that are more satisfying. Such observational learning can be programmed by the behavioral therapist in psychodrama, in which a family enacts various scenarios that apply to their relationships—but in the safe confines of the therapist's office. Sculpting—the construction of family attitudes and incidents in bodily positions—is another method. Perhaps the most common method of all is also the most subtle: provision of a demonstration of how to behave by a less troubled person—that is, the therapist. Through guided performance and positive reinforcement (encouragement), counselees in behavior therapy can learn and practice new behaviors under conditions close to those they experience in "the real world."

Aversive therapy is of quite different nature. It involves negative reinforcement (a behavioristic term for punishment). The reverse of desensitization with its gentle movement into new and improved states, aversive therapy can be sudden and startling. Punishing stimuli may be chosen among chemical or electrical stimuli as well as the more innocuous punishments of restraints, removal of privileges, or discouragement of certain acts. Aversive therapy is used for recalcitrant cases of drug abuse and in sexual anomalies.

Operant conditioning stems from the significant work of B. F. Skinner, the outstanding living authority on behaviorism. In this modality, the behavioral therapist will reinforce certain spontaneous actions of the counselee. The therapist waits for the action, and only after it occurs is the person rewarded. This method has been used by parents and teachers for centuries, but in less sophisticated ways. When one learns what significant others like to reward, that person modifies behaviors or speech to bring such reward. In the give-and-take of marriage relationships, operant conditioning can be a powerful motivation; and it is used in marital counseling a good deal. Sometimes labeled "shaping," this work is designed to gradually extinguish the undesirable behavior and to increase the desired behavior by means of a variety of reinforcements such as rewards, approval, commendation, punishments, disapproval, and the like. After a time, the changes that take place can be toted up and progress can be measured. Gradually, the number of therapeutic interviews can be reduced and the time lengthened between them until they are discontinued altogether.

Techniques in behavioral therapy are based on the bald assumption that whenever behavior, whether desirable or undesirable, is followed by a rewarding consequence, the possibility is increased that such behavior is going to be repeated. Behaviors are strengthened when they are reinforced. The husband who voices his appreciation for the spice cake his wife has baked is likely to discover spice cake again for dessert. Such selective reinforcement (via compliments, warmth and affection, or thanks) comprises an important learning device in behavioral psychology and in day-to-day living. "The most available, useful, and important consequences are those such as praise, touch, attention, and smiles. These are simple things. They occur hundreds of times each day" (Patterson, 1971).

Within the five therapeutic types discussed above, a variety of techniques can be brought to bear by the behavioral therapist. A few typical examples will illustrate ways such therapists work to modify behavior.

1. *Keeping records.* To be consistent in reinforcing some behaviors and ignoring or punishing others, it is necessary to collect and record all observations. " 'Just making up your mind' is not sufficient for most parents, particularly when they are first learning" (Patterson, 1971, p. 29).

Nothing is more characteristic of behavior modification than the quantification of behaviors. The therapist, working with a fighting couple, may require them to keep a record of how many shouting matches and arguments ensue each day and week. In habit correction, such as smoking or overeating, the count might require a total of the number of cigarettes smoked per day or a running account of one's daily weight.

2. *Progressive relaxation.* One of the simplest techniques utilized in behavior modification, progressive relaxation is of aid to tensed-up people. It involves breathing exercises accompanied by the suggestion of pleasing images (spoken by another person in a soothing voice), to influence a new state of calm. Family problems may stem from nothing more than the "high strung" attitude of a nervous individual. That attitude could be the result of conditions that are not easily touched by relaxation therapy; but in a large number of cases this technique, and others related to it, are effective.

3. *Easy achievement.* One way of encouraging depressed or unaccomplished people is to offer them achievable assignments that they cannot fail. To set tasks beneath the person's ability will not only build confidence, but will create a climate of counter injunction as the person soon comes to want to do more than is being asked (Kovel, 1976, p. 213).

4. *Contracts.* Contractual agreements have come into wider use among family therapists in recent years, and not only in behavior therapy. The *quid pro quo* arrangement of a battling husband and wife may begin to bring some sanity into ther relationships. For her to agree to his weekly night of bowling in return for another night when he will take her out on a date can make all the difference between a state of war and a reign of peace in their home. Contracts require mutual agreement, fair conditions, and a built-in understanding that alterations can be made.

5. *Time out.* Time out from reinforcement will make a difference in how we behave. A young child can be removed from an environment that reinforces poor behavior to one that allows no such reinforcement at all. A couple can take a weekend away from

familiar and tension-producing situations and have "a second honeymoon" in new pleasure. Time out of the usual reinforcement can speed up behavioral change. Perhaps the simplest form of taking time out of reinforcement of unwanted behavior is to ignore it, a practice that has been used on children by canny adults for many generations.

6. *Kind firmness.* The calm, even pleasant insistence that tasks be accomplished regardless of complaining, or that agreements be fulfilled despite resentment, is a powerful technique. It has the virtue of offering an alternative model of behaving in time of stress, and yet keeping the original principle or standard intact and without compromise. (It may be somewhat more effective with the discipline of children than in negotiating with a mate; but it has application in both areas.)

Behavior Therapy in Pastoral Ministry

When the mid-marriage crisis hit Dave and Del Daniels, the rector soon heard about it, as did the entire congregation. Del saw to that. It was her complaint, in fact, that brought them to see Father Deer soon after the forgotten birthday.

It had been Del's forty-fourth, a number about which she was not very happy to begin with. Dave had made no mention of the date as it approached, and Del began to hope he must have a surprise planned for her. That afternoon she carefully dressed for dinner out and a night on the town, in case that was to be the surprise. When six o'clock passed and Dave had still not arrived, she began to fret. At six-thirty, he did telephone, but it was to say he had just returned to the office after a quick sandwich at a fast food restaurant, that he had to work late to revise an office manual due for committee review the following day.

Del, now agitated and disappointed, exploded in tearful rage. Denouncing Dave with loud indignation, she called him selfish and hateful and declared their marriage a mistake. Although Dave, now unable to complete the manual, hurried home, there was no peace to be had at the Daniels' house that night.

The next morning Del was in Father Deer's study. Her question was couched in traditional terms: "Can this marriage be saved?" Careful questions about the problem elicited the information that as the years had advanced, Dave had become more immersed in his career and less interested in romance. The gradual deterioration of their marriage relationship, and their growing failure to communicate, had already brought Dave and Del to partial separation in terms of activities and emotional attachment.

Faced with this challenge of broken relationship and decreasing companionship, the rector invited Dave, contrite and unresisting, to attend appointments too. Father Deer first went to work on helping the couple rebuild romance in their marriage. To sensitize them to their situation, he assigned them the task of keeping a tally of the number of minutes they were together ("*really* together") when awake each day. Later he moved them onto a count of doing *anything* together: chores, chats, trips, or dates.

When they had become somewhat more aware of the pattern of infrequency in their companionship, and the slippage of their relationship, the rector discussed with them the possibility of a contract for their interchange of contacts. They were ready now for such a step: Dave agreed to forego some of his business activity to help their marriage, while Del volunteered to accompany him to the company parties she had loathed and long boycotted. They themselves suggested that a time be set aside each evening for meaningful talk. In time they learned that, alienated and hurt though they had been, they cared for each other. They still had a way to go in rebuilding their neglected relationship, yet the rector's canny use of sensitization about their behavior patterns and movement toward ready goals led them from self-centered wandering to a growing toward each other again.

FAMILY THERAPISTS AND THE MINISTRY

The four groups of family therapists heretofore described are not discrete entities, but have considerable philosophy and practice in common. Nonetheless, each has a distinctive emphasis; and from this we, in the ministry, can learn.

One cord that ties all four together is their common reliance on the educational method. Thus, from the problem-oriented school, we learn not only that clear communication is a mighty aid to improved relationships, but also that communication skills can be taught. From the psychodynamic group we can take a lesson about "related individuation" and realize that people can learn both to be themselves and to have meaningful relationships without conflict. The intergenerational therapists enable us to see how the wider context of family relations, including grandparents and ancestors, plays a large part; and that troubled people can be tutored in better understanding their families of origin. Finally, the behavioral therapists' emphasis on encouraging new acts and contacts of counselees enables us also to appreciate better ways of working with people. As clergy, we can indeed derive from the family therapists valuable methods to adapt in ministry.

4. Interviews and Interventions

In responding to human pain we risk what is known for what is yet to be known. We give up safety for searching. We lose life for the sake of life. If we are to respond, then we must risk that risk.
—JAMES B. ASHBROOK, *Responding to Human Pain*

THE PROCESS OF INTERVIEWING

Interviewing (literally, "seeing between") is the major tool in the therapist's kit. Although it has many forms and uncounted variations, a therapeutic interview invariably involves a therapist who guides counselees through a conversation concerning their problems. From that point on, it can cover a spectrum of types —from the "talking cure" of psychoanalysis to primal scream therapy.

Any interview begins with an initial signal for aid from counselees. Frequently, this is a request made through a telephone call; and the way we answer this cry for help sets off the quality of the relationship that follows. Even in that limited opportunity we can accomplish four significant objectives. We can show enough interest to communicate some hope to the caller. We can arrange a definite time to see the counselee soon, always an encouraging lift to one in distress. We can elicit enough of the affect of the caller to catch just a little information about the seriousness of the problem. And we can, even at this early date, suggest one specific task (e.g., take a walk away from the house, avoid all arguments about the issue until the appointment, or sit down and write a list of the issues to be discussed).

When the counselees come to the church study, we do not simply hear family relations described; we also witness how the family interacts. (Even if the interchange takes place in the supermarket, we can be observant.) We watch how the couple or the family enter the office, listen to how they address each other, see how they look at one another, and note who speaks first and who habitually answers, notice with what confidence or lack of confidence they walk, whether they choose chairs in a pattern of relating to or distancing from certain others, and so on. We seldom have to reconstruct a full description of their quarrels; if quarreling has been their habit, they will in time stage a quarrel right in the counseling office. Nonverbal gestures and body language will tell much about their regard for each other; it is not necessary for us to ask a plethora of questions about their ways of relating. Their concerns and attitudes of love, of fear, of hate, of worry, and a host of other emotions will come through in one short hour of intensive work. However, if the therapist wishes to delve more deeply into some of these relational emotions, it is feasible to do so by means of a variety of techniques such as role playing, sculpting, empty chair work, communication games, and the like.

As therapists, we should not only watch and listen as if we are objective spectators. We should always be what Harry Stack Sullivan (1954) dubbed *participant observers.* In family therapy we also act and intervene, intrude to facilitate change, tell one to be silent awhile and invite another to speak, direct someone to remain outside the interview, invite another in, set a new appointment, and define how many are to come to it. The point is obvious: family therapists are active in their interventions. Far from the tradition of nondirective counseling (which does have a rightful place in certain cases), the bulk of family therapy calls for a therapist who is more than a listener, more than an observer, and surely more than a reflector. The therapist actively enters the family system in order to enable the family to make changes more efficiently. Like an honorary relative, the therapist joins the system and plays a purposeful part in negotiations for a better adjustment.

THE FIRST INTERVIEW

From the outset it is possible, and it is important, to convey a sense of interest and of encouragement through willingness to be of help. Few counselees ask for aid until they have tried all the ways they can think of to solve their problems, and have failed. Typically, they first attempt to meet their own needs privately. Failing that, they turn to friends, then to us clergy, and finally to psychotherapy or hospitalization. By the time they reach that third step of consulting us, they may be quite despairing, even depressed. They want to know that there is some hope for them. They may not be asking for assurance that we can remedy their difficulties; and we ought not to promise that. But we can hold out an offer to be with them, to listen understandingly, and to be supportive in their time of trouble.

The conduct of an initial interview will differ according to whether we are meeting with a couple or with an entire family.

With a husband and wife in marital therapy it is highly desirable, if at all feasible, to urge them both to be present from the outset. It is not impossible to work with one person alone to change a marriage; but it demands more skill than most pastors have, and the results are less effective. In some cases, only one partner appears willing to come to the opening interview (in our culture, more often the wife than the husband); and the therapist will need to persuade that one to bring the spouse to the very next interview. In the event only the wife is present, she may demur that her husband refuses to come to marital sessions. But her hesitation may be traceable to fear, to misjudging his willingness, or even to a desire to exclude him. In these circumstances, I offer to telephone or write him an invitation to the next session. Such a message makes three succinct points: (1) that his wife has sought me out to discuss a marriage problem; (2) that she has given me her perception of the marriage and its difficulties; and (3) that I need also to know how he views these difficulties. In nearly every case, the husband is on hand at the following meeting in order to present his view. Note that the language here is about how he *views* his marriage, as if we are looking at a picture rather than about hearing his "side" of a competition. There is already enough side-taking and adversary spirit in their relationship without hearing the therapist's language confirm such feelings.

When both spouses do arrive together, however, therapy begins with their very greeting. The experienced pastor would note their attitude and demeanor through their tone of voices, their facial expression, the firmness of their step, the erectness of their carriage, and the strength of their handshake. These will give off cues as to the depth of their depression or their resiliency. These observations guide the therapist in how to respond to their felt needs. This, certainly, is no appropriate time for the ministerial heartiness of which we see so much. This is a time for quiet calm and a cheerful but subdued greeting.

My own pattern is to begin with some identification to their feelings of pain and awkwardness at having to come for aid in their marriage. The simple observation that this must have been a hard decision for them will suffice to open. If this is our first encounter under such conditions, I go on to ask if they have previously been in any kind of therapy. From this I will learn whether the current crisis is one step in a long series of crises for which they have sought help, or whether it is something more recent. In either case, I go on to tell them very briefly how I work with a couple and what they can expect in the hour and a half ahead. (In common with other marriage and family therapists, I find that the first interview is apt to take longer than those that follow.) I describe my methods, something of my philosophy, attempt to communicate a bit of hope again ("We'll sort out the issues together here, and try realistically to see what they mean"), and promise a tentative evaluation at the close of the interview.

These preliminaries past, I move them toward description of their presenting problem: "No one ever phones me the first time they become troubled about their marriage. It usually takes a special jolt. Tell me what had happened before you picked up the telephone to call me." This will uncover a first, perhaps superficial description of some conflict. Although it may not be the underlying relational difficulty, it will need attention; and it must be dealt with sometime during this first session. Positive attention to the opening complaint can open the way to working in depth.

Next, I query them very briefly about their family history. If I do not already know anything about their past, I'll ask about how and where they met, how long they had known each other before marriage, whether their families had approved of this marriage, how long they have been married, what children they have, their ages, their condition of health, and any other particulars they believe I ought to know. This is not an exhaustive inquiry. Many other facts about their background, their employment record, and their families of origin will unfold as our conversation continues; and I tell them this. In the main, it is profitable to learn from them those details that they feel are worth knowing and volunteering. They themselves will fill in many of the gaps.

From past history we move into current history. "What," I ask them, "is going on in your marriage right now?" By this I mean not just their general relationship during recent weeks, but the present moment in this very interview. My purpose is to update our collective information about emotions and expectations, and to open their awareness as well as my own to the interactions they experience at home and in this new system of couple and therapist. This brings on a full discussion that has to be arrested at some summary point with an assurance: "We'll want to come back to this topic for another go at it. For now, I'd like to turn our attention to a different question."

Then, because I need to learn what methods they have used to attack their problem and want them to be aware of their patterns too, I say, "No couple ever comes to see me about their marriage until they have tried a number of remedies of their own. I wonder how you have tried to work on your problems." Sometimes they are stymied by this query, being unaware of the turnings and defenses they have constructed in their conflict. Sometimes they are reluctant to talk about the ways they have dealt with their situation; for they may have turned to physical coercion, to drugs, or to mate-swapping rather than to advice or reading. It is useful to probe with easy leads: "Some people in such a hassle thrash around for any number of methods to handle their stress—jogging, drugs, alcohol, spending sprees, prayer—what's yours?" Bit by bit they will recall and admit to their mechanisms of defense, a minor exercise in catharsis and a valuable stage in self-understanding. It also assists a therapist to learn what measures the couple has tried and found wanting. These can be augmented or discarded now.

Rather soon thereafter I move the interview into individual sessions, dismissing one spouse to an outer office or some other room, and then asking them to change places in order to see the second spouse also alone. These private sessions, I explain, are to give each person a chance to speak of concerns that are difficult for them to discuss in front of each other. Sometimes they need the privacy to express anger and resentment they fear will bring an eruption in the three-person session. Sometimes they bear a secret they are not yet ready to divulge to a partner. Sometimes they simply need a period of personal attention without the tension that they feel in the presence of the other. I may agree to keep confidences that they entrust in me at this time, at least until they can be readied to level more courageously with each other. Not a few therapists, whose opinions I respect, decline to hold any confidentiality in family therapy, contending that this practice obstructs the process of trust and openness. My own position is that couples must be given opportunity to work out their feelings about secrets and their plans of how to divulge these without confrontive pressure. It is in this setting that someone may admit to a clandestine extramarital affair and begin the painful process of squarely facing its incongruity in the marriage.

After these two necessarily brief sessions in private, I bring the couple together again for a closing session. It consists of summary, evaluation, and an assigned task. All the while during the interview, I will have been pegging points of the process that will be itemized in the summary. But this is a group project, not mine alone. Together we sum up what has happened in our time together. Invariably, they will recall items or see significance in details I would not have cited. From this summation I pull together a tentative evaluation, and ask for their participation. It touches on our perceived seriousness of the conflict, the chances and methods for its correction, the arrangements for further sessions, if needed, and some word of hope, if at all feasible.

Last of all, I leave them with some task to fulfill and to report in the next week or fortnight. This could be a communication exercise, a dinner date, a record to keep, or any of a number of constructive assignments construed to compel them to work on their problem. Then I take their hands or touch them on the shoulder, bid them goodbye, and usher them to the door.

A first interview with a family group is necessarily different. Parents and children coming together present a mixture of greater complexity. Yet it resembles the configurations with whom a pastor is accustomed to working in situations of wedding rehearsals, baptism arrangements, board meetings, or funeral plans—circumstances in which it is necessary to keep contact with a number of people simultaneously. Alertness to responses, careful listening, and prayerful preplanning will pay off here.

Again, it is of value to note how they enter the room and how they conduct themselves. If you give them no instructions about where to sit, you can observe who chooses to be close to whom, who is practicing some avoidance, who is uncertain, who is aggressive. Initial behaviors will tell you much that mere questioning would take a long time to reveal. Keys to their family system will soon be shown by who talks to whom and how, whose remarks habitually follow someone else's, which person corrects the reports of others, those who comply and those who disagree.

It is productive, I have learned, to open the family session with a round report on the problem that brought them in. To this collective report, everyone, no matter how young or old, is invited to contribute. "Tell me, won't you, how you see the problem your family is having," is an easy way to begin. I ask this of someone who is likely to be a bit reticent in response (an adolescent, if present). Insofar as possible, I try not to pose this question first to the most articulate (who could drown out all the others in a sweeping report), nor to the identified patient (thereby seeming to confirm the family's scapegoating), nor yet to a young child (who may be unready for such a challenge until he has observed how others handle this query). From that initial answer, the question rotates to every other person in turn until each has given his or her variant response. Now we're into the work.

Although it might seem fitting to follow these revelations and contradictions with a level of deeper probing, there is wisdom in changing the subject to a positive note after the first round. I find it useful now to say, "But I know that family life is not all problems. There is also fun and good times and strength. Tell me about the better side too." Directing this question to the sons and daughters, and firmly holding back any promptings from parents, one can learn quickly not only where there are strengths on which to work, but also the methods of amelioration that have appealed to this family. Once again, this query makes the rounds until everyone has had opportunity to reply.

As therapist, evaluating even while collecting data, I can begin now to gauge the depth of this family's conflict, whether they are passing through normal but disruptive events at this stage, are upset but in a steady condition, or have plunged into a crisis that leaves them dysfunctional. The very exercise of sorting through the problem, followed by rehearsing their strengths and good memories, would have opened up some minor insights and suggestions of their own unless they are so conflicted as to have arrived at a place of despair.

In any case, it is time now to pose the standard inquiry of what remedies they have already tried for their troubles. Knowing what has been attempted without success will help to eliminate useless approaches and to alter the partial or temporary solutions. This phase also can awaken the family members to the realization that they have already been working on their problem and that there may be hope if they change some methods. Families frequently come into therapy with two implicit messages: (1) we need help, and (2) nothing can be done about our mess; we've already tried and failed. Any therapist, aware of this ambivalence of hope and despair, can identify with their dejection, but also hold out hope for their own resources to meet their problem; for they have demonstrated to themselves that they do have some strengths. The truth behind this optimism is that all families, even the most dysfunctional, go on solving some problems day in and day out.

Because we work with a system when counseling a family, the process itself can be of greater import than the content of their problem. Occasional checking to inquire what is going on in this very session will keep therapist and family alike aware of process. The family system is already undergoing some change when it is exposed to a new, therapeutic setting. A new, intrusive personality has been introduced into their family homeostasis and put it out of balance. It should occasion no wonder that they are ready to fight me as therapist to protect their customary ways and to avoid any change.

The major objective of this first family session is not to eradicate all their pain and problems (as if that were possible), but rather to be of support to these anxious parents and to establish rapport with these pained and resistant children. In the first session, there will be little time to move beyond the introductory stage at which I get acquainted with the family members and they with me. Especially if the number of people involved is large, or if the network of three generations has come in together, it requires time to cover all persons with the questions. Nevertheless, some interventions into the family difficulty must be made at this meeting.

In this instance, as in marital therapy, it is useful to close the opening session with some simple assignment that alleviates their angst and pulls them together. I search for some activity they have not tried for some time: a whole-family picnic, a visit to some congenial relative, planning an event such as a vacation together, or even—if it is unusual for them—eating dinner together. On this they are to report back at the next session two weeks or so in the future.

From the first interview with any family, it behooves a therapist to take firm hold of the proceedings. If the family gains control, the prognosis for change is poor. You are in a position to guide the session through the topics you choose, the questions you ask, the subjects you terminate, the people you call on, and the people whose interruptions or domination you check. There can be no standard model of interview for a complete family because of the variability of types and the multiplicity of concerns they bring into therapy. But there is a common form of the direction you will seek: to gain first a clear picture of the major problem behind their conflict, and second to ascertain what they wish to change. That there should be congruence between these two is obvious; but the family members may not be able to see it that way nor agree on just what changes they would make. This very possibility of disagreement is the stuff on which therapy may proceed; for stress of that dimension is easier by far to deal with than an apathy that excludes both dissonance and resolution.

The first interview is an occasion for emphasizing relationships and possibilities for change. This session can be kept on an intellectual level, minimally contentious and at moderate depth until some understandings are squared away and some principles established.

SUBSEQUENT INTERVIEWS

By the second and following interviews, we do well to begin with inquiry about what has happened in the interim. If they move immediately into expression of their feelings, I would still hold that off and keep them a little longer on a factual level: *what is happening?* Soon thereafter, I inquire about how they carried out the task I assigned at the close of our first meeting. If they succeeded at this, I encourage them to talk about it and to wallow in some satisfaction over their success. If they have failed, I make sure that they do not assume that they have somehow failed me but that they realize it is their family they have failed. They are given a new chance to meet the assignment, adjusted if need be, but matter-of-factly reinstated as their continuing objective.

From that point we move on to a consideration of their family background and history. The point here is not so much to assemble a genealogy as to demonstrate their commonality of origin, to discover homeostatic patterns, and to enable them to see, as Virginia Satir notes, that nothing has happened in their tradition by accident. Astonishing as it might seem, they learn facts about one another they had never realized before, and they become interested in their roots and their forebearers. A very useful form for eliciting this history is the use of a genogram, a diagram of family events and relationships that spans as much time and as many people as possible. This will be discussed in detail in Chapter 6.

The children have much to gain from history taking. They make discoveries about their parents; and the parents themselves can come to new understanding about their own parents.

In all this process, I as therapist do well to keep impressions and assumptions tentative; there will be turnings and alterations ahead. This is, in fact, a time to listen for indirect messages and to observe their interactions. I will not need to ask a series of penetrating questions about the patterns of interaction in the family; for these now become apparent to any observer.

At this stage, families begin to sense a few breakthroughs. They may want to revise their estimates of what they wish to change at home. They may begin to stiffen and show new resistance, which is not a bad sign at all when they feel themselves moving into a new pattern. They may even begin to relate to each other in new ways. To such signals a therapist must remain vigilant.

You will want to bring a master plan to your work of family therapy. Particularly if you already know the family, you can draw that plan with fitting details for their situation. The plan will allow for establishing rapport at the outset so that therapy is feasible. It should permit time for careful questioning in order to ascertain where the actual problem or problems lie. It must clarify the difficulties and bring to them some aids toward solution. It will include a clear objective for each session as well as the general objective for the series. It will offer supportive help and procedures to reduce anxiety so that the family is free enough to mobilize their strengths.

Family therapy tends to be short-term treatment. The Family Service Association of America reports that their family cases average only about six interviews. Yet on those half dozen and sometimes fewer occasions, therapy can pass through overlapping but identifiable stages. The first stage, we have seen, involves a struggle for agenda and some history taking.

By the third interview, the therapist is usually ready to help the family to redefine the presenting problem in relational terms. This systemic move will sideline the identified patient, and the therapist can now begin to treat the family as the patient. This is the time for assessment and evaluation of the conflict. This therapist asks one person after the other, "Why are you here?" and then moves on to the question, "If you could change one thing in your family life, what would it be?"

Promptly, the therapist moves on to a new stage: to involve the entire family in working for change. In an intergenerational situation, parents must be put in charge of the coming change. The therapist begins to back off of authority and to place it on the father and mother; for if the family is ever to make a positive alteration in their system they will have to carry it on themselves. Focusing on the present setting (here and now), the therapist may turn to a choice of several interventions. One technique is "sculpting," which will be explained in detail in Chapter 6. Another is to program some agreement they are to reach on an essential issue.

The goal of working through the refractory middle of the process is to complete a change in the family system. More resistance will be encountered at this new stage; and the therapist will need to keep sometimes unwilling counselees at the task. For any family to move into new levels of development requires some flexibility; but flexibility is what troubled families lack. In point of fact, the more dysfunctional the family is, the more rigid it is likely to be, since it has established some homeostasis at a level of rigidity. Still, if therapy is to succeed, each person in the family will now be enlisted to help change the system, and will be asked to make a personal contribution to that therapeutic process. The interaction of family members now is of utmost importance. The therapist's task is to keep them open to each other, to encourage every change they are able to make, and to reinforce their progress with positive feedback.

This "working through" phase, loaded though it is with conflict and resistance, often turns out to be the most promising stage of all. It leads to resolution and termination in those cases that succeed.

The long-term goal of every therapist is to free the family of the need for a therapist. When the family has shown some progress in handling its presenting problem and growing toward the change that will make repetition unlikely, it has reached a stage where it can arrest therapy for the present. In the event the family has been unsuccessful, the time may be at hand to make some new intervention; perhaps a decision to continue for another series of interviews in a new contract, or a referral to another type of therapy.

INTERVENTION

An intervention, from the Latin *inter-venire,* literally means a "coming between." As used in therapy, it consists of some method the therapist uses to wedge a new perception between the counselees' current perception and their subsequent behaviors. Crisis interventions are used to meet emergencies in quick order, but interventions can also be introduced into ordinary therapy sessions.

The examples of intervention that most often come to mind are *confrontation* and *clarification;* and there are many others. Interventions can be brought into the process as brief segments of a long-term objective. Direct confrontation of denial, for example, might be used sparingly in a continuing relationship whose objective is the building of self-confidence. Interventions, to be effective, must be firm enough to break through phony rationalization, yet affirming enough to maintain a good relationship. Whatever the need to intervene, the therapist aims to keep the door open for continuing work; knowing that people cease cooperating when they feel hurt.

Typical interventions in family therapy, chosen among a large number, are the following:

- Confrontation: this "calling a spade a spade" puts the issue squarely to the counselee. "Yet only last week you were saying just the opposite."
- Clarification: "No, our job is not to find someone to blame in this family, but to get you to the place that you're all working together again"—when an identified patient is being blamed.
- Relabeling: "Sam certainly does act belligerent; but I have an idea that he may be scared."
- The indirect approach: "Marty, you understand Bob better than I do; would you tell me what he is saying?"
- Focus on here and now: "What is passing through your head just now as you listen to Gene describe his plans?" is preferable to asking counselees to recall their reactions of the previous Thursday.
- Exploration of the depths: "Shut your eyes a minute and try to relive the experience. What do you remember?"
- Nonverbal cue: the purposeful frown, grimace, or encouraging smile that silently intervenes to signal concern or approval.
- Setting the topic: changing to a new subject, or bringing the counselees back to the subject they had avoided: "Let's shift back to that question of the money."
- Probing: "Let's linger a bit longer on that one. Tell us what you did when you first learned she was unfaithful."
- Explication: "Paint a picture of that" is a request to develop the report more fully.
- Staging the next interview: "When we get together again on the nineteenth, we're going to turn our attention to how discipline is handled in this family."
- Context: scheduling of interviews; inclusion or exclusion of

certain members of the family; arrangements of the room: all of these are potent interventions.

Directives

Directives are a type of intervention used by therapists to move persons toward changing their methods or timing in the way they manage their living or relate to others.

Jay Haley relates how he once directed a young man to organize his work and his relations with people. Although the man wished to become a great novelist, he could not bring himself to sit down at the typewriter and write. He was also afraid of women. In his late twenties, he had never had a real date.

The therapeutic strategy was obvious: when posed with two symptoms, one should be used to cure the other. I asked the young man to specify how many pages per day he should write, and he said he should write one page per day of 250 words. I directed the young man to write six pages per week (he negotiated one day off). If he did not follow the directive, then the following week he had to ask young women for dates until he went out with three women that week. The next week if he did not write six pages, he must arrange three dates again. Rather than ask a woman for a date, the young man sprang to his typewriter and methodically wrote a minimum of six pages per week. Later the problem of dating young women was resolved. (Haley, 1976)

Directives come in six different styles. (1) A therapeutic directive may be as subtle as a nod or a smile that encourages some action. (2) It may, on the other hand, be an outright request. (3) It may be directed toward either a small and limited change or (4) a larger, more ambitious one. (5) It may be an inconspicuous request attached as a rider to another point; or (6) it may be a paradoxical directive.

The purpose of any directive, like that of therapy in general, is to influence people to change their behaviors. That it also alters relationships among family members and with the therapist is counted as an additional boon. When the therapist assigns family members to a task, a new dimension of intensity is introduced to their interactions.

The problem-oriented therapists, who use this method widely in their work, have developed standard ways of getting into their directives. They tend to assign them authoritatively: "I want you to do thus-and-so; I have my reasons, but I'm not going to discuss them." They lay out the task clearly. They choose tasks that involve everyone in the family, if possible; and they set a time in the future to review how the directive was accomplished.

In our training of ministerial interns in family therapy at the Divinity School, we set them to devising directives for their families they work with. For example:

1. One therapist worked with a middle aged couple whose twenty-five-year-old son was a dependent, idle, maturing "flower child" in a distant city. The directive was to cut off funds for the young man to help him to grow up—and, what is more, to help the parents to let go.

2. Another, confronted by a married couple who had cooled the romance in their marriage, directed them to arrange a series of dates for dinner, theatre, visiting, and so forth, on the theory that the Lange-James (James, 1918) theory is valid in its contention that the more we act in a definite way, the more we are inclined to feel that way.

3. Others devise directives around reading certain assigned materials that pertain to their problem ("bibliotherapy"), or to the keeping of diaries to be shared in the counseling sessions. The more literate counselees respond to these directives, which would be lost on some others.

4. Another directive, designed to bring some order into the communication of a family where interruptions were the rule, specified that family members were to practice talking and listening to one another without interruptions of any sort. The task was practiced during the interview, with the therapist acting as coach until they got it right. Then it was rehearsed at home until the next session.

Paradoxical Directives

One clear November afternoon in Palo Alto, I sat behind a one-way mirror in an observation room at the Mental Research

Institute (MRI) observing a young married couple in therapy. The problem was the issue of the husband's drinking. It was becoming excessive, and his wife resented it. She was an attractive, alert young journalist, he a somewhat languid young man who resented her resentment. The therapist was working through a paradoxical directive that had been set up with MRI's Brief Therapy Center team, who were now watching its progress with me.

The directive was tough. The therapist warned the couple that he doubted they could succeed. The husband was actually to continue his drinking (no abstinence was attempted), but under his wife's control. On Mondays, Wednesdays, and Fridays she was to phone him from her office and prescribe for him the number of bottles of beer he was to drink. On Tuesdays, Thursdays, Saturdays, and Sundays he was to set his own quota. If he ever exceeded the agreed-on quota, he was to down six bottles of beer in a two-hour period the next Sunday afternoon (thus exaggerating the behavior), then begin the controlled quotas again the next day. The couple accepted the task and agreed to return in two weeks for an evaluation.

Without realizing it, they were faced with a paradoxical directive. If they followed it to the letter, they would be agreeing to a regime of controlled drinking. If the husband rebelled and set his own quota on Mondays, Wednesdays, and Fridays, he would already be in charge of his drinking. If he exceeded the quota, he would have to drink the punitive quota of beer on the following Sunday and thus prove true the therapist's warning message of, "I don't think you can do it." But if he began to control his drinking within the fortnight, he would confound both the therapist and his wife.

Paradoxical directives are made of such no-lose situations. While they vary in detail, they generally involve these five characteristics: (1) a prescription to continue some behavior already begun; (2) a built-in mechanism to produce the opposite effect of the directive; (3) a device to con the counselees (sometimes with their own collusion); (4) an authoritarian preempting of the procedure by the therapist; and (5) a gracious disclaimer for any credit at the end by the therapist if the paradoxical directive succeeds. Let's explore these points in more detail.

1. The use of paradox in therapy nearly always involves "prescribing the symptom." In some way or other, the therapist directs the counselee(s) to go on doing what they are already doing. The order to "continue what you are doing" has been applied to problems of school phobia, sexual aberrations, marital quarreling, and depressive behavior. One of our students, for example, was struggling with a family case in which two middle-aged parents were at their wits' end with a grown son who lived at their home and refused to get out of bed before noon or to look for a job. The student therapist attempted a number of interventions without success, and then consulted her supervisor who suggested that she try a directive that prescribed the very symptom: namely, that she direct the young man to continue lying in bed not only until noon but until three o'clock each afternoon, and that the parents make no comment about it whatever. The paradox succeeded; and within a week the young man, sick of the confinement to his bed, was out seeking employment.

2. The reversal in a paradoxical directive is the built-in provision for an opposite effect. A depressed, self-flagellating mother sighs, "I guess I'm hopeless." The therapist may respond mockingly in kind, "I guess you are." Then the woman may get up some spunk and flip over her helpless complaining and defend the opposite: "Well, I'm not exactly hopeless. I guess I have some pretty strong points too. It's just that I don't seem to be able to pull them together very often."

Charles H. Kramer lines out the workings of this rolling with the resistance:

Part of the considerable power of the strategic therapist comes from the technique of always agreeing with the patient, actively working toward solutions, readily willing to quit whenever an impasse is reached, and refusing to take credit for even small beneficial changes.

This approach is especially effective when clearly definable symptoms or problems can be identified and the family is motivated to change after having failed to change through their own efforts or through previous therapy. Paradoxical interventions work best with chronically oppositional people with a dramatic and disabling problem. It is an exciting method which is often startlingly effective. It can be fun for the therapist to concoct an intervention and even fun for the family to carry out the directive in a spirit of, "We've tried everything we could think of without success, we can't lose much by trying this crazy suggestion." It requires a therapist who is capable of looking at the situation from a fresh perspective. Often the interventions are novel, creative, even brilliant.

Some of the pitfalls are that: the method often appears slick, pat, and manipulative; strategic therapists often take an attitude toward their work and patients which is considered by others to be cynical, flip, and insincere; paradoxical interventions are complicated to devise . . . it remains to be seen how well some of the symptom changes stand up over time. (Kramer, 1980, p. 148)

3. A paradoxical directive contains a built-in device to hoodwink the counselees, sometimes even with their own connivance. This element of deception would make the technique too risky to use, were it not for the suspicion that many an intelligent counselee accepts the paradox with tongue in cheek. Paul Watzlawick, a master of paradoxical therapy, once counseled a conflictual married couple who together operated a small restaurant business. The wife wished that her husband could competently manage the restaurant so that she could spend more time at home, but she was so critical of how he did it that she was constantly at him to change his ways, directing him and disputing. The therapist found that they both arrived simultaneously at 8 A.M., and that she unlocked the door while he parked the car. He changed their life by directing that the husband was to come along in the morning and open up, giving his wife an extra half hour to tidy up the home and come later to begin her takeover. But the result was that he got the day's routine under way, made the preliminary decisions, and was already in charge by the time she arrived. She, on the other hand, began coming over later in the morning and leaving earlier in the day as she enjoyed her home and had

less to complain about at work (Watzlawick, 1978). It is possible, is it not, that such a woman realized what was happening in the new order, but colluded with it in order to find a way out of the impasse without losing face?

Carl Whitaker has practiced some of his more absurd therapy with paradoxical manipulation of feelings. Faced by a teenaged girl who had attempted suicide, he once deglamorized the fantasies he knew had fascinated her: fantasies of the crowd of mourners, the banks of flowers, the grieving crowd. He matter-of-factly suggested to her that her workaholic father would probably have been too busy to leave his office to attend her funeral. Crude but effective, such statements have a paradoxical bent both because they are contrary to what the counselee expects to hear, and also because they have a good chance of producing an opposite effect, (e.g., causing the depressed, suicidal person to consider the prospect from a new and startling perspective). The counselee is entitled to smile ruefully and to realize she has been teased into a fresh, different position.

4. The therapist who uses paradoxical interventions will need to be ready to anticipate resistance by a preemptive introduction. Introductory clauses that serve this purpose tend along such lines as, "There's an astonishingly easy solution for this problem, but I doubt that you will like it"; or, "This is certain to sound ridiculous to you; nevertheless I believe it is valid."

Still another twist on the preemptive introduction is used by Paul Watzlawick in the familiar social device of denying responsibility for a statement even while making it: "If your wife were not here, I would say . . ."; or, "Somebody less desperate than you I'd probably tell quite frankly that I consider this problem to be rather trivial. . . ."

"Reframing" is yet another use of paradox. By means of this intervention, the therapist can set a task off in a new setting so that it is both felt and handled in a suddenly new way. Watzlawick tells of the child who continued sucking his thumb well into later years and could not be stopped until a therapist told him in the presence of his mother that in a democratic society every finger deserves just as long a chance at being sucked as the thumb. He was assigned then to suck each of his other nine fingers just as long as he had sucked his thumb; and his mother was to time this exercise. It required only a short while for the boy to give up this annoying chore as well as the original problem of thumb sucking.

5. Finally, the therapist who uses paradox graciously disclaims any credit for its success, but ascribes this only to the clever resourcefulness of the counselees. "You certainly fooled me!" was the disingenuous exclamation of the therapist when the indolent young man who lay abed until noon now began to arise at eight. When the alcoholic man finally was able to drink moderately, the therapist could say, "I never thought you could do it."

The major reason for giving credit to the counselees is that it is with them that responsibility lies. It is a *sine qua non* in all counseling that the therapist cannot take over responsibility for the lives of counselees. They must be set free to solve their problems and take charge of their own lives. If they have a relapse and cannot maintain the new improvement, the relapse is genuinely their own and cannot be laid at the door of the therapist. Neither should the tribute for improvement be the therapist's. The improvement should last longer and the chance for a relapse should be less if the counselees feel that they are in charge of their own lives now—for the credit as well as the work.

5. Therapies and Theories

> We are not proposing that families are the only or the best support system, or that all families should be held together—only that families are mostly what we have to work with.
> —GINA OGDEN AND ANNE ZEVLIN, *When a Family Needs Therapy*

WHAT THE COUNSELEES BRING INTO THERAPY

Troubled families seeking help will have already attempted a number of solutions for their problems, attempts which, like as not, have now added something to their accumulated stress. They have come to the conclusion that they cannot work out their difficulties alone. When they at last come to the pastor for assistance, dragging along their identified patient, they are confused, fearful, humiliated, and reluctant. Their feelings of helplessness are mixed with an expectation of relief; their pain is commingled with hope, their gratitude with resistance. For the minister to have been a counselee in therapy will prove of immense value now. Such experience brings a deeper appreciation of what counselees are feeling and going through. It makes the clergy more sympathetic to know some of the hazards and barriers of the process, the ambivalence and sense of failure, as well as the feelings of dependence and expectancy. For this reason, though not for this alone, training programs for therapists include arrangements for them to receive some therapy themselves. In the future, such experience may stand them in good stead for ministering to families.

Experience helps the therapist to realize that the couple or whole family coming into therapy will arrive wrapped in a huge, buzzing confusion of mixed emotions. It is the system itself, the family relationship—whether they know it or not—from which they crave escape. Their very interdependence, once a source of comfort and support, can now be the ground of conflict. Regardless of their misery, they will maintain a loyalty to their rules, their rituals, their secrets, and their relationships. We have seen that individuals in a family are capable of achieving very little change in themselves, unless they receive support from the family system. But therapy directed at the relationship rather than at individuals will make it unnecessary to challenge the family's invisible loyalties, and make it possible to use their family connectedness as an aid to therapy itself.

The contrast between therapist and counselees is wide. The family is more disturbed, the therapist less. The family is frightened; and the therapist is not, or at least not very much. The therapist, indeed, has to work with that initial fright and reduce it sufficiently to allow therapy to proceed. This you do by asking your questions matter-of-factly, building the self-esteem of the counselees, and handling their delicate concerns with care. Your objective is to lessen threat by your modeling of calmness in the face of the difficulty, by monitoring their interaction and checking it when it gets out of hand, and by helping them to assume responsibility for their decisions. Any therapist will hold up a figurative mirror to counselees and help them to see how they appear both to themselves and to others. Such a program gradually brings a family around to a new concept of itself, a hopeful step on the route to change.

Families that are no longer able to cope with some disabling problem experience heavy stress, both between members and within each person. To exacerbate this condition, they are also likely to feel a sense of shame and failure; for normative folk myth has it that families are expected to solve their problems by their own strength and goodness. Just as the ocean is supposed to wash itself, so families have been supposed to overcome their own difficulties; but when the pollution is too great for seas or for families, such expectations dismally fail. Indeed, it is possible through a rough sort of measurement to score the impact of stress on individuals and families through a "stress test" that has been circulated by the National Mental Health Association. In it, a stress quotient of more than twenty points may indicate mounting emotional or health problems for troubled persons or families. Its categories make a useful check list in counseling; and its scoring can be informative, as long as it is understood that the test is a simple and inexact instrument that would reflect differently according to people's other strengths and weaknesses.

Table 2. The Stress Test*

Stressful Situation	Points
Minor law violations	1
Vacations	1
Change in residence	2
Foreclosure of mortgage	3
Change in financial status	3
Being fired	4
Pregnancy	4
Marriage	5
Severe injury or illness	5
Death of family member	6
Jail term	6
Separation	6
Divorce	7
Death of spouse	10

*SOURCE: The National Mental Health Association. Used by permission.

A first remarkable note about the test is how much a person or persons might have withstood before accumulating 20 points. But it can also be predicted that family members under stress will enter a therapy relationship defensively, rationalizing their actions and complaints with excuses and explanations, blaming each other for the problems they cannot overcome, and tending to make one of their number a scapegoat for their accumulated stress. Given such a predicament, it should occasion no wonder that they tend to protect their status, no matter how painful it may be. More comfortable with the troubles they are accustomed to than with the unknown solution they might adopt, they resist any jostling of their precarious balance. The homeostasis they have found, painful though it be, is to be preferred to any new change in their equilibrium, or neostasis. Change, in fact, will be fought by the entire family system. Even a fractured family can rally and close ranks to battle an intruder (and they may perceive the therapist as just that instead of a welcome house guest). If they feel a massive threat, they are inclined to flee therapy even more readily than would an individual.

Beginning therapists are frequently astonished to discover that some of their early encounters with troubled families become contests. Family members will automatically try to do to the therapist what they have been doing to each other; that is, they will attempt to manipulate you, and they will test your strengths. Time-consuming and wasteful though it appears, they will often seek to avoid facing reality and to fend off assistance toward solving their problems. That they may deny some difficulties or faults in order to keep your good opinion can be taken for granted; and their intense reactions to family disclosures, or to your questions may sometimes catch you off guard. They may even lie to you and to each other, withhold important information, or subvert therapeutic procedures. And why not? Family therapy, if it is to be at all effective, will stir up old anxieties and foment painful insights, challenge rituals. The process, as Augustus Napier notes, is like a surgical incision—there is the capacity to heal, but there is also the certainty of pain.

It is not enough for the therapist to be reasonable, benevolent, and mature. Only a strongly personal power can make the almost surgical incision through the family's layers of denial and avoidance, exposing the profundity of their pain and the immensity of their power. This must be a special kind of force, one guided by a caring intent. (Napier and Whitaker, 1979, p. 184)

And that caring intent is an important input from the family therapist in the interviews.

WHAT THE COUNSELOR BRINGS INTO THERAPY

To reflect on what the couple or family bring into such counseling is but half the story. You, as therapist, also bring into this relationship your own baggage of emotions, skills, concerns, and wariness, along with a different perspective. Ministers who enter the family area are well advised to do so with the complementary attitudes of caution and confidence.

Any therapist enters a new case with some measure of hesitation and watchfulness, with certain feelings of personal inadequacy and unfulfilled needs. It may be that you are asked to aid families in their brokenness at a time that your own family is going through some unresolved pain. It is not required that you have all your marital and family problems solved before you intervene with some other family's dysfunction. What is required is that you have come to realistic terms with your own marital and family status, that you know both where you stand and how to work on your human condition.

Not to have faced your own family background and condition with honesty can be folly; for it can lead to two gross temptations. On the one hand you may be tempted to project your own family difficulties, ghosts, and worries into the counseling situation and try to solve your own problems through this relationship—a hope foredoomed to failure. In order to deal empathetically with families, the personal life of the minister must affirm a dignity and worth of its own. Only if the minister has other gratifications and can avoid using the therapy session to replace personal dissatisfactions will it be possible to give to the family rather than take from it. Clergypersons need intimate supportive relationships of their own to offset the tendency to use families in therapy to fulfill their own needs. If your own satisfactions are sufficient, you may be whole enough to be empathic to others, to understand feelings as well as words, and to communicate an attitude of caring.

On the other hand, you might heedlessly foist your own value system upon another family and attempt to influence them to reconstruct their family system on your own model; that too is bound for failure. The pattern of your family life is distinctly your own and might be altogether impossible for another household to adopt. Legend has it that, when Woodrow Wilson was president of Princeton University, he once warned the faculty that they were not to try to make over their students to be imitations of themselves. "For you know, and I know, and God knows that one of you is enough," he added.

At best, family therapy is a risky discipline; and no one can always be successful, understanding, and giving when working with families in difficulty who themselves are difficult. Even the mellow, avuncular approach to joining a family cannot hold out indefinitely with a sweet spirit. Family therapists have learned to disclose themselves as they are—fallible, struggling people without claim to perfection. That stance is no novelty to pastors.

Therapists, in fact, may have some family problems of their own. Who of us has all our family relations in order, all past problems solved, all "ducks in a row"? A minister may come straight into a session with a fractured family from some regretted quarrel with a spouse. The pastor who faces a trying situation with a guilt-ridden person may realize that there remain unreconciled problems with his own father. We, too, are wounded healers.

The experienced family therapist enters into the family system, adopting some of their language, observing their rituals, and seeking to understand some of their myths. As in Salvador Minuchin's "joining maneuver," the therapist invades family relationships as a relative, perhaps like a concerned uncle or aunt. In such a position, the therapist begins to model family behavior almost at once: showing patience with a hysterically manipulative mother, demonstrating calm firmness with a glowering and tough father, or lending support to the pregnant daughter as she tries to explain her needs to her parents. Therapists model more open communication than most troubled families are accustomed to; this they do by asking for clarification, by checking out messages to make sure they have heard correctly, and by correcting erroneous perceptions.

In time the minister, acting as family therapist, learns to operate on several different levels at once, watching body language to test its congruency with people's words, listening to the feeling tone of what they are saying, working into and out of their family system, and moving back and forth between their interaction and an assessment of what is going on.

Two Persistent Myths

Clergy owe it to themselves and to parishioners to give up two persistent myths if they are to become effective family therapists. One myth is that our profession comprises a continuing rescue operation. In training programs of the clergy, it is difficult to dispel this myth. A long tradition of seeing ourselves as rescuers of the perishing has fed the idea that we must save those who are imperiled, and that in this service we are indispensible. That can be a messianic complex. Yet we cannot make decisions for our people; that they must do for themselves. We cannot save them from their errors and their faults. To attempt to do so would put us in charge of their lives. We cannot do their work for them, believe for them, or shield them from the results of their actions. The detachment that is part of our professional stance prevents such interference in the lives of others, no matter how well-intended.

The second myth, widely spread and devoutly believed by many, is that you who fulfill your ministry as therapists are capable of doing some irreparable harm in the lives of people. Perhaps the caution seems well taken insofar is it reflects a conscientious concern for the welfare of counselees. But in too many cases it is a cover also for timidity or an alibi for the diffident pastor. I have observed that priests and ministers tend too quickly to refer marital or family cases to psychotherapists rather than to labor through the counseling challenge themselves. It may be that they consider themselves too busy to take the protracted time necessary for such work; but in that case we must ask what ministerial task it is that takes priority over helping troubled families. It may be that they modestly consider themselves unskilled in such work; yet there are ways to improve aptitudes for this ministry (see the Resources for Family Therapists section in the Appendix). I know of very few cases where pastors are accused of doing harm to people through counseling; and even in those situations there are other factors so involved that we cannot assume that it was the counseling itself that caused the effect that is cited. That some difficulty sequentially followed counseling does not logically infer that the difficulty occurred *because* of the counseling. That presumption has long been exploded by a famous proverb: *Post hoc, ergo propter hoc?* (After this, therefore because of this?) It is true that our counseling may leave people unimproved. It may be that we shall only console or encourage, but not cure the pained and the troubled. It may be that our sole ministry will be a support and empathy for the traumatized parishioners of our church; but even being present to their pain is no small boon, and it could be the key that unlocks some of their own powers. To deal compassionately with the wounds of families without intruding our domination or our expectations, and to hold out to them hope and understanding in their time of trouble may be all that we do—but that is a significant contribution by which no one is harmed. How to do that, and how to make referrals to other specialists in situations where our own ministry needs augmentation, will be discussed below.

USING YOURSELF AS THERAPIST

Any minister acting as family therapist may well approach this task with awe. It is appropriate even to be frightened a bit; but you will still not be as frightened as some members of the family you meet. You enter this ministry as a whole person, probably far less disturbed than the family in pain, and with greater authority in their eyes than you are ever likely to suppose. They come into the encounter with expectations of help and healing; and those very expectations become positive aids toward improvement. In the hour or hours that lie ahead, your clinical training, diagnostic skills, or psychological information may count for less than your genuineness as a person. It will be your caring, your openness, your personal balance, and your experience in mediating redemptive possibilities that make the major difference. Indeed, unless your ministry goes beyond the level of mere technique and intervention, you may be little more than a mechanic. Worse, you might be a manipulator of people. Essential though knowledge and abilities are, the way that you use yourself is your most important therapeutic tool.

This, I believe, is why it has sometimes been possible to enlist untrained and unsophisticated persons as effective family therapists: they have learned to use themselves as genuine instruments of empathy and caring. They possess what envious professionals have come to refer to as "factor X"—that is, affective empathy. Young adults from the ghettos of Philadelphia have been successfully coached to become family therapists. Businessmen, homemakers, and custodians have been recruited as effective therapists. A desire to be helpful and an understanding heart are, of course, not sufficient in themselves; but much of the necessary training and experience can be achieved on the job. So much the more then, the seminary-educated minister or priest who is a concerned, capable, and supportive person can grow into a family therapist. Theological education and clinical pastoral experience, now augmented by daily work among real families, have readied them for such ministry.

The availability of the therapist as a whole person makes possible a full range of responses to the problems of pained families. In an instructive recollection of one event, Donald A. Bloch reports an intervention from the heart that produced dramatic effect.

In the course of a family interview, a male therapist began to become aware of his own growing anger at the father of the family who seemed to be using deft, humorous, self-deprecating remarks to reduce awareness of painful feelings and so as not to notice pleas by other family members for support and love. The therapist in an irritated tone said that he did not like being "fobbed off" by the father. There followed an intense moment of silent eye-to-eye contact, after which the father said, "I don't want to fight with you." More silence followed and the father added, "Either we would destroy each other or I would have to back down, and I prefer to back down." The therapist became aware that his own anger was replaced with a profound sense of sadness; tears welled in his eyes and he said to the father, "Would this be the only possible solution?" The two men continued looking at each other; not a sound was to be heard in the room. After a moment, the therapist became fully aware of the emotion that had been moving him and so said to the man, "I know what it feels like to be an isolated father." As he said this, tears began to stream down the father's face. Throughout, the family watched this display in silence. (Bloch, 1973, p. 5)

In therapy, Gregory Bateson once observed, the heart can do more to heal than the intellect. The intellect is often naive; for the mind learns tomorrow what the heart knew today.

Such emphasis upon the personality of the therapist is hardly meant to denigrate conscientious preparation and study for becoming a family therapist. That kind of anti-intellectual slur you would hardly expect from one who teaches in a graduate program for family ministries. But it is meant to encourage working clergy to use themselves caringly and cannily in this ministry. Maturity will count for much: your capacity to love, your ability to discipline emotions and words, your firm touch with reality, your capacity to relate to others with generosity and consistency, your willingness to remain flexible and open to families in pain.

THEORY OF FAMILY THERAPY

What makes family therapy succeed—when it does? That question, discussed and debated through many a learned paper in convention and classroom, has given rise to a library on theory. But in the long run, experience is a better guide than theory; and theories are good only insofar as they are practical, can be used as predictive aids, or will explain the situations we encounter. Family theory, when effective, teaches us to work with the ordinary stuff of family developments and crises: entrances and exits, communication challenges, and ambivalent love/hate binds. Family theory differs, as it should, from therapist to therapist; for it is not an absolute scientific formula but a construct of knowledge that enables individual helpers to understand what they are doing and why.

Any theory is an explanation of the principles of a body of knowledge. It is to enable the theorist to do just what the original

Greek *theoria* implied—to contemplate. Although my next door neighbor, Andy, says that a good theory is often upset by brute reality, it does have its contribution to make. Jay Haley, criticizing theories of family therapy, has written that any theory should provide an orientation that leads a therapist to success, should be a guide to action, should generate hope both in the therapist and the family, should define failure when it occurs, and should be simple enough for the average therapist to understand (Haley, 1978, p. 67). He goes on to note, "A theory of therapy seems to be more helpful when it focuses upon real people with real problems in the real world and takes the social context into account whenever explaining human nature" (Haley, 1978, p. 80).

SOME LESS EFFECTIVE APPROACHES

Our question about what makes therapy succeed can be asked from the obverse: what prevents family therapy from being effective when it stops short of success? Our theory ought also to instruct us about what will be less effective, and therefore to be avoided. I believe that I now know a half dozen ideas that do not contribute to success in family therapy, at least in my own experience and observation. That they may have validity for other modes of therapy, I will not argue; but with families, I contend, they are not very productive.

1. *It does no lasting good for the family therapist to work out solutions, no matter how wise, on behalf of families.* Unless family members come to their own solutions of problems and agree on them, such remedies cannot long endure and they will soon revert to their homeostasis. It is far better for them to arrive at their own partial or inadequate decision when it is their own, than to accept a superior but imposed plan from the therapist. Our objective should never be to take over the decision-making prerogative of the family, nor yet to deprive them of their initiative; but to free them up to make more effective decisions on their own.

2. *Too much time spent on diagnosis can be time ill-spent in family therapy.* However essential a clear diagnosis may be in a medical

examination, its laborious introduction into a family session could cool the relationship and bring therapy to a premature end. A pronouncement that this adolescent is "a parentified personality with borderline paranoid tendencies" adds to the problem rather than to the solution. We do need to evaluate the family's condition, of course; but such evaluation proceeds simultaneously with our interventions in effective therapy.

3. *Counselees' insight is of limited value in family therapy because it lacks the power to change behaviors.* If a woman is brought to the insight that she has been treating her family in an unconscious imitation of the regrettable pattern her own mother adopted a generation ago, it does not follow that she will learn from that insight to alter her own behavior. Many people possess impressive insight into their personality structure without acting on it at all.

4. *Interpretation by a therapist is an overrated form of intervention in family practice.* For the minister to interpret and make explicit an underlying hostility is less helpful than aiding the family to resolve the transactions that spark such hostility. Difficult as it is to keep silent about our own brilliant interpretation of a behavior, it is the better part of family therapy.

5. *Promoting or even allowing family conflicts and hassles during therapy interviews is of little worth; indeed it is often a detriment to treatment.* To be sure, it permits the therapist to witness "live" the level of dissension among family members and demonstrates how serious this can be. Yet a little conflict goes a long way; it is hardly necessary to do anything more than sample the conflict for a brief minute before quelling it. Although some experienced therapists "escalate the stress" to enable a therapeutic intervention, this can be risky business. For most of us, open conflict in therapy sessions is a waste of time and a hardening of the negative behavior that brought the counselees to us in the first place.

6. *Conducting family therapy by the bits-and-pieces method is undisciplined, and can be destructive to the outcome.* We may be pressed to deal with new crises and sudden anxiety attacks over the telephone or in the church parking lot. Indeed, those settings may be the only ones available in some cases. However, we do better

to request the supplicant to defer the topic for a more appropriate setting, or to schedule a session when the related parties can be brought together. A controlled and regular approach to family therapy brings better results than the disordered rescue attempts that answer each emergency call with new assistance.

Although these methods contribute to limited effectiveness in family therapy, some other measures are more promising. Among these are the therapist's own input, the influence of the context, and the use of process.

THE THERAPIST'S EFFECTIVE PART IN THE THEORY

A first requirement for effective therapy is the establishment of a helping relationship between therapist and counselee.

Any theory of family therapy in pastoral ministry must take account of the person who is acting as therapist; this remains a most important factor. Therapy will be substantially advanced when the minister acting as therapist is genuine, warm, and caring. A genuine attitude on the part of the therapist awakens a reciprocal genuineness in the family; when they experience you as an honest person willing to lower your mask and reveal your own strengths and weaknesses, they feel encouraged to do the same. Your ability to communicate warm, friendly, but unobtrusive interest in counselees will inspire them to an openness and a trust in the process; and this at once moves them toward confidence that conditions will grow better. Finally, because people in trouble are usually suffering (at least temporarily) from low self-esteem, the recognition that someone important to them—indeed, the minister—cares about who they are and what happens to them lifts their self-image and contributes to their gains.

The therapist's empathy is essential to family therapy. Empathy (from the Greek *empatheia,* "suffering in") is a way of putting yourself into the psychological frame of reference of the family members, and even to share and understand what they are feeling. You can voice it: "You sound angry, and I know how that feels too"; or, "I've been there, and know how it is to be depressed." Empathy is essential in ministerial counseling. It goes deeper than sympathetic sayings, farther than compassionate glances. It involves the whole person. Your empathy consists of "being with" the couple in marital strife or the family in grief, of entering into their emotions with them and staying by them rather than attempting to pull them out to a cheerful level too soon. Yours may be "affective empathy," the "factor X" that is inborn and natural. Or yours, like mine, may be more a "cognitive empathy," learned and practiced through experience and evaluation. In training seminars, we structure exercises in cognitive empathy so that clergy can test their proficiency in this area and learn better how to relate to others empathically. True empathy enables pastors and theologues to get past their sometimes regrettable tendencies to become judgmental, moralistic, or timid in the face of people's problems. True empathy will also save them from maudlin sympathy in the "I know just how you feel" fallacy.

Knowledge about emotional relations is necessary to make psychotherapy work.

Any theory about what makes therapy effective must also take account of skills. It is not enough to be oneself—genuine, warm, caring, and empathic; the experienced therapist also knows how to use interventions, how to respond to desperation, how to conduct interviews, and how to help families practice new ways of living with each other. Such skills do not come automatically or quickly. Encounter with actual families in pain is the best education for learning such skills. To be doing real family therapy under supervision and to be in simultaneous study is the recommended way. And one can also pick up pointers and guidance in workshops and in reading on one's own (see Resources for Family Therapists in the Appendix).

The therapist needs more self-understanding and self-knowledge than most people, as well as a deeper understanding of people and what makes them act as they do. In text books of psychology, this understanding is known as theory of personality. In everyday business, it is known as interpersonal competence. As therapists, we are better in this work if we already realize that anger can be a mask for fear, that blustering may cover a feeling of inadequacy, that seductive behavior may be a maneuver for power. All this begins, however, in a better understanding of yourself, in a candid examination of who you are and how you operate under different conditions. That alone will not make you sophisticated about the conduct of others, because self-awareness could lead you astray in attributing to others your own projected wishes and motives. Nevertheless, it can aid your appreciation of how others feel about their own identity and self-protection. It is part of personality theory.

A Whole Armor: Trust, Assertiveness, Objectivity

Like St. Paul's armamentarium in the sixth chapter of Ephesians, the characteristics brought into therapy by the pastor constitute a protective and effective attire. The shield of *trust* is a piece of this armor of therapy. As ministers, we shall need to have trust in ourselves and in our potential to be of help. We shall also need to exercise trust in the families we counsel. Trusting family members to fulfill homework tasks to make the changes they say they will make, and to work during the interviews, is essential to therapeutic progress. Even when they let you down—and they will—to maintain such trust opens the way to remedies and corrections. Trust enables us to withstand the shock of startling revelations or deep disappointments; at the very least, it aids us to retain our openness to counselees as worthwhile persons. Trust in the redeemable potential of people keeps the way open for growth to occur, a growth that is not only theirs but ours as well.

Ministers who act as therapists also need a breastplate of *assertiveness;* for there will come times when we must struggle with families for authority and power in therapy sessions and we need a base from which we can work effectively. Even shattered families can unite to fight off an outsider who threatens their homeostasis. They may try to control the therapeutic plan and to decide how it is to be carried out, which is to say they would like to make sure that no changes will be brought about. Family therapy differs in several respects from individual therapy, and client-centered approaches are less effective with family groups. Family therapy demands a more intensive *use of the self* on the part of a therapist. Not merely an observer and commentator about the family and their dynamics, the family therapist becomes a participant observer who can interrupt, can alter the direction of the communication when necessary, can intervene to protect someone from attack by another member of the family, or perhaps even to spur one who is too passive into more aggressive action. As ministers we have to realize that we exert considerable power with families. They look to their pastors for leadership (perhaps too much for some of us), for some solutions for their dependence and their problems, and also for strength.

Minister-therapists will also carry the sword of *objectivity.* Objectivity also enables us to cut through some of our more refractory problems. It will, for instance, assist us to maintain a stance of detachment. For even though our empathy is encouraged, a certain degree of detachment is also necessary in order to respect a family's authority and to allow them to handle their own responsibilities. In addition, objectivity is a boon to interpersonal relations in our therapy, lest our own ego needs and satisfactions get into the way of our professional integrity. It is not unheard of for therapists to become overly involved in the lives of their counselees—sometimes, indeed, to fall in love with or to become deeply involved with someone who had first come for counsel. The very modality of family therapy, however, reduces the danger of dependent, destructive, or sexual behaviors in the process. Although everyone has heard of some incident of improper intimacy between professional helpers and patients in individual treatment, such misconduct is rare among family therapists. The very method of working with several family members at once makes such improprieties unlikely.

THE CONTEXT OF FAMILY THERAPY

Any theory, to be comprehensive, must also take account of contextual elements. In family therapy as conducted by the clergy, the context includes the religious faith of the parties, their degree of confidence in the outcome, and their capacity and desire to change.

The faith of the minister who is acting as therapist is a key element in this mix. Approaching the family with a conviction that God heals and redeems our broken relationships, we believe that our human limitations in skill and insight can be strengthened by power beyond our own. Coming into such a challenge from prayer and a belief that God accepts and improves upon our own finite abilities, we enter into partnership with him and a confident meeting with the family coming into therapy. There is an ineffable element about this ministry; yet everyone who has been surprised by grace will know what it means to discover that our possibilities have been exceeded by a power we did not know we had.

The degree of confidence that the therapist and the family have in the process will make a substantial difference in the outcome. The very act of seeking out help for family problems is a first therapeutic step on the way to their solutions. The fact that a couple now is ready to acknowledge that they can use guidance in their problems and that they are willing to ask for it, is used to advance their cause. If counselees enter with some confidence in the minister as well as in the process of conjoint therapy, the chances become better for a propitious outcome. Although some clergy are awed and embarrassed by the trust parishioners sometimes place in them and the power they ascribe to them, this can aid progress in therapy. On the other hand, if counselees come with doubt and pessimism, this can work into a self-fulfilling prophecy that can lead toward failure.

The desire to make necessary changes in one's own ways of relating to others is another major factor in the context of any family therapy. It is not uncommon for wives to press for changes in their husbands, or husbands in their wives. Change seldom comes about that way, however. It is important to correct such imperialistic expectations with a cautionary word: "Of course you would like to change Henry's [or Henrietta's] ways. But it is fiendishly hard to influence someone else to change according to our own preferences. The only person you can change profoundly and readily is yourself. Let's work on that goal, each of you." And of course change *is* the goal of any therapy. Even when counselees are willing to assume responsibility for change in themselves, it will not come about easily. We seldom produce alterations in our habits simply by making up our minds to do so. The process may call for a manipulation of environment, some behavioral modification, or a support group to abet the change.

THE IMPORTANCE OF PROCESS

Alertness to what is happening within and during the interview is essential to effective therapy.

As a therapist, it will be your objective to keep the family away from overemphasis on issues of content (e.g., what kind of housekeeper Nellie is, or how much Jerry smokes) and focused on their own processes of relating to each other. Beginning therapists can be led astray by the mere facts of a case. Spending more time and attention on who did what and who said what than on the feelings and relationships of the people, they risk an early and unsatisfying termination. If we do not move couples and families away from a recital of grim details, they may not remain in therapy long enough to work through their conflicts. Unless we get them beyond their destructive ways of relating to each other (and to us), they can interpret our permission to review their many complaints as a support for their negative patterns. It is no wonder then that some drop out of the counseling interviews, too frightened to continue. Any valid theory of what makes family therapy work must credit attention to process. Process includes not only an analysis of interactions with one another, but also repeated reminders of what is happening in the therapy session itself.

A therapeutic group of counselees and minister is a community system of its own. The rapport that is built within it can contribute to the efficacy and the speed of therapy. To maintain a friendly, yet detached position in regard to families in therapy can inspire their confidence and improve their efforts to work on their relationships. In some respects this is a teaching-learning transaction, an educational event in which you as minister are the mentor and they the learners, studying new ways of relating to each other.

The more people learn about solving their own problems, the more likely it is that they can use their problem-solving techniques as they encounter new challenges. A chain reaction of improvement in family therapy extends to issues and to relief not originally envisioned. This is often dubbed "the ripple effect," and it can touch outlying problems that had never been mentioned in therapy sessions at all. A modest change in one aspect of people's interrelationships can be extended into other aspects and can contribute to healthier family life. It is never necessary, therefore, for families to seek therapy for every crisis that arises. Quite the contrary, it is preferable to place families on their own after a brief series of interviews, and to make of them their own family therapists. Indeed, *our goal is to put ourselves out of work as their therapists.* Through learning to solve one relationship problem, families can learn to solve others; thus leading to the prevention of still others that might have arisen.

INTERACTION IN THE SYSTEM

Modeling open communication will teach blocked families to be open.

Central to family therapy is the goal to improve relationships among family members. As soon as possible, therefore, the experienced therapist moves them from addressing him or her to talking with each other. This simple exercise in communication makes a valid point: they must learn to get along together without talking through an interpreter.

Communication is improved more by modeling clear messages than by talking about it. To ask a mother, "What do you understand your daughter to be saying to you?" is preferable to translating the message yourself.

Even in dealing with the sensitive question of an identified patient's place in family life, direct experience beats indirect description. To get in to the family system, therapists must get the confidence of the I.P. To the family, the I.P. has become no longer a person, but is identified with some unacceptable function. This is a crucial point. When the therapist begins to treat the I.P. like a person instead of a function, it becomes possible to challenge some behaviors as unacceptable; and, what is more, to express confidence that such behaviors can be controlled better than has been the case in the past. Such a therapeutic maneuver begins to drain some of the emotionality out of the relationship, relabeling the problem as a function rather than as an individual. It becomes a first step toward showing the family what their input is in contributing to the I.P.'s troubles. A major task of the therapist, in fact, is to lift the label of patient from one designated member and place it on the family system where it belongs.

Taking emotionality out of the therapeutic relationship and replacing it onto the family where it belongs is a common procedure of such experienced therapists as Murray Bowen. If Bowen begins to feel himself getting angry at an obdurate husband, he will turn to the wife and ask her what she does when she finds herself in the same position. If, for example, the husband has made an aggressive verbal attack on the therapist, it can be safely assumed that this is the way he behaves at home when he feels threatened. Counselees tend to treat the therapist the way they treat each other, it will be remembered. If you, as the therapist, are able to view the attack not so much a personal assault as a function of the man's relationship, you can then work with the family system in which this behavior occurs. By entering yourself into that system, you have become part of the family and are in a position to introduce a variety of interventions.

GOALS OF FAMILY THERAPY

No discussion of theory in family therapy could be considered complete without reference to other goals for which it is designed:

- A primary goal is to treat the specific problem or problems that have motivated the family to consult the pastor in the first place. Through improved functioning, family members may avoid some new complications spreading throughout the home.
- To achieve release from dysfunctional behavior, so that the family can better cope with their living among themselves.
- To work out such relief of pain that family members can be gratified by the improvement and encouraged to grapple anew with their difficulties.
- To aid each person in the household to learn how to say (and mean) yes and no, and how to express openly what she or he wishes.
- To discover how the presenting problem they brought into therapy was linked to their family system, and to demonstrate through the interviews how family members are involved with one another.
- To aid the family to become independent of the therapist so that it can depart with autonomy.
- To leave open the door for future returns if the family needs a check-up or additional help.

6. Seventeen Often-Asked Questions About Family Therapy

> The old joke that, after psychoanalysis, a Van Gogh would still cut off his ear, but would know why, is, as Freud points out, the revelation of truth in humor. The marriage fails; the patient has insight, but his behavioral contribution to the failure does not change. It is important that changes in behavior become the outcome criteria of therapy, not just inner understanding.
>
> —FREDERICK J. DUHL, "Learning, Space, and Action in Family Therapy"

TIME after time, in ministers' workshops and divinity school courses, certain predictable questions are raised. Seventeen of these are gathered and treated in this chapter.

1. *Sometimes I get stuck and don't know how to keep an interview going. What openers can I use to make an interview progress?*

Sometimes, of course, a period of silence in an interview can be an advantage to the process. But for restarters, the following will help:

- Probes for deepening the relationship:
  - What do you think about . . . ?
  - How do you show your feeling when . . . ?
  - What happens when you . . . ?
  - How do you suppose your family ever came to . . . ?
  - What did you hear him saying just then . . . ?
  - Can we check that out?
  - If I had been there, what would I have noticed?
- Procedures for keeping interviews moving:
  - At tense moments it is wise not to say things like, "Now

don't become anxious." Instead, avoid approaching a feeling directly by turning to queries of specificity (who, what,
when).
- Assure families that your office needs to be a safe place in
  which to express themselves; therefore they may not use
  against each other anything that is said there.
- Caution families not to fight at home during their series of
  interviews. This could bring them back to therapy emotionally black and blue. Encourage their openness—and
  their quarrels—under controlled conditions in the interview. "It is," as Augustus Napier notes, "an anxious step,
  inviting a family to bring all their long accumulated tension
  into your office. But then, where else can they take it?"
  (Napier and Whitaker, 1978, p. 34).
- Keep some tension in the interview. By any means, avoid
  languor and sloth. Comfortable interviews drift.
- Move descriptions of problems from the concrete to the
  affective; that is, from sheer recital of content over to the
  feeling level of the process.
· Helpful procedures that therapists use:
- When a dead silence descends upon the group, one that is
  not productive, repeat the last sentence that was uttered.
  That will often get the interview moving again. It also
  enables speakers to hear what they have said and to check
  out whether they were heard correctly.
- Occasionally translate what people are saying to each
  other. In slightly altered language, it will sound different
  to them; thus they may be motivated to work on communication.
  Change the subject when the emotional load is too great to
  bear or too heavy to produce a therapeutic effect. There is
  nothing wrong in allowing people to be uncomfortable, and
  it can be quite helpful at times; but it is counterproductive
  to have their anxiety block the process.

2. *What is the technique of relabeling and what does it accomplish?*
Relabeling at once puts a different light on a trait by calling it

by a different name; it has the virtue of using the converse side of a statement to make a positive out of a negative.

For example, anger may be interpreted as pain, hatred as fear, or interference as concern. A therapist may say to a counselee, "I'm glad, in a way, that you are depressed; it shows that you care."

Sometimes relabeling enables the therapist to remove an uncomplimentary label on a person and place it instead on a rule (e.g., the problem may not so much be in Henry as a person as in the rule that he is to empty the trash before 8 A.M. When that kind of relabeling is executed, we aid both Henry and Henry's parents to maintain a higher sense of self-worth).

3. Under what circumstances is it better not to recommend family therapy?

Family therapy, of course, is not the only form of psychotherapy to use, nor is it a panacea for all forms of emotional trauma. There will be occasions when family therapy is not indicated at all, and when some other form of therapy would be better applied. Moreover, there are times when family therapy is exactly right for the situation, but when certain forms of it are not appropriate for pastors to use.

A number of conditions may indicate that family therapy is not the treatment of choice. Among these are:

a. Any severe pathology in which one or more family members have excessive fear about exposure before the others.

b. A destructive motivation in one or more people, which may lead to some violence.

c. A progressive paranoid condition in one member of the family.

d. The presence of a confirmed criminal or psychopath in the family group.

e. A mixture of family members, some of whom are incapable of honesty and who deal in deceit as their way of interaction.

f. Illness or disease that prevents participation of a key person in the family.

It is generally agreed, on the other hand, that certain conflictual conditions in a family indicate that family therapy might be of real value. Among these are friction between parent and child; conflict that is repeated without any adequate awareness of its causation; marital quarreling; an interest in therapy and a willingness on the part of the counselees to use their strengths to make changes; or a situation of generalized family dysfunction, although there has been a previous ability to cope.

Several of the forms of family therapy, used by some of the best known therapists, may prove to be not recommended, even unusable, for the clergy.

a. The use of the more stringent paradoxical directives is not recommended to pastors. Not only do they take considerable skill and practice to execute, but there is the distinct possibility of confusion on the part of congregants when they come to realize that they have been led into the paradox by the clergyperson they had previously been taught to trust. The forms that clergy do use with effectiveness include reframing and preemptive introduction.

b. Likewise, the escalation of stress in order to provoke a therapeutic family crisis is seldom indicated for pastors; it is risky for the type of relationship most clergy have with their counselees. Although there are times when a pastor might justifiably escalate stress, those times must be chosen carefully and the condition must be induced gingerly.

c. In addition, the psychotherapy of the absurd (as practiced by Carl Whitaker and others) is hardly appropriate for most clergy to use in their family therapy; it is too prone to being misunderstood, and the relationships of the minister are too vulnerable to benefit from that method.

d. The social network method of assembling a group for family therapy is effective and commendable; yet its very complications and massiveness make it less than ideal for most clergy to handle. An aggregation of thirty or so relatives, friends, and neighbors make up a potentially unruly group for any but the most experienced of therapists to handle—and then better with the aid of some cotherapists.

4. *What is "a voyage home" to one's family of origin, and how does it work out?*

Some therapists, in a dramatic contradiction of Thomas Wolfe, insist that you can—indeed, you must—go home again. Murray Bowen, for instance, sends his patients back to their families of origin on "a family voyage" to trace their roots and to reopen their contacts. He coaches them on the time and the content of these visits to parents, grandparents, siblings, cousins, et al. They are assigned to inquire about the family past, to retrace relationships, to notice family patterns, and to rediscover their own selfhood (Bowen calls that step "differentiation") on such voyages. What is more, they will begin to see new aspects of their own choices, roles, relationships, and patterns of conduct as they notice their family members. When successful, a family voyage repairs old fractures in relationships and opens the way to more effective family therapy.

Counselees, in such a period, go back to their families for gradually increasing periods of time. The therapist, meanwhile, helps them to remain calm and objective enough to analyze the experiences that affect them most strongly.

Counselees are admonished to deal with only one parent at a time in any depth. Parents can be very skillful at fending off encounter if they are together and can exercise their practiced defenses.

The objective is also for the counselees to experience their families of origin and how they interact with them. In this pursuit, the counselees should be patient listeners and try to get their parents to talk about their own backgrounds. If the parents are now dead, then the counselee is sent to other relatives. Gradually, through this process, adult children gain the strength to differentiate themselves and thereby also to accept their parents. At the same time, the parents are allowed to accept their children as adults.

The voyage is particularly indicated in cases where adults have never felt emancipated from their parents and have never been able to grant autonomy in any respect to their own children;

where adults have become so enmeshed with their families of origin that they are unable to be effective spouses or parents themselves in maturity; where adults have so cut off their families of origin that they show signs of over reaction by having abandoned them. To such people, the therapist might put the crucial question: "What do you want to clear up with your parents before they die?"

A second kind of family visit can be held in the pastor's study. When the older parents are visiting in the local area, or when they can be persuaded to come into a family therapy session (and they are often astonishingly willing to do so), a couple in marital conflict might be joined by the parents of either spouse, or on rare occasions, the parents of both. Such two-generation events, though freighted with emotion, can turn out to be the breakthrough in a difficult case of marital conflict.

A symbolic imitation of the voyage home, developed by Florence Kaslow, is the survey of a family photograph album for the couple to tell about the people pictured there. From that explanation may come surprising revelations of secrets, memories, skeletons in closets, rules, meaningful relationships, and much more.

Therapists themselves can gain much by returning to their own homes for a voyage. This feature, in fact, is required in some training programs. Reasonable facsimiles of the experience are found in assignments to write one's autobiography in the context of the family system; this is practiced in many training centers including ours in Rochester. The resulting realization, revelations, and insights are astounding to many budding therapists; and, what is more, serve to make them into better family therapists. They come to the realization that we are all a little confused, even somewhat strange; they come to accept some of the oddities in their own families of origin, and subsequently to understand better some of the aberrations in their cases. Above all, they gain ability in helping people to free themselves because they have had the experience of gaining freedom.

5. *How can our pastoral visitation assist in family therapy?*

In some denominations, the long-respected pattern of home-calling by pastors has fallen on difficult times. Pressed by the multitudinous duties of ministry, many clergy today confine their pastoral calls only to the sick, the troubled, and to those with whom they have specific and current business, such as planning a church program. It is somewhat ironic, then, that members of other helping professions (e.g., social workers and psychotherapists) have taken up the practice of home calls and promote it as a valuable work.

Typically, such a psychotherapist makes an appointment to go to the home of a family under treatment and schedules the visit as a regular interview; this is to be a professional rather than a social event. Upon arrival, the therapist gets acquainted with all members of the household (including pets), and asks for a tour from top to bottom. The objective is to understand this family in as natural a situation as possible. The impact of experiencing events firsthand cannot be matched by mere description given at the office. Therapists on home visits have made unexpected discoveries: eight-year-old Jerry and his grandmother occupy the same bedroom; couples who are always well-groomed for office visits live in a state of disarray and dirt at home; or gloves-off fighting is a regular occurrence in the household; or there is present in the home a previously unacknowledged person.

Pastors have a natural passport into the homes of parishioners. They can take the initiative and, without being invited or even making an appointment, may call on the homes of the parish. As Henri Nouwen notes, "The pastor takes initiatives and can even be considered as an aggressive practitioner who wants 'to proclaim the message, welcome or unwelcome, and insist on it' (2 Tim. 4:2)" (Nouwen, 1971, p. 55).

The pastor can follow up reports or hunches about the difficulties in a family, and drop by to ask if all is well or if it is possible to be of help. The pastor can schedule routine pastoral calls in a neighborhood and, if alert to feelings, can pick up vibrations about family problems. The pastor can use the home as the locus for family therapy, choosing an evening hour when everyone is available. Thus the clerical caller has, through such easy entry, an advantage in family therapy.

6. *What is the importance of history-taking in a family interview?*

That the therapist must learn something about the history of a family in treatment is without doubt. What is questionable, however, is the amount of time that should be spent on this phase of therapy and the method that should be used. Theories and techniques vary widely according to the philosophy of the therapist and the context of the case. My own preference, taught in the Colgate Rochester Divinity School training program, is to spend minimal time on history-taking—but always to include some aspect of it in an early interview.

The advantages of history-taking are impressive. It helps family members to realize that there are connections with their past, and that former occurrences have a bearing on their current situation. It can uncover some of their patterns of secrecy and mystification. History-taking also aids a frenetic family to get under some control in that first anxious interview; it has a somewhat disciplinary effect. Virginia Satir (1964) notes that the historical questioning manages to connect current bad times with past good times, show the linkage between parent-child patterns and families of origin, and bring the present state of the family into a wider perspective. She reviews days of early courtship with couples, because "persons are first interested in each other because of their sameness, but they remain interested because of their differentness. Periodic loneliness is a natural outcome of being a separate person." Thus, by taking up the past and commenting upon its connectedness to the present and what this might mean, it may hold out the hope that good times can come again.

The disadvantages inherent in history-taking are nearly all problems of excess. It can be time consuming if the family and therapist get bogged down in too much detail or too many interesting stories about the past. Such digressions can be used as rationalized delays and resistances either by the family or by the therapist to keep from getting on with the counseling.

One argument against the formal history-taking has been that most of the pertinent facts will emerge in the case anyway; and when the family gets around to telling them, they may be more timely and significant than they would be if they were elicited by the therapist. Another argument, sometimes advanced by those whose historical research has led them astray, is that explorations of what has happened in the past lead a therapist into a bog where only the family knows the ground. In such cases, the reference to some obscure event in the past can detain by detail until the therapy all but grinds to a stop. Only an alert and determined therapist will be able to push a family beyond this point.

7. *What is a genogram, and how is it used in family therapy?*

One standard device for organizing a family's history is the genogram (pronounced *jeen-o-gram*). It originated in a research project at Harvard under the direction of Florence Kluckhohn, Norman Bell, and John Spiegel. The form now used by most family therapists is a simplified version designed by Murray Bowen.

The genogram covers not only the family's current history, but also reaches back through previous generations—at least to the grandparents of the adults. Together with the family, the therapist plots the generations and significant events, meanwhile keeping aware of the family's patterns of interaction as they discuss people and places. This device can be used to discover details about health, religious and ethnic background, deaths, divorces, relationships, moves, transgenerational patterns, broken relationships, scandals, strengths, traditions, and family ghosts. If children are present at this session, they may learn for the first time that their family has a history.

Background questions are asked about names, ages, dates of marriages, births, deaths, and other significant events. The therapist will be alert to tones and nuances in the reportage, to off-hand references and incidentals, to indications of how the family system works, and to how the generations have gotten along together. Soon the "toxic issues" that poison their relations may emerge. From this inquiry about the organization of characteristics and circumstances, it is possible in a relatively brief time to detail the major problems of the family. For the sake of convenience, a genogram utilizes a series of standard symbols (see Figure 1). Figure 2 shows an example of a genogram as it might be plotted for a particular family.

Figure 1. Symbols used in a genogram

☐	Male	**/ D**	Divorce
○	Female	**M**	Marriage
B	Birth	——	Horizontal Marriage Line
X	Death	|	Vertical Generation Line

In Figure 2, we see a four-generational genogram. Charles and Rachel are the couple in therapy. Married in 1943, they have now come into a later stage of marriage where new adjustments must be made. They have had three children during the country's "baby boom" in the 1940s; each of those children is now grown and married, and there are grandchildren as well. Both Charles and Rachel have a living parent, the elderly survivors of this family. Charles' parents were divorced in 1940; and his mother died in 1966. Rachel's father died in 1972. Their children were born in 1945, 1947, and 1949. Each of them married (e.g., M. '71, M. '68, etc.). They, in turn, bore children (see the bottom generation line).

Far from being a simple, mechanical device, the genogram is a counseling tool that opens up a number of topics and feelings. The minister can prompt counselees with a few leading questions as the generations are filled in: "How would you like to have a marriage like that of your parents?" "How did that come about?" "Do you still have strong feelings about it?" "Who are the pow-

Figure 2. An example of a four-generational genogram

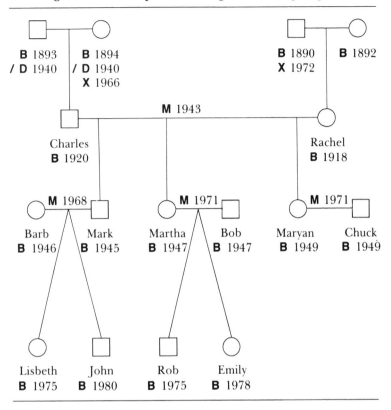

ers in this chart?" These queries can lead into significant areas. The genogram then becomes a doorway into a deeper level of therapy, and a source of pertinent information for that stage.

8. *I get stopped by resistant counselees. What can be done to meet their resistance?*

To the inexperienced counselor, it is always puzzling to learn that people will ask for help and then rebuff it. The specter of resistance is hard to understand. That people who have asked for assistance would omit some facts on purpose, explain away others, or lie outright seems incomprehensible. Yet, in order to maintain the therapist's esteem, some counselees believe they must cover their traces with fiction. They may even be voicing their fables to fool themselves.

Resistance can take many forms. Families may cancel their appointments at the last minute. They may refuse to carry out some assigned task. Some may balk at responding openly in the session itself. Others may arrive late or declare that they must leave early for an important appointment.

Many resistances, however, are not so bald. They are present in the form of bullying, manipulation, helplessness, threat, negativism, or even compliments. Confronted with these, the family therapist counters with polite firmness and a reminder that all of us are in charge of our own lives and cannot fob the responsibility off on another.

Bullying of the therapist by an individual, or sometimes even by the entire family, is not unusual. It has to be handled promptly and calmly: "My job here is not to debate with you until one of us wins the debate. What I can do is to let you know what I see and hear and feel in your relationships and what I perceive may be going on among you."

Compliments, which superficially appear to be affirmation, may be a form of stiff resistance. "We both know that you are the finest marriage counselor in the city," is said with a winning smile, but can mean the beginning of noncooperation. A therapist who is caught in this situation might respond, "Thank you for your compliment, but it makes me feel uncomfortable. I don't know why. Can you help me figure out why it should?"

Helplessness plays directly into the hands of the minister-as-rescuer; and many of us get caught by it. "I'm feeling some signals of helplessness from you," might be the frank rejoinder to this resistance; "It makes me feel that it's up to me to work it out if we're going to make any progress. But is it really?"

Threats, in their outright and naked form, are seldom encountered in family therapy. When they do come, they are frequently references to dropping out of therapy because it isn't doing any good. The therapist might reply, "Perhaps you do need to consider carefully whether to come back again. I see it differently; but you are the final judge on its value." Do not defend yourself against such accusations; it only invites further attack.

Negativism about their family living, their own worth, or even about life itself needs to be countered with an intervention that places responsibility squarely on the counselees. "I would look foolish trying to argue that you have more possibilities than you realize. What we can do together is to evaluate whatever is stopping you from getting satisfaction out of life."

Anger is a highly useful and intimidating tool for those who lack any smoother form of negotiation with others. Such people, of course, will exercise it on you as the minister-therapist. Stop such a person and ask, "What happened inside you just before you became angry?" This gets down to the triggering feeling and helps to relive the experience. If the counselees go on to mount accusation on top of indignation and say, "You made me angry," assure them that no one else can really make them angry; they make themselves angry. A Gestalt therapist might go on and ask them to analyze the experience with "How did you make yourselves angry?"

Distancing is a common device people use to control others. Such counselees pull away emotionally and make themselves unavailable for contact. To pursue distancers is folly; they may only withdraw to ever-farther positions. Instead, pull back yourself, and allow the distancer to stop and to return part way for reestablishment of the lost contact. Try a new topic with the counselees; if that does not succeed, frankly acknowledge the impasse: "Evidently, you don't really want to work on the issue today. Shall we just stop?" (Not a little of this resistance in therapy sessions is matched by a similar resistance in the corporate life of a congregation. Ministers have found that the skills they learn to exercise in counseling can be transferred to organizational relationships in the parish [see Dittes, 1979].)

As therapists, we are not limited to countering resistance as initiated by counselees—we can do much to avoid it in the first place. The very manner in which we pose and pursue our questions will make a difference. To press repeated questions to reticent or tired counselees produces feelings of pressure that they may feel compelled to defend. The persistent inquisition is not unlike a police officer's action in seeking to trap a suspect, and will inevitably promote resistance that might easily have been avoided with courtesy and skill. We must beware that we do not promote unwanted resistance by our own methods. Who can blame them for getting their collective resistance up? "After all," as Augustus Napier writes, "this system—these people, this subtle language and tonality and pattern derived out of years of life invested together—is all they have. It is the central continuity of their lives, the bridge between their past and their future" (Napier and Whitaker, 1978, p. 81).

9. *What is brief therapy?*

Brief therapy is, of course, a relative term; and the inquirer has reason to ask, "Relative to what?" In psychotherapy, the brevity to which it refers is considered in contrast to psychoanalysis, which sometimes stretches into three and more years. Family therapists mean by brief therapy a series of interviews that range from three to twelve sessions.

It is generally agreed that the termination of a brief series ought to include a follow-up arrangement for quick access to the therapist if further difficulties arise (see question 17 below). Thus crisis intervention may follow this brief sequence.

Brief therapies also build in a time for brief evaluation. The very least that must be delivered in a short span of interviews is a partial assessment of the couple or the family and some objective view of their tangled relationships.

10. *What is a contract in family therapy?*

"Contract" is a loose term in family therapy. It is meant to cover whatever agreement family and therapist make about their arrangements to work with each other. A contract will usually cover the understanding of who is to come for therapy sessions, how often sessions will be scheduled and when, what problems are to be discussed, and what fee or gift, if any, is expected.

More involved contracts in family therapy go on from this point to cover aspects of number of minutes per interview, completion of assignments, the method of termination, and much else.

11. *What records does a pastor keep in doing family therapy?*

Record-keeping in family therapy is a must; but it can be held to a minimum. It is hardly necessary to keep a word for word transcript, except for those segments of an interview whose very phrases and responses you wish to preserve. A serviceable record for each case consists of its own separate file in a folder or an individual section of a loose-leaf binder. It should include vital information on the family, their genogram (see question 7), and a note about agreements understood between the family and the pastor (see question 10). It should also include the planning sheet for each session (i.e., a paragraph that lays out your plan of treatment and objectives before you meet the family). There it can contain a short summary of each session together with the expectations for the following session (assigned tasks that will be recalled, topics to be resumed, and so on).

Finally, it should be emphasized that such records are to be locked safely away from prying eyes. It is unnecessary to enter into the summaries the most dramatic revelations; you recall those easily. But even the ordinary stuff of family life must be kept confidential in records; and a safe place and some code for names are essential.

Writing down our experiences is important not only to stimulate our memory about particulars, but also for us to learn from our ministry and to be able to bring theological reflection to bear on the nature of our work. Keeping records keeps us reflective.

12. *What are the rules of confidentiality in family therapy?*

Some family therapists insist that they will not keep any secrets and that all information must be shared openly from the outset. I can agree with their ideal, but find the rule too doctrinaire. There are cases where some item vouchsafed to the therapist is too painful and potentially disruptive to be brought out of the past for exposure.

Others, and I am among them, attempt to get individuals to share some of their secrets with the family as a means of cementing relationships and preventing splits. In the mean time, the therapist may be keeping the report confidential until the time comes for the individual to divulge it. Still others accept some confidences and keep them secret from family members while turning aside other secrets, depending somewhat upon their nature and the circumstances.

The *sine qua non* of confidentiality is that the pastor will not divulge the problems and circumstances of the family to anyone else without the family's express permission. Permission is sometimes requested for a conversation with the physician, a report to one's supervisor, or a consultation with a social worker involved in the case.

Beyond that, it behooves us to remember that dredging up old secrets, while freeing some families, may harm others. The minister will want to keep confidential whatever is told in confidence, for this is an essential ingredient in establishing trust. Some court decisions in recent years appear to have eroded clergy privilege in regard to confidence, and state laws differ. But Kentucky's law, for example, decrees that no minister can be forced to testify in court about matters told him or her in confidence. The situation is open to change and disputed interpretation and should be followed closely.

13. *What exactly are referrals, and how are they made?*
Referrals are any conveyance of counselees to some other helping source. One may refer a counselee to a psychiatrist, a physician, a financial advisor, or any of a large number of specialists, as needed. We know that it is time to make a referral when the counselees' needs are not only urgent but also beyond our abilities to aid.

The pastor should introduce the idea of referral gradually. The initial step may be no more than observing, "That particular problem is one I won't be able to help with," before moving on. The next may be a more direct, "We'll come back to that. I think

I know someone who can aid you in it." In most cases the referral arrangements should be made in the presence of both marital partners or, for children, in the presence of a parent. The pastor should also brief the specialist who is to work with the counselee.

Pastors generally refer to mental health professionals in this order: marriage counselors, physicians, psychiatrists, rehabilitation and guidance counselors, social workers, and psychologists (Fairchild, 1980, p. 90). It is a good idea for clergy to become personally acquainted with local people in the helping professions, and with the quality of their work, in order to make appropriate and confident referrals.

Generally, pastors will refer to psychiatry those people who: (1) have some chemical dependency beyond the reach of verbal therapy; indeed, where psychopharmaceuticals may be needed; (2) need long-term psychotherapy beyond the skill and resources of the work-a-week pastor; (3) show clear suicide risk and may be in need of hospitalization; (4) exhibit evidence of unmanaged schizophrenic and paranoid disorders;* and (5) tend to violence and antisocial acts that endanger others.

14. *What is family sculpting and how is it done?*

Family sculpting has been used for more than a decade as a means of getting around some of the limitations of language by physically placing family members in positions that graphically illustrate the nature of their relationships. Devised and developed by David Kantor, Fred and Bunny Duhl, and Peggy Papp (Papp, 1976), it aids the less articulate in expressing their feelings and thoughts; it also prevents some of the use of language as a defense to deny, avoid, rationalize, and cover up secrets and alienations.

For example, the therapist asks a ten-year-old girl to "sculpt"

---

*The referral of a person with paranoia requires special handling. Nancy Andreasen advises that this person should "never be characterized as paranoid but should be told sympathetically that he is unhappy and uncomfortable about the rebuffs which he feels he has experienced and that a medical doctor may be able to provide a medication which will help him feel less painful and unhappy" (Andreasen, 1977, p. 200).

her family by placing her parents in the symbolic positions in which she most often experiences them. She takes their hands and puts one at one end of the room, the other at the opposite. She turns their faces from each other and toward her in the third corner position of a triangle. The therapist then asks her to place them in a position she would prefer. Slowly, hesitatingly, she takes them by hand and brings them together and places their arms around each other in an embrace. She herself stands at their side with her hand on their arms. Silently, they reach down and include her in their embrace. Everyone's eyes become moist as her feelings are made poignantly clear.

In fact, the message is clearer than it could have been if everyone had been asked to describe the situation verbally. The way is now open to work with that family system.

A variation on the family sculpture technique is a development Peggy Papp now calls "choreography"—an emphasis in sculpture that involves more movement and discussion than the tableau seems to encourage. The family members often shift their positions and remain in motion when choreographing their relationships.

15. *How is role playing used in family therapy?*

Role playing in family therapy is not different from its use in education. Family members are asked to assume assigned roles in order to test their feelings about themselves and to better understand the issues that brought them into therapy. Some of the more common role situations are:

- *Reenactment:* a married couple may be asked to reenact some previous misunderstanding or conflict. In several run-throughs, they can (1) show how it happened; (2) practice how it might have developed if they had altered their responses to each other; and (3) experiment with some totally new concept of relating to each other.
- *Rehearsal:* family members may act out a situation they expect to face soon, so as to gain some proficiency in handling the problems they anticipate. One family, for example, tried out

several different approaches to welcoming a difficult grandmother who was arriving to live with the family.

- *Recollection:* people may be invited to rid themselves of pent-
up toxic feelings by speaking to some dreaded being as if
that one were there. Thus a woman might, in line with a
famous Gestalt technique, address an empty chair as if her
father were sitting in it.
- *Reversal:* two people can be asked to take each other's roles
and speak through them in order to gain a deeper appreciation of the alternate viewpoint. A counselor might ask a
father to play out his daughter's role, and the daughter to act
out his as a means of aiding them to understand each other.
This is role reversal.

16. *How are homework assignments used in family therapy?*

Homework tasks are often assigned by family therapists because they keep the family working on the problem, and also
because more progress can sometimes be made by families between interviews than during them. Guided projects in those
intervals can be therapeutic. Typical homework tasks include an
assignment to work out peaceably some family project such as a
weekend trip; to schedule an evening date for parents who have
not been away from their children in months; or to keep a written
diary or chart of certain behaviors.

It is important that the minister who assigns such tasks to keep
notes about it and to ask about it at the next session. If the family
has failed to complete the task, it is simply expected to fulfill it
before another session.

Homework assignments, like all directives, have to be chosen
with care and assigned with discretion. Haley believes that if we
wish to get a family to behave better, it is important to give them
a directive so small that it appears trivial to them. Moreover, it
helps immensely if the directive joins some impulse the counselees already feel; to ask a man to take his wife out to dinner
succeeds best if he is already moving in that direction.

17. *How do we know when to close out a series of interviews in family therapy? What are the signs that we have completed therapy?*

You're coming toward termination when the first suggestion of ending therapy is voiced. It may be you as minister and therapist, or a family member, or both who mention it. The signs will be there; perhaps the family is now communicating more openly and freely; or they can allow individuals to be themselves and even to be different without its causing conflict; or they have made a change or two in their relationships and actually like the effect.

The end is predictably in sight, of course, if you and the family have contracted for a definite number of sessions and the final one is approaching. This means either the end of the series or a necessary stop for evaluation and review to reset a new number.

Termination is also indicated if the couple or the family have taken the proverbial "flight into health." Whether you believe that this marvelous improvement is permanent or not, you have little recourse but to end the therapy in the face of their claim that everything is coming up roses. You might, however, leave the door ajar for their easy reentry in case they require a subsequent "check-up."

To leave such an arrangement is wise in any case. It should be possible for counselees to return for additional help and without embarrassment when they recognize the need for assistance. A simple assurance that "the door is open for you to come back for a chat when you like," is adequate invitation for most.

That spirit, in fact, will assist the entire process. An open stance on the part of the pastor, holding out the promise of a continuing relationship beyond the counseling, will ease any separation anxieties. An open stance will also allow counselees the freedom to speak up when they are dissatisfied and wish to leave therapy instead of dreading that they may be in it *ad infinitum.*

7. Pastoral Theology and Family Therapy

> It is not so much that I bring the good news of the possibility of reconciliation to the family, but that I discover the power of God working in the helping process.
> —A. J. VAN DEN BLINK, "Family Therapy and Pastoral Care"

PASTORAL theology presents difficult and vexing questions to clergy engaged in family therapy. If we are to develop a competence in family therapy, how are we also to maintain our theological commitment? How can we remain faithful to our task as theologians and still enter into the specialized work of therapists? These two questions are effectively the same, and it is to them that we turn in this chapter.

No minister could be simply the mirror image of the secular psychotherapist. We carry with us, as few psychotherapists must, dynamic theological convictions, the ineluctible material of our Christian faith. It is therefore manifestly impossible for us to bracket off our theology and set it aside while we are at work as pastoral therapists. To be sure, many clergy attempt to do just that; but the attempt fails, and their presuppositions break through in spite of themselves. In any case, clergy can hardly be true to their vocation if they try somehow to be nontheologians just at the very time they are working within their own helping profession.

Our experience at the Divinity School, in placing theological students in family social agencies for supervised training, has sometimes fomented just such a crisis of confused identity. Some trainees, unsure of themselves, have denied the theological side of their profession in order to better imitate a model of psychotherapist. Because this has so often led to embarrassment with counselees, the doctoral seminar now features role playing and discussion of this very difficulty. Taking off from a real incident, one trainee (playing the part of a counselee) abruptly challenges another (who is playing the part of family therapist) with, "Say, what are you—a priest or something?" With one's cover blown so precipitously, the pastor *qua* family therapist must quickly come to terms with this dual identity and deal with it on the spot.

As pastors, we have many roles. We are preachers, educators, liturgists, evangelists, counselors, administrators; yet we cannot disavow we are primarily theologians. Our theology is applied theology, grounded where life is lived and where issues are real.

THEOLOGY IS INESCAPABLE

Obviously, there is no escaping theology even if we wish to. It is not possible for anyone, let alone the minister, to avoid thinking along theological lines; we all fall into the habit in spite of ourselves. Everyone, even the unreflective, comes to moments of asking questions about the nature and destiny of life. Basic theological questions occur within the fleeting sentences of even casual conversations. Far more, then, will theology show itself in the thinking and speech of the clergy. Christianity is a thinking faith; the "God talk" of theological perspective is at its very foundation. It must perforce play an integral part in our practice of counseling.

In the main it will not be our diagnostic skills, our technical training, or our understanding of personality theory that alone make us effective in family therapy, but, as Thomas Oden (1974a) suggests, our ability to mediate actual redemptive possibilities. Those redemptive possibilities do not reside in us; rather, they are to be found in the grace of God, over and above our counseling skills and our therapeutic practice. As ministers, we will understand the family members to be God's creations in need of, and entitled to, his grace. Even more to the point, as ministers we also stand in need of God's grace, and are keenly aware of it.

So we not only pray *for* the troubled family in our intercessions, but at church worship we also pray *with* them in the general confession; for we all stand in the same need of God's forgiveness (Brister, 1978). This acknowledgment of our collective sin and failure is a part of our Christian theory of personality. Troubled people are God's people too; and although we may be ministering to persons more disturbed than ourselves, our human condition is much the same. In fact, it is while working through the relationships we have with people and offering whatever help we can that we begin to realize the far-reaching implications for our own personal lives.

PSYCHOTHERAPISTS AND CLERGY ONLY *LOOK* ALIKE

In some ways, of course, psychotherapists and ministers resemble each other. So like the time-worn examination question to "compare and contrast" two entities, our quest leads us now to identify both the similarities and the distinctions between psychotherapists and ministers. At the outset, we are impressed more by their commonality than by their differences. Exemplifying Harry Stack Sullivan's famed one-genus theory that we are all much more nearly alike than we are different, these two helping professions appear as lookalikes. They do have characteristics in common: both are supportive of measures that make for health and prevent disease, both care about persons and their development; both are educators in their own ways; both know that values are inevitably involved in counseling; both promote personal integrity, foster positive relationships, and confront dysfunctional behavior.

Paul Tillich (1952, p. 77) noted how both clergy and psychotherapists take on each other's specialities. In discussing the relations between the two, he pointed out distinctions in terms of how human anxiety is seen and treated:

Neither the medical nor the priestly function is bound to its vocational representatives: the minister may be a healer and the psychotherapist a priest, and each human may be both in relation to the "neighbor." But the functions should not be confused and the representatives should not try to replace each other.

One goal of both the medic and the priest is to help people to reach their full self-affirmation; or, in Tillich's own phrase (1952), their "courage to be." It was his observation that psychiatrists and clergy struggle with each other over the best ways of healing anxiety. This, he felt, was a useless contest: for anxiety is a universal condition and psychotherapists and theologians need each other's cooperation in their mutual work. He saw no reason for ministers to aspire to become medical types; for the ministry has a unique task of its own.

Pastoral Therapy Has Distinctive Aspects

While it is undeniable that members of all helping professions share in similar motivation and mutual work, there remain distinctive aspects of ministry that mark us out with significant differences from our colleagues in the psychotherapeutic specialties. These involve the observation that pastors are a preferred choice as counselors; that they are specialists in unraveling the ultimate meaning of life; that they are convinced of the capacity of people to change through conversion; that they can view family relations as convenantal; and that they are committed to a goal of reconciliation.

A First Stop for Therapy

Pastors, whether we choose it or not, are often the first resort of aid for people in distress. A host of people seeking counsel for personal and interpersonal problems show a strong preference toward consulting ministers over other helping professions (Fairchild, 1980; Mudd and Peterson, 1968). A survey by Richard Kulka and his research team at the University of Michigan in 1979 shows that clergy lead the list of physicians, psychiatrists, social workers, and others to whom troubled people turn. Even if their ulterior destination is psychiatric treatment, many churchfolk prefer to find their referral via the pastor's study. Nor is this tendency confined to church members; numerous neighbors of the community, and those who belong to no church at all, frequently turn first to the clergy in time of stress. Through experience and tradition they have learned that a caring ministry is to be found in the church. It is generally trusted, widely available, and usually free or inexpensive.

Sometimes, of course, it is the pastor who takes the initiative and seeks out the troubled family. Frequently aware of conflicted conditions in parish homes even before they reach the crisis stage, ministers are in a position to render aid to families who might otherwise not get any help at all. As ministers, we may be needed more than we realize.

The Search for Ultimate Meaning

Pastors, through their vocation in the cure of souls, serve as specialists in theological questions. Without making an issue of it, we must remain alert to the theological questions that distressed people continually ask. It is essential for us to be able to recognize these theological queries when they emerge; for they are seldom posed in pious terms or metaphysical vocabulary. Yet, as Reinhold Niebuhr (1946) reminded, the most urgent challenge raised for theology is a basic question as to whether life has any meaning. It is the self-same problem posed by William James in his famed essay, "What Makes a Life Significant?" (James, 1912). It is the concern raised by thousands of people whose despair has led them into therapy. (Even preschool children repeatedly voice questions that are essentially theological; and they must be treated, needless to say, with respect and seriousness. Such questions as "Where did Grandpa go when he died?" "Why are some people so bad that I am not allowed to ride with them?" "Does God have a big house?" are a typical sample of queries that can open a profound teaching opportunity.)

Sometimes, indeed, the presenting problem from a counselee about a family difficulty may be but the thin cover of a deeper religious concern. (The opposite may also be true: a parishioner bringing a religious question to a pastor may be masking a personal problem of difficult dimension.) Carl G. Jung (1953) was convinced that the majority of people who turn to their pastors for help in solving personal problems are actually seeking assistance in some aspect of religious or moral self-evaluation. More especially, he believed that those past middle-age are seeking religious certainty whenever they request personal counseling; maybe, because as Paul Tillich (1951) believed, the threat of nonbeing increases with age.

Seminary training in therapy, therefore, involves the education of theologues to hear questions about meaning and value, and to become more aware of their own capacity to assist troubled people with troubling questions. Indeed in their systematic theology, ministers are also being prepared for such counseling. Theology comprises an attempt to order our God-talk and our conceptualization of the elements of faith. Systematic theology, in fact, is a deliberate organization of doctrines that impart meaning to existence and illumination to our human condition; for example, considerations of sin and salvation, of redemption and reconciliation, impinge directly upon the very problems of human relationship that counselees bring to clergy. For what is theology but "the attempt to speak consistently about the human predicament, the possibility of deliverance from the predicament, and the means of implementing that new possibility" (Oden, 1974a, p. 48)?

The pastor who begins to comprehend how counseling and theology blend in ministry comes to see its encouraging impact on a sense of our worth and work. Henri Nouwen (1971) has identified this as creative ministry and noted that, when a minister discovers the ability to give life to people by enabling them to face their real condition without fear, the minister will at the same time cease considering this work on the periphery of reality. Such a minister, instead, is at the very center; and theological competence is a *sine qua non* for such counseling. We must be the kind of practical theologians who can bring theological understanding into significant relation for human experience. "At the very least," as C. W. Brister (1978) writes, "our Christian approach to therapy can be characterized by theological richness in congruity with Christian tradition. [Such an approach can impart] a vision of spiritual wholeness rooted in the promise of the Christian faith."

Therapy, though it can deal effectively in the depth of personal trauma, remains unfinished unless it also reaches the counselee's anxiety about meaninglessness, emptiness, and guilt; for even after therapy sessions are completed, one still retains questions about life and about death. When ministers are operating as therapists, their work with a family is not over when the presenting pain is assuaged; there is still work to be done in personal growth and in the strengthening of faith. Ministers acting as therapists are also specialists in meaning and, as such, are not permitted to forget that Jesus is ever Lord of our life and of our times, and that his lordship stands over our plans and decision-making, our family loyalties, our vocation, and our counseling.

The Possibility of Personal Conversion

The minister-as-therapist retains a pervading and realistic optimism about the capacity men and women possess for making personal changes and even experiencing conversion in their attitudes and habits. Of course, all therapists everywhere believe that change in affect and in personality are possible; else they could not be in the work. The very idea of therapy, like the very essence of education, is that change is not only possible, but that it can be programmed. Such a concept of mutability is essential to the practice of family therapy.

Now if the secular therapist believes in change, the minister will be even more confident in change. For the minister is acquainted with religious conversion and its tremendous power to alter lives. More than that, the minister is convinced about the working of God's grace in human lives, and has faith that God can do abundantly more than we can ask or think to bring about transformations in people and in their relationships.

The goals of changing individual conduct, of changing the ways people regard each other, of changing dysfunctional family systems: all these are central to the concept of family therapy. Nothing could be more integral to Christian faith. Christians know that dramatic change and conversion are possible; they have been witness both to the amazing turnabout in lives of people they know, and also to the witness of the Bible concerning repentance and conversion. They have a name for the new relationship that makes so great an alteration possible: salvation. Those in Christ, St. Paul assures, become entirely new creations (2 Cor. 5:17), transformed by the renewal of their minds (Rom. 12:2).

In Christ, God reveals what we are to become—new beings altogether. In his law of love, we are given a new birth. Our calling as God's children, our calling in our sexuality, our calling in our particular marital status, and our acceptance as forgiven but fallible persons: all these are possible because of God's grace. In the Incarnation, we have seen the ultimate length to which God will go to grant us salvation and to transform us into new beings. In such a massive change even the threat of death, the specter of meaninglessness, and the burden of unalleviated guilt are overcome. The miracle of the Incarnation, as Origen once put it, means that God became like us so the we might become like him.

Change in therapy remains small change when compared to the mystery of conversion. The minister-as-therapist lives and works in the expectation of both.

The Covenantal View of the Family

Pastors bring into the practice of family therapy a distinctly biblical conception of the family. The view that the family is covenantal sounds odd to modern ears; still, this notion from the scriptures remains valuable for contemporary life. The vows that we make, our mutual decisions, our renegotiations, and our obligations of marriage and family life remain covenantal today for Judeao-Christian traditions.

There are distinctions, of course, between the contemporary family and the biblical family regarding covenantal relationships. Nevertheless, the biblical example remains normative. The family in biblical times was always intergenerational; the tight nuclear family we know today would be unthinkable to ancient Israel. The complex relationships within the family were covenanted: the central issue in marriage was lasting fidelity; the obligation for parents was nurture and discipline of children; the ties of brothers and sisters were meant to preserve the family tradition and estate for following generations. In such a system, the entity of the entire household becomes a phalanx of solidarity against threats from the world outside.

Biblically grounded pastors, realizing that they are working with a covenanted relationship, proceed differently from the secular therapist. That could be, in part, the result of regarding the marriage vows so seriously; a regard that moves the pastor toward a bias for reconciliation.

The Tilt Toward Reconciliation

Finally, ministers who do family therapy will invariably reveal a stronger commitment to reconciliation than their colleagues in the therapeutic professions. Called to a ministry of reconciliation from the outset, pastors bear this calling into all parts of ministry. In the pulpit we preach that central theme of biblical theology: "God was in Christ, reconciling the world unto himself and entrusting to us the message of reconciliation" (2 Cor. 5:19). Thus Christian ministers, with a divine example to inspire them, cannot afford any privilege of neutrality in respect to whether to try to repair a broken marriage or allow it to split. The clergy will, first of all, always explore the possibility of reconciliation. If we are wise, we will not attempt to press a husband and wife into a relationship of continuing and hopeless hostility wherein they can destroy each other; we cannot prescribe reconciliation whatever the cost. We will, however, search out those positive clues that could lead to rebuilding once firm and living ties. Reconciliation is an integral part of our function because ours is a ministry of reconciliation. Our doctrine of sin makes us realistic; our faith in God keeps us hopeful.

THE MINISTERIAL MODEL FOR COUNSELING

We clergy differ in another respect from other helping professions in that our model for family therapy is ministerial. In the helping professions, on the other hand, it is the medical model that long has served as a standard in counseling. Because psychiatrists are physicians, and because theirs has been the eminent example for all forms of psychotherapy, their model has carried prestige and dominated the style for many imitators. Many social workers, marriage counselors, personnel officers, and, of course, clergy have, at one time or another, adopted this medical model. They have mimicked the techniques of examination, diagnosis, probing, prescription, and treatment. They have appropriated something of the doctor-patient relationship. They have used medical terms, and have conducted their business practices much as psychiatrists do.

Because many of the clergy have picked up medical terminology and mannerisms from clinical pastoral education in hospital settings, the medical model has been taken over without sufficient critical thought. The manifest incompatibilities between an internist's waiting room and a pastor's study seem not to have occurred to some. Yet the trappings of white coat, diagnostic procedures, and billing arrangements have small place in the church.

Nor is the industrial model of counseling used by the personnel officer of any direct value in the church setting either. It carries along with it an employer-employee nexus with inferences about assignment, advancement, and income that are irrelevant to much of our work. Similarly, the educational model of guidance counseling (despite its features of problem-solving, teaching of interpersonal skills, and mentor-student transactions) cannot quite serve as the model for ministry.

Ours, quite simply and necessarily, is the ministerial model in therapy. It is theologically based in Christian convictions about the value of people created by God and reconciled in Jesus Christ. It is informed by our understanding of a fallen humanity in shocking need of salvation, and in our faith that men and women are redeemable despite everything we know about their fallible nature and original sin. The pastoral model of counseling knows the grace of forgiveness and the practice of our forgiving each other, grounded in the conviction that God has already

forgiven us. The ministerial model contains a confidence in Prov-
idence and the bountiful gifts from a God who cares too much
for us to allow us to stay down where we, in our heedlessness,
have stumbled. It places realistic emphasis on healing as restora-
tion to wholeness of life and health; this is theological derivative
from our concern for the cure of souls. The ministerial model
assumes that a far higher power than our own pastoral skills is
operating in redeeming the lives of women and men, and that
God's grace can greatly improve upon our ministerial techniques
of working with his people.

Operating within these convictions, the ministerial model has
some distinctive characteristics. The setting is generally to be
found within a church building; and that context itself contributes to the expectations and effectiveness of the therapeutic situation (Hiltner and Colston, 1961). In this model, the therapist-
minister often is acquainted with the individuals or family, and
can bring to bear previous knowledge from church and community on the their relationship. Bearing on the acquaintanceship,
the minister can also refer back to previous experiences together
(e.g., a confirmation class or another counseling time) and carefully ask about the spiritual health of counselees, their practice
of prayer, and their faith; these being integral to the therapy
itself. The minister, who comes into the therapy situation as a
wounded healer, is able to suffer with counselees and understand
their grief. The minister can share, where appropriate, faith statements and witness with families in stress. On these respects the
ministerial model is unique.

CAVEAT CLERICUS

Let the clergy beware: we have peculiar temptations in our
counseling. Irrespective of our distinctions as therapists and of
our pastoral model in the practice of family therapy, we ministers
must be alert for three potholes of difficulty in our work with
families in distress. We shall need to guard against (1) an unwanted pious approach in family therapy; (2) against any unreal-

istic acceptance of human sin; and (3) against naive assumptions that fail to take account of the problem-centered tradition of our family theology.

First, some of us have a prevailing temptation to exhibit our religious stance in unwanted ways when we are counseling. That we are primarily theologians ought, by now, to be undeniable. Nevertheless, there is good cause to exercise caution in regard to displaying either our theology or our sacerdotal style when dealing with the family problems of our people. When wife and husband seek us out to discuss their conflicted marriage, it is hardly the time for even a short discourse on the eighth chapter of Romans or a review of St. Augustine's ambivalence about marital relations.

At its worst, some self-conscious explication of theology could impel us into the gross error of actually preaching to a troubled couple. The place for sound preaching is in the pulpit. Even if preaching during therapy resulted in a good homily, such conduct is irrelevant to the immediate pain and problem, no matter how apt the topic might be. The dangers of tumbling headlong into moralism and judgmentalism are already so great in our pastoral processes that we must take elaborate care to avoid any and all inappropriate theologizing in that setting. In any event, as Dietrich Bonhoeffer once noted, we are not expected to be more religious than God.

Likewise, the use of spoken prayer in a therapy session with couples or families will call for careful, critical decision. It is not our silent intercession for strength and wisdom, nor the general confession in the service of worship that cause the trouble. These have their undisputed place. The difficulty is that it is not unheard of (I wish that it were) for a minister to close a counseling interview with a prayer in which a forgotten point of advice or a neglected insight is now added, or even wherein a heretofore client-centered interview now becomes blatantly directive through some word to God, on the side. Of course, explicit prayer does have its place in the interview if the couple requests it, if the tone is one of humble access, and if it is not to be used as heavy-handed persuasion on the counselees themselves. Moving into prayer in therapeutic situations calls for care and compassion.

Nor are we called particularly to underscore our status as theologians when we are engaged in counseling. The public already know us as clergy anyway; the families who consult us will hardly have forgotten our vocation. They probably have already seen us in one of our other functions where our cloth shows through plainly, as in our leadership of divine worship or delivering the invocation at a Rotarian luncheon. In any case, it is all too likely that our nonverbal symbolism of clericalism will leak through at times, no matter what we do to stanch it. (The use of video tape in our training program for family therapists has helped trainees to discover quickly how their unconscious attitudes and mannerisms show through body language, when they screen the tapes that depict them counseling.)

At this point, a caveat about our caveat is in order: it is possible to lean over backwards in a resolution to avoid religiosity in the counseling interview. That could result in an awkwardness equal to the problem we were trying to correct. In no case are we expected to mask our faith affirmation or to disguise our setting. To do that would indeed erase whatever distinctions lie between us and secular family therapists. It would then seem true of us, as a now-famous study of psychiatrists found it was true for them, that "very few therapists, regardless of their religious affiliation, ascribe a religious motivation to their conducting family therapy" (Group for the Advancement of Psychiatry, 1970, p. 3).

Occasions do arise, of course, wherein it is proper in interviews to share openly our faith in God in Christ. "We do share, eventually, something of our response to the parishioner's story," Gaylord Noyce writes. "We even, by manner or words, tell a story of our own faith, as parishioner and pastor together we face the dilemmas that oppress the one seeking help. . . . Together we can acknowledge the resource we both share: the guiding word and caring love of God" (Noyce, 1978).

There is a wide middle ground between these two extremes of

larding piousness over the counseling interview at one pole, or denying our foundations in faith at the other. We need walk no fine line to maintain such a balance. Rather, we need to reflect that some people more easily respond to the language of faith than others, that some are threatened by our witnessing while others are comforted by it. Most of all, we must never assume that we can compensate for any lack of counseling skill by assuming a pious demeanor. In such a displacement we might be practicing what Lewis J. Sherrill declared to be "theology as escape" (1955, p. 208).

Second, the pastor-as-therapist can make another type of error by leaning too heavily toward one pole or the other in considerations of morality. If we are unwise enough to assume that ethical standards are synonymous with prohibition, and that therefore the only way to describe Christian duty is in terms of "don't," we shall probably not be bothered by very many troubled people seeking us. Or if we suppose that unless we are punitive in our remarks and condeming in our sterness that we are somehow encouraging immorality, we shall confuse more than we clarify. It is not our privilege to encourage sin; but neither is it our task to spread the heresy that persons who prudently stay out of trouble are morally superior to those who test pharisaical standards of prudence. In the recent past, the clergy often communicated to their parishioners that sins of the flesh are the most heinous of all; but they would have been well advised to recall Dorothy Sayers's *bon mot* that there are six other deadly sins (Sayers, 1949).

But if our professional group has at times made a fetish of condemning sin and overemphasizing the dangers of sexuality, there are current indications that some others may have become more permissive about immorality than objectivity requires. It is ironic that the reminders about our duty to help people realize their duty have lately been coming from the directions of psychiatry, recalling the clergy (of all people!) to their rightful work. It is among the psychotherapists that we have been hearing calls for the reminder that ethics play a definite part in mental health. Karl

Menninger (1973), Hobart Mowrer (1961), and Paul Pruyser (1976) have been pulling our attention back to a truth that we ought to have been retaining all along: that it is therapeutic for men and women to be held accountable for their ethical decisions. A misdirected application of our objectivity and a missapplied emphasis on acceptance of troubled people can sometimes lead us to disguise our ethical convictions. It is one thing to avoid a judgmentalism that condemns and depersonalizes the fallen; it is quite another to seem to approve unethical practices and to pretend that our own stand is a neutral one. There is no neutrality in therapy; values bleed through every therapist's work, sometimes consciously, often unconsciously. Nothing is lost in the counseling transaction if we say, "Now that you mention the issue, I must say that I could not approve of that myself. But I am staying by you and trying to understand your position."

It is not incumbent upon us to abdicate our own standards of Christian value in some new stance of antinomianism (i.e., the idea that we are not obligated by the rules of ethics) in order to counsel families. As pastors, we remain committed to a core of Christian beliefs and to the ethical style integral to our faith. The point is not all that obscure: we are to hold to our own moral convictions while at the same time accepting our counselees for the persons they are.

Third, pastors may become tempted to base their practice of family therapy upon unrealistic and naive presumptions about the normative Christian family. If pastoral counselors work out of an image of some ideal standard for marriage and family (one that clergy homes themselves seldom fulfill), they may appropriate a vision that informs their counseling expectations with a perfectionism that unnecessarily complicates the dynamics of therapy. Therapy is already complicated enough!

Actually, theological teachings about family have usually grown out of problems and polemics. These doctrines arise from turmoil and times of dissonance. If we look to the Bible, for instance, as a charter to guide family therapy, we must learn to deal with tangled threads of guidance. There is no self-evident system to the references; and they have frequently erupted from sharp encounters. Marriage and divorce are discussed by Jesus in the context of a direct challenge by his detractors (Mark 10:2 ff.). Interfaith marriage is considered in some anxiety to keep Israel's heritage unaltered (Ezra 10:4) or in the strained circumstances of the early church that worried Paul about this problem (1 Cor. 7:12 ff.). It is just as problematic to consult the writings of the church fathers for their theological understandings of marriage and the family. They also wrote and spoke out of the pressures of their particular times. How could they have done otherwise? Thus Augustine formulated some of his influential dogma about sex and marriage while in the midst of polemic with one Jovinian, a tractarian who might otherwise not be remembered at all. Jovinian had attracted the ire of conservative ecclesiastics by publishing a tract that upheld a rationale for the sex act in marriage as a gift from God. If God created our alimentary canal for the digestion of food, did he not also create our reproductive organs for copulation?

Jerome, who is credited with the opinion that the good of marriage is that it produces new virgins for the world, made an attempt to debate with Jovinian. Augustine, dissatisfied with Jerome's attempt, got into the act by asserting that, although marriage is not exactly evil, virginity is the higher good because it promotes spiritual dedication. He could testify, in addition, that considerable experience had taught him that flesh is pitted against spirit and that marital sex, while a minor sin, is nonetheless a sin. With this negative view of sexuality Christianity was saddled for centuries.

The point is that our theological doctrines emanate from our problems; and they may still carry vestigial remnants from the types of problems which gave them rise. The romantic picture of a tranquil thinker secluded in an ivory tower and writing theology with a quill pen must give way to the truer one of theologians wrestling with their contemporary problems. Our theological dogmas come to us, for better or for worse, from turmoil and from pressures. As surely as the Westminster Confession of Faith reflects views of its Cromwellian era, or Barth's church dogmatics reveal the context of Europe affected by world war, our family theology is shaped by the family difficulties of particular eras. Theology inevitably arises out of living.

Theology also arises after we do our living. First we live; then we do our theology. Theology represents an afterthought to life. The moral standards of sexual fidelity and marital stability surely were codified after violations of such ethics had become a problem. Family joy and family pain, lived out by ordinary people, surely preceded theological reflection about such matters. It should occasion small wonder that Christians are alert to questions about sexual behavior and family living in these times; for these issues are difficult and problematic for our particular day. Theological statements characteristically arise from the difficulties faced by Christians; they tend to be related closely to the challenges of the times. In an age of ferment, like this fourth quarter of the twentieth century, or the years of the early church mentioned above, people are impelled to raise queries about family order. It is only when we are pressed by problems that we stop to consider what God's intention may be for this period of history. Certainly, in those periods when families were (by contrast) more stable (yes, there have been such periods), the theological and ethical literature of the day are devoid of any consistent references to marriage and sexuality.

This afterthought aspect of theology may account for the largely uncoordinated nature of family teaching in Christian history. Life precedes reflection. The church lived in and through its home for ages, taking them for granted before theologians began to theorize about the family, its being, and its purpose. First we live, then we reflect. Before we seek order, we grapple with disorder. Before we solve our problems, we are beset by the problems. Thus we humans move from questions toward answers, from life to theology, from the particular to the general, from the inductive to the deductive. We don't even bother to think until we are challenged by a problem, John Dewey taught. So it is that families seldom seek out assistance until there is pain. And we ministers are seldom inclined to search out a theological rationale for our counseling until we begin to wonder what we have been doing.

THEOLOGY INVOLVES FAMILY RELATIONSHIPS

Our pastoral counseling practice with families as well as with individuals is grounded in our theological convictions about relationships. One way that we learn to know God and God's truth is through our family relationships. Such an assertion admittedly will be unthinkable to those whose homes have fostered earthly hells of battering, abuse, and exploitation. But there are numerous pathways to God; and for many of us, family life has served as a *via divina*. It was in the home we first knew of God's saving grace.

We began to find our way to God through our family relationships. The Lord as revealed in biblical times was sometimes dubbed "the God who speaks." How is he understood as speaking? Sometimes in direct speech; but, more often, God speaks through others and our relationships with them. In various times and places God spoke to our father through the prophets; but climactically he spoke to us through his Son in the Incarnation (Heb. 1:1 f.).

God also speaks through history. This fundamental conviction of the Judaeo-Christian tradition means not only that God has made his disclosures through the events of biblical times (e.g., the travail of Israel or the missions of St. Paul), but also in the events of our own personal current history.

His message of revelation has come to us through many contacts, some of them quite ordinary folks who have heard the word and passed it on. Typically these people have included parents. In the family, the oncoming generation is instructed through a process labeled socialization. Through a language of relationships, through emotional overtones and undertones among habitual actions and rituals, and in the provision for needs, socialization takes place. It is in this matrix, for good or for ill, that we are also grounded in our faith. Religious faiths, with a clearsightedness born of experience, consider the family as integral to the preservation of their tradition. Parents transmit their convictions in the ways that they talk with their children, walk with them, put them to bed and greet them in the morning (Deut. 6:7).

The centrality of the family as a locus for religious faith is so well established in tradition and commitment that, were it not for our contemporary situation it would need no reminder here. Today, religious practices in the home are as honored in the breach as in the observance. Historically, however, the Jewish family has understood the home as a place of prayer and worship. The Roman Catholic family, with its start in a marriage regarded as a sacrament, can believe its tradition has a salvific effect. Protestants, with neither of these formal recognitions from their religious communities, nonetheless have sometimes envisioned their homes as little churches within the church *(ecclesiola in ecclesia)*. Therein "the God who speaks" may get the message to us through those who relate with us.

Much of our theology is devoted, as therapy is, toward establishing order out of our broken relationships, many of which are family oriented. In family life we try to fulfill the hope of Dietrich Bonhoeffer who, while realizing that not all inflicted wounds could be healed, maintained "what matters is that there shall be no further wounds" (Bonhoeffer, 1955, p. 54). The doctrines of sin and of grace both have to be understood relationally. How else could they be conceived? Neither can be experienced apart from other persons, and indeed the person of God. "By the family you were broken, by the family you will be healed," speaks as much of our God-given relationships as it does of therapy. One veteran in the ministry testifies that it is family therapy that has opened his eyes anew to theology and helped him to understand what had been for him abstract doctrines. Previously, he had framed his theology in terms that were overly individualistic. Now he knows that to deal only individualistically with needs, wishes, will, and conflict is to hold an inadequate concept of sin, guilt, and salvation.

THE HOME IS A THEOLOGICAL SEMINARY

If the clergyman mentioned above found it difficult to appreciate theology's abstract terms until he experienced them in relationships, then so much the more will the laity be confused by some of our doctrinal pronouncements. Unless Christians can begin to conceptualize such doctrines as redemption in interpersonal terms, they stand light-years away from conceptualizing them in metaphysical terms. We are not permitted to suppose, of course, that when we understand relationships on a human level that we then, by a cosmic leap, know the mystery of the Godhead. In the main, however, all our language about God must necessarily be analogical because all language about everything is analogical; we habitually think in a series of metaphors (see Sayers, 1949). To be sure, an analogue about redemption through human friendship will miss the full truth about God's redemptive act in Christ; but if we have never known anything about minor redemptive experiences we are even less prepared to apprehend any truth about God's redemption.

Or consider the exchange of love between parent and child. The child is taught to love by the example of the parental love. Indeed, the psychoanalyst may be correct to contend that it is at the mother's breast that the infant learns love, just by being fed. The infant's response, then, comes because the mother has taken the initiative. The baby can love back. So it is that this child can some day better comprehend some element of the love of God; we love because he first loved us (1 John 4:19). If, however, children are deprived of love when they are infants, they may also be handicapped in their ability to give and receive love later on. They may also be unable to achieve abstract thinking about God's love, and thus be out of reach of much current teaching of systematic theology on this topic (Bowlby, 1973).

Scripture helps us continually with this relational emphasis. God is a father to us all; and we are therefore his sons and daughters. We are then brothers and sisters to each other because we are first of all brothers and sisters to Christ. Ours is the family of God; it is the household of faith. Paul's letters to the early churches are peppered with the language of family relations. Indeed, there is not one book of the Bible that lacks family allusions.

Likewise, children learn what forgiveness is by being forgiven as well as through forgiving themselves and others. There actually are parents who say to their children, "I can never forgive you if you do such-and-such," implanting into these young minds that they are not worthy individuals. When, as adults, these same people arrive at the pastor's study to confess that they have committed the unpardonable sin, or that they feel that a spouse or God cannot possibly forgive them, the pastor will do better to discuss with them their personal memories of unforgiving experiences than to reason with them about dogma.

Moreover, it is in family relationships that the child will learn what reconciliation is. Experiencing broken relations from time to time with members of the family, the child comes to grasp what acceptance and reconciliation are when such splits are healed, and self esteem is strengthened.

To argue that love, forgiveness, and reconciliation as practiced in the home will be crucial to understanding these theological doctrines is not to suppose that the human sphere and the divine are identical, or that one can take a grand jump from family life to spiritual realms and equally apprehend them both. Rather, it is to argue that God's reconciling the world to himself is a loving act of which our earthly experience partakes, at least in this small measure. It is to assert that the knowledge of reconciling love and forgiveness in family relations does prepare one better to understand basic theological teachings. Without the analogical experience in our own relationships, we are handicapped to know much of theological truth.

Our educational efforts in church and synagogue will reach farther when they are integrated with the daily living that goes on in the homes of members. It is an ideal difficult to achieve; but that in itself hardly warrants dropping such a curriculum as many churches have done.

"God Is in the Midst" (Ps. 46:5)

Our vocation as ministers has set us into the midst of people who are struggling with life's deepest meanings: the meaning of existence, the meaning of death, the meaning of our interrelationships. It is with these questions, including all their ambiguity, that our people, and we ourselves, wrestle. We—all of us—partake of the human condition with its inevitable limitations, all the while knowing that, even as we are dust, we can be valued as a little lower than the angels (Ps. 8:5). We are children of Adam, yet children of God (Luke 3:38); limited, yet free; guilty and yet redeemed.

In the midst of our therapeutic service we ministers and priests are simultaneously theologians. When we are doing theology we have opportunities to act as therapists; when we are practicing therapy we have no call to obscure our work as theologians. If ever we lose our way theologically, while trying to perfect our work as counselors, it is because we have neglected our directional signals; we are turning the wrong way. It is then that we struggle with saving people as if their healing depends solely upon us. Once again, it becomes time to recollect what our vocation is and recall that we did not choose this way, but were chosen; that we are not responsible for finding meaning in the lives of people but that God has set us all into the midst of meaning and has imparted to his whole family in heaven and earth his reconciling love.

In the midst of our family therapy sessions, we shall often know the guidance of God. Even dysfunctional and troubled families who seek us out for counsel are among those who, in the words of John Calvin, "introduce spiritual values into a world that is not spiritual." When we come into this pastoral task of family therapy, even as when we come into the sanctuary to celebrate with the congregation the liturgy of worship, we come into the presence of God. It is not as if we introduce God into the counseling session; no, God is already in the midst.

References

Ackerman, Nathan. *The Psychodynamics of Family Life: Treatment of Family Relationships.* Basic Books, 1958.

Ackerman, Nathan. *Treating the Troubled Family.* Basic Books, 1966.

Andreasen, Nancy C. "Deciding Who Must See a Psychiatrist." In *Klemer's Counseling in Marital and Sexual Problems,* 2d ed, edited by Robert F. Stahman and William J. Hiebert. Williams and Wilkins, 1977.

Ashbrook, James B. *Responding to Human Pain.* Judson Press, 1975.

Bane, Mary Jo. *Here to Stay! American Families in the Twentieth Century.* Basic Books, 1976.

Bell, John E. *Family Therapy.* Aronson, 1975.

Berger, Milton M. *Beyond the Double Bind.* Brunner/Mazel, 1978.

Berne, Eric. *Games People Play: The Psychology of Human Relationships.* Grove Press, 1964.

Bloch, Donald A., ed. *Techniques of Family Psychotherapy.* Grune & Stratton, 1973.

Bonhoeffer, Dietrich. *Ethics.* Edited by Eberhard Bethge. SCM Press, 1955.

Boszormenyi-Nagy, Ivan. *Invisible Loyalties.* Harper & Row, 1973.

Bowen, Murray. *Family Therapy in Clinical Practice.* Aronson, 1978.

Bowen, Murray. "Theory in the Practice of Psychotherapy." In *Family Therapy,* edited by Philip Guerin. Gardner Press, 1976.

Bowlby, John. *Child Care and the Growth of Love.* Penguin, 1973.

Brister, C. W. *The Promise of Counseling.* Harper & Row, 1978.

Buber, Martin. *Between Man and Man.* Macmillan, 1948.

Burgess, Ernest. *The Family: From Institution to Companionship.* American Book Co., 1945.

Calvin, John. *Institutes of the Christian Religion.* Edited by John T. McNeill. Westminster Press, 1960.

Caplan, Gerald. *Principles of Preventive Psychiatry.* Basic Books, 1964.

Casler, Lawrence. *Is Marriage Necessary?* Human Sciences Press, 1974.

Cassell, Carol. *National Family Sexuality Education News,* September 1980.

Christensen, Harold T., ed. *Handbook of Marriage and the Family.* Rand-McNally, 1964.

Christie, Agatha. *Appointment with Death.* Dodd, Mead, 1938.

Clinebell, Howard. *Growth Counseling for Marriage Enrichment.* Fortress Press, 1975.

Cobb, John B., Jr. *Theology and Pastoral Care.* Fortress Press, 1977.

Corfman, Eunice. *Families Today: A Research Sampler on Families and Children.* 2 vols. Department of Health, Education and Welfare, 1979.

Couch, Elsbeth H. *Joint and Family Interviews.* Family Service Association of America, 1969.

Cuber, John F., and Peggy Haroff. *The Significant Americans.* Appleton-Century, 1965.

Dittes, James E. *When the People Say No: Conflict and the Call to Ministry.* Harper & Row, 1979.

Donzelot, Jacques. *The Policing of Families.* Pantheon, 1979.

Duhl, F., D. Kantor, and B. Duhl. "Learning Space and Action in Family Therapy: A Primer of Sculpture." In *Techniques of Family Psychotherapy,* edited by Donald A. Bloch. Grune & Stratton, 1973.

Erickson, Gerald, and Hogan, Terrance eds. *Family Therapy: An Introduction to Theory and Technique.* Brooks/Cole, 1972.

Fairchild, Roy. *Finding Hope Again.* Harper & Row, 1980.

Fairchild, Roy, and J. C. Wynn. *Families in the Church: A Protestant Survey.* Association Press, 1961.

Ferber, Andrew, Marilyn Mendelsohn, and Augustus Napier. *The Book of Family Therapy.* Science House, 1972.

Flügel, J. C. *The Psycho-analytic Study of the Family.* Hogarth Press, 1960.

Foley, Vincent D. *Introduction to Family Therapy.* Grune & Stratton, 1974.

Freud, Sigmund. *The Complete Psychological Works of Sigmund Freud.* Hogarth Press, 1955.

Friedan, Betty. "Feminism Takes a New Turn." *New York Times Magazine.* November 18, 1979.

Friedan, Betty. *The Feminine Mystique.* Norton, 1963.

Glick, Paul. *Marriage and Divorce: A Sociological and Economic Study.* Harvard University Press, 1976.

Goldman, Harvey. "Role Clarification in the Jewish Two Career Family." D. Min. thesis, Colgate Rochester Divinity School, 1977.

Greene, Bernard L., ed. *The Psychotherapies of Marital Disharmony.* Free Press, 1965.

Group for the Advancement of Psychiatry. *Treatment of Families in Conflict.* Science House, 1970.

Guerin, Philip J., ed. *Family Therapy.* Gardner Press, 1976.

Gurman, A. S., and D. P. Kniskern. "Research on Marital and Family

Therapy." In *Handbook of Psychotherapy and Behavioral Change,* 2d ed., edited by S. Garfield and A. Bergin. Wiley, 1978.

Haley, Jay. "Ideas Which Handicap Therapists." In *Beyond the Double Bind,* edited by M. M. Berger. Brunner/Mazel, 1978.

Haley, Jay. *Problem Solving Therapy.* Jossey-Bass, 1976.

Haley, Jay, and Lynn Hoffman. *Techniques of Family Therapy.* Basic Books, 1967.

Harper, Robert. *The New Psychotherapies.* Prentice-Hall, 1975.

Henry, Jules. *Pathways to Madness.* Random House, 1971.

Hiltner, Seward, and Lowell Colston. *The Context of Pastoral Counseling.* Abingdon, 1961.

Howard, Jane. *Families.* Simon & Schuster, 1978.

James, William. *On Some of Life's Ideals.* Henry Holt & Co., 1912.

James, William. *The Principles of Psychology.* Henry Holt & Co., 1918.

Johnson, Dorothy, and Mary A. Vestermark. *Barriers and Hazards for Counselees.* Houghton Mifflin, 1970.

Jones, Susan L. *Family Therapy: A Comparison of Approaches.* Robert J. Brady Co., 1980.

Jung, Carl G. *Two Essays on Analytical Psychology.* Meridian Books, World Publishing Co., 1953.

Kaplan, Helen. *The New Sex Therapy.* Quadrangle, 1974.

Kempler, Walter. *Principles of Gestalt Family Therapy.* Desert Press, 1974.

Keniston, Kenneth. *All Our Children.* Harcourt, Brace, Jovanovich, 1977.

Knox, David. *Marriage Happiness: A Behavioral Approach to Counseling.* Research Press, 1972.

Kopp, Sheldon B. *If You Meet the Buddha on the Road, Kill Him!* Science and Behavior Books, 1972.

Kovel, Joel. *A Complete Guide to Therapy: From Psychoanalysis to Behavior Modification.* Pantheon, 1976.

Kramer, Charles H. *Becoming a Family Therapist.* Human Sciences Press, 1980.

Kulka, Richard, Joseph Veroff, and Elizabeth Donvan, "Social Class and The Use of Professional Help for Personal Problems." *Journal of Health and Social Behavior* 20 (March 1979).

Laing, R. D. *Politics of the Family.* Pantheon Books, 1971

Lantz, James E. *Family and Marital Therapy: A Transactional Approach.* Appleton-Century-Crofts, 1977.

Lasch, Christopher. *Haven in a Heartless World: The Family Besieged.* Basic Books, 1977.

Lederer, William, and Don Jackson. *Mirages of Marriage.* W. W. Norton, 1968.

Lewis, Jerry M. *No Single Thread.* Brunner/Mazel, 1976.

Lewis, Jerry M. *To Be a Therapist.* Brunner/Mazel, 1978.

Liberman, Robert P. *A Guide to Understanding Behavior Analysis and Therapy.* Pergamon, 1972.

Lidz, Theodore, and A. R. Cornelius. *Schizophrenia and the Family.* International Universities Press, 1960.

Luthman, Shirley G., and Martin Kirschenbaum. *The Dynamic Family.* Science and Behavior Books, 1974.

McLuhan, Herbert Marshall. *War and Peace in the Global Village: An Inventory of Some of the Current Spastic Situations That Could Be Eliminated By More Feedforward.* McGraw-Hill, 1968.

Madanes, Cloe, and Jay Haley. "Dimensions of Family Therapy." *Journal of Nervous and Mental Diseases* 165 (1977): 88–98.

Madanes, Cloe. *Strategic Family Therapy.* Jossey-Bass, 1981.

Menninger, Karl. *Whatever Became of Sin?* Hawthorn Books, 1973.

Miller, Arthur. *Death of a Salesman.* Viking Press, 1965.

Minuchin, Salvador. *Families and Family Therapy.* Harvard University Press, 1974.

Minuchin, Salvador, and H. Charles Fishman. *Family Therapy Techniques.* Harvard University Press, 1981.

Mowrer, O. H. *The Crisis in Psychiatry and Religion.* Van Nostrand, 1961.

Mudd, Emily H., and James Peterson. *Marriage and Family Counseling: Perspective and Prospect.* Association Press, 1968.

Napier, Augustus, and Carl Whitaker. *The Family Crucible.* Harper & Row, 1978.

Niebuhr, Reinhold. *Discerning the Signs of the Times: Sermons for Today and Tomorrow.* Scribner's, 1946.

Nouwen, Henri. *Creative Ministry.* Doubleday, 1971.

Nouwen, Henri. *The Wounded Healer.* Doubleday, 1972.

Noyce, Gaylord. "Has Ministry's Nerve Been Cut by the Pastoral Counseling Movement?" *Christian Century* (February 1, 1978).

Oden, Thomas. *After Therapy, What?* C. C. Thomas, 1974a.

Oden, Thomas. *Game Free: A Guide to the Meaning of Intimacy.* Harper & Row, 1974b.

Ogden, Gina, and Anne Zevin. *When a Family Needs Therapy.* Beacon Press, 1976.

O'Neill, Eugene. *Long Day's Journey into Night.* Yale University Press, 1956.

Papajohn, John, and John Spiegel. *Transactions in Families.* Jossey-Bass, 1974.

Papp, Peggy. "Family Choreography." In Philip Guerin, ed., *Family Therapy: Theory and Practice.* Gardner Press, 1976.

Parker, Beulah. *A Mingled Yarn.* Yale University Press, 1972.

Parsons, Talcott, and Robert F. Bales. *Family Socialization and Interaction Process.* Free Press, 1955.

Patterson, Gerald. *Direct Intervention in Families of Deviant Children.* Research Institute of Eugene, Oregon, 1969.

Patterson, Gerald. *Families: Applications of Social Learning to Family Life.* Research Press, 1971.

Pattison, E. M. *Pastor & Parish: A Systems Approach.* Fortress Press, 1977.

Pauling, Linus. *No More War!* Dodd, Mead, 1962.

Pincus, Lily, and Christopher Dare, *Secrets in the Family.* Pantheon, 1978.

Pruyser, Paul. *The Minister as Diagnostician: Personal Problems in Pastoral Perspective.* Westminster Press, 1976.

The Report: Listening to America's Families: Action for the 80's. White House Conference on Families, 1980.

Ricoeur, Paul. *Interpretation Theory: Discourse and the Surplus of Meaning.* Texas University Press, 1976.

Rimmer, Robert H. *The Harrad Experiment.* Bantam, 1973.

Sager, Clifford, and Helen S. Kaplan, ed. *Progress in Group and Family Therapy.* Brunner/Mazel, 1972.

Satir, Virginia. *Conjoint Family Therapy.* Science and Behavior Books, 1964.

Sayers, Dorothy. *Creed or Chaos.* Harcourt, Brace, 1949.

Seward, Rudy Ray. *The American Family.* Sage, 1978.

Shah, Idries. *The Way of the Sufi.* E. P. Dutton, 1970.

Sherrill, Lewis J. *The Gift of Power.* Macmillan, 1955.

Skynner, A. C. Robin. *Systems of Marital and Family Psychotherapy.* Brunner/Mazel, 1976.

Stahmann, Robert, and William Hiebert, ed. *Klemer's Clinical Counseling in Marital and Sexual Problems.* Williams and Wilkins, 1977.

Stewart, Charles. *The Minister as Family Counselor.* Abingdon, 1979.

Stierlin, Helm. *The First Interview with the Family.* Brunner/Mazel, 1980.

Strauss, Anselm, ed. *The Social Psychology of George Herbert Mead, 1863–1931.* University of Chicago Press, 1956.

"The Stress Test." *In Touch.* National Mental Health Association, 1979.

Sullivan, Harry Stack. *The Interpersonal Theory of Psychiatry.* W. W. Norton, 1953.

Thornton, Edward E. *Theology and Pastoral Counseling.* Prentice-Hall, 1964.

Tillich, Paul. *The Courage to Be.* Yale University Press, 1952.

Tillich, Paul. *Systematic Theology: Reason, Revelation, Being, and God,* vol. 1. University of Chicago Press, 1951.

Toffler, Alvin. *Future Shock.* Random House, 1970.

Toffler, Alvin. *The Third Wave.* William Morrow, 1980.

Toynbee, Arnold J. *Surviving the Future.* Oxford University Press, 1971.

Tolstoy, Leo. *Anna Karenina.* Random House, 1939.

Tuchman, Barbara. *Practicing History.* Knopf, 1981.

van den Blink, A. J. "Family Therapy and Pastoral Care," *The Journal of Pastoral Care* 28:183.

von Bertalanffy, Ludwig. *The Meaning of General System Theory.* Braziller, 1968.

Watzlawick, Paul. *The Language of Change: Elements of Therapeutic Communication.* Basic Books, 1978.

Whitaker, Carl. "The Hindrance of Theory in Clinical Work." In *Family Therapy: Theory and Practice,* edited by Philip Guerin. Gardner Press, 1976.

Wiener, Norbert. *Cybernetics or Control in the Animal and the Machine.* M.I.T. Press, 1961.

Williams, Tennessee. *The Glass Menagerie.* New Directions, 1945.

Winter, Gibson. *Love and Conflict.* Doubleday, 1958.

Wynn, J. C. *Pastoral Ministry to Families.* Westminster Press, 1957.

Wynne, Lyman C., "The Study of Intrafamilial Alignments and Splits in Exploratory Family Therapy." In *Exploring the Base for Family Therapy,* edited by Nathan Ackerman. Family Service Association of America, 1967.

Wynne, Lyman C., et al. *Nature of Schizophrenia: New Approaches to Research and Treatment.* Wiley, 1978.

Zelnik, Melvin, and John F. Kantner. "Sexual Activity, Contraception Use, and Pregnancy Among Metropolitan Teenagers, 1971–1979." *Family Planning Perspectives* 12, no. 5 (Sept.-Oct. 1980).

Zuk, Gerald H., and Ivan Boszormenyi-Nagy, eds. *Family Therapy and Disturbed Families.* Science and Behavior Books, 1967.

Appendix. Resources for Family Therapists

PROFESSIONAL ORGANIZATIONS

For those doing family therapy, membership in a professional association can offer benefits. Some of these organizations certify therapists. Nearly all offer opportunities through continuing education, conferences, periodical journals and newsletters. For details about membership, fees, and benefits, apply to the offices listed below.

American Association for Marriage and Family Therapy, 924 W. Ninth St., Upland, CA 91786. This foremost professional association with rigorous standards for certification (including comprehensive educational background, experience in counseling, and a minimum of two hundred hours supervision) has numerous clergy members.

American Association of Pastoral Counselors, 300 Connecticut Ave. N.W., Suite 300, Washington, D.C. 20008. A prestigious organization that promotes professional competence among pastoral counselors. Membership standards require clinical pastoral education, experience in ministry, and wide experience in counseling (under supervision).

American Family Therapy Association, 15 Bond Street, Great Neck, NY 11021. An organization for professional family therapists, many of whom are in private practice or teach in family therapy. Still a young organization, its membership is not large, yet includes leaders in the field.

National Council on Family Relations, 1219 University Ave., S.E., Minneapolis, MN 55414. An old and learned society of teachers, counselors, researchers, and clergy who are engaged in the wide spectrum of family studies. The Council's publications feature several quality journals and numerous monographs.

American Association of Sex Educators, Counselors, and Therapists, Suite 310, 5010 Wisconsin Ave., N.W., Washington, D.C. 20016. A comparatively young group that grew out of the startling need our society has for education and assistance in human sexuality. It has grown rapidly into an organization that certifies specialists, schedules conferences, and publishes pertinent titles in the field.

American Personnel and Guidance Association, 1607 New Hampshire

Ave., N.W., Washington, D.C. 20009. An organization of organizations, this group includes counselors in guidance, personnel work, vocations, rehabilitation, and much else. In recent years, their publications and films have reflected a growing concern in family therapy.

Family Service Association of America, 44 E. 23rd St., New York, NY 10010. A venerable organization that includes both contributing individuals and community social agencies as members, its numerous publications have long featured family therapy as a specialty.

Association of Couples for Marriage Enrichment, 459 S. Church St., P.O. Box 10596, Winston-Salem, NC 27108. An international organization of married couples that promotes better marriages. It offers training programs for couple leadership, conferences, and publications in marriage education.

Resources in Supervision

Ministers who are looking for supervisory teaching to guide them as family therapists may find that local mental health centers, hospitals, universities and colleges, and social agencies will have staff personnel who can supervise a pastor's cases.

If the pastor seeks one-on-one supervision, it is advisable to arrange approximately twice-a-month sessions with the supervisor. Sometimes such a person (a psychotherapist, family therapist, social worker, or pastoral counselor) may be a member of the church and willing to donate time to this service as a contribution. Some clergy barter a trade of their volunteer staff time at a family agency in exchange for supervision time. Others are prepared to pay a professional fee for the supervision, the amount matching the supervisor's regular fee for therapy.

Group supervision can also be of considerable value to clergy. Several clergy, together with a supervising teacher, can organize a case conference wherein each takes a turn at presenting cases for criticism. The advantages of group supervision of course involve its prorated lower costs and the rich input that comes from one's peers as well as from the supervisor.

In either case, whether in individual or in group supervision, the pastor will need an outside opinion about her or his progress in the work of therapy. To go on counseling families and individuals without periodic guidance can be unwise.

Malpractice Insurance

Professional and personal liability insurance of several kinds is available to those engaged in personal counseling and family therapy. Policies ordinarily cover either alleged malpractice or personal negligence. The general objective of such insurance policies is to have legal assistance available for defense in case of a lawsuit.

The Church Mutual Insurance Company of Merrill, Wisconsin, has been offering riders on multiperil church policies to cover pastoral counseling. Coverage of up to $300,000 liability is available for about $25 a year.

The American Home Assurance Company of Amityville, New York, insures clergy and pastoral counselors for coverage up to $300,000 for $50 a year. Higher limits of liability are available at larger premiums.

The American Personnel and Guidance Association Group Trust in Washington, D.C., offers a $200,000 policy for $25 a year to APGA members.

Atlantic Insurance Companies, Inc. of New York has added malpractice riders to its nationwide policies for the Lutheran Church in America and the United Methodist Church.

The Preferred Risk Mutual Company of Des Moines, Iowa, covers those in the United Presbyterian Church and the Church of the Nazarene.

The Western World Insurance Company in Keene, New Hampshire, handles $300,000 policies at $206 a year for the Chicago Board of Rabbis.

WORKSHOPS IN FAMILY THERAPY

Many people in the helping professions now update their continuing education in family therapy through the numerous workshops offered throughout the nation. These opportunities offer a brief course, often expertly taught, that includes lecture, discussion, videotaped cases, and sometimes even practice sessions for participants. The following list of available workshops has been chosen from the large number available. It is not intended to be comprehensive, but to illustrate the sorts of workshops that were available in a recent season:

Midwest

Topeka, Kansas: The Menninger Foundation; "Marriage and Family Counseling Applied to the Context of Ministry," a four-day workshop.

Chicago, Illinois: The Center for Family Studies (Family Institute of Chicago); "Helping Families to Change," a two-day workshop.

Wisconsin and Minnesota: The University of Wisconsin Extension Education; "Strategies in Dealing with the Alcohol Impaired Family," a one-day workshop.

West Coast

La Jolla, California: Center for Studies of the Person; ten-day workshops.

Watsonville, California: Western Institute for Group and Family Therapy; week-long workshops.

Palo Alto, California: The Mental Research Institute; frequent training and workshop opportunities.

Seattle, Washington: The Strategic Therapy Training Center of Chevy Chase, Maryland; Strategic Family Therapy, a two-day workshop.

Eastern United States

Philadelphia, Pennsylvania: The Philadelphia Child Guidance Clinic; Structural Family Therapy workshops.

Chevy Chase, Maryland: The Strategic Therapy Training Center; Strategic Family Therapy workshops of two days and longer.

New York, New York: The Ackerman Institute for Family Therapy offers continuous training in workshops.

New Rochelle, New York: The Center for Family Learning; four-day workshops in the Bowen Theory of family therapy.

Washington, D.C.: The Institute for Comprehensive Family Therapy; "Theory and Practice of Family Therapy," a three-day workshop.

Saratoga Springs, New York: Skidmore College; "Structural, Strategic, and System Therapies," a four-day workshop.

Canada and Europe

Toronto, Ontario: The Toronto Family Therapy Institute; "Workshop in Intergenerational Family Therapy," two-day workshop.

Zurich, Switzerland: The Jung Institute; "Jungian Winter Seminar," two weeks in January.

BASIC BOOKS ABOUT FAMILY THERAPY

A host of books for family therapists is now published annually. The following list is meant to be basic in its selection and brevity, and it reflects somewhat my own taste and appreciation.

Family Therapy: A Comparison of Approaches by Susan L. Jones (Robert J. Brady Co., 1980). Of first rank among the one-volume surveys, this study covers the field comprehensively.

Family Therapy by Philip Guerin (Gardner Press, 1976). A well-chosen selection of original essays by ranking family therapists, edited by one of them.

Conjoint Family Therapy by Virginia Satir (Science and Behavior Books, 1964). If there's a classic in this still new field, Satir's spare, basic study must be it.

Family Therapy Techniques by Salvador Minuchin with H. Charles Fishman (Harvard University Press, 1981). In this volume, one of the superstars of family therapy reveals how he does it.

The Family Crucible by Augustus Napier and Carl Whitaker (Harper & Row, 1978). Whitaker is an old pro; this book, prepared with his cotherapist, guides the reader through a course of skilled therapy with one family.

Problem Solving Therapy by Jay Haley (Jossey-Bass, 1976). Haley, the most entertaining writer in this genre, lays out the practical steps of strategic therapy; but let the reader beware—it sounds easier here than it is.

Becoming a Family Therapist by Charles H. Kramer (Human Sciences Press, 1980). Admirably organized and candidly written, this study is written straight from the author's training program in Chicago.

The Language of Change: Elements of Therapeutic Communication by Paul Watzlawick (Basic Books, 1978). The use of language in therapy makes a fascinating study at the hands of an ingenious and clever writer-therapist.

PERIODICALS FOR THE PASTOR

Family Life. Bimonthly. 5287 Sunset Blvd., Los Angeles, CA 90027. A small and venerable paper that includes opinion, statistics, book reviews, conference notes, items on couple communication, marriage enrichment, and so on.

Family Process. Quarterly. 148 East 78th St., New York, NY 10021. The leading journal in family therapy; Lyman C. Wynne is chairman of the editorial board.

Family Relations. Quarterly. 1219 University Ave., Southeast, Minneapolis, MN 55414. The National Council on Family Relations. Readable articles related to counseling and educational themes (e.g., "Premarital Counseling for Minors").

Journal of Christian Counseling. Quarterly. P.O. Box 548, Mt. Pleasant, MI 48858. Evangelical viewpoint on the crucial issues.

Journal of Family History. Quarterly. 1219 University Ave., Southeast, Minneapolis, MN 55414. Seldom about counseling, these articles deal with historical data on family life the world over.

Journal of Marital and Family Therapy. AAMFT. 924 W. 9th St., Upland, CA 91786. A competent, solid journal. Practical articles about experiences in family therapy.

Journal of Pastoral Care. Quarterly. Suite 450, 475 Riverside Dr., New

York, NY 10027. A superior periodical with ever-pertinent articles that deal with pastoral psychology, theological concerns about *pastoralia,* and specific issues such as family therapy.

Journal of Pastoral Counseling. Semi-annual. Iona College, North Avenue, New Rochelle, NY 10801. Scholarly and occasionally recondite, this largely Catholic periodical also treats family themes.

Journal of Psychology and Theology. Quarterly. 13800 Biola Ave., La Mirada, CA 90639. Family studies get their just attention here, and from a conservative theological stance.

Journal of Religion and Health. Quarterly. 3 West 29th St., New York, NY 10001. Minor space is given to topics about family, sex, and marriage.

Journal of Sex and Marital Therapy. Quarterly. Human Sciences Press, 72 Fifth Ave., New York, NY 10011. Chiefly concerned with sexual therapy. Sample title: "Sex Therapy As An Aid to Marital and Family Therapy."

The Journal of Sex Research. Quarterly. 208 Daffodil Road, Glen Burnie, MD 21061. Valuable data from the Society for the Scientific Study of Sex.

Marriage Guidance. Quarterly. N.M.G.C., Little Church St., Rugby, England. A valuable little magazine published for the volunteer counselors in the National Marriage Guidance Council. Helpful articles on counseling details, research, and publications.

Pastoral Psychology. Quarterly. Human Sciences Press, 72 Fifth Ave., New York, NY 10011. This long-established journal publishes quality articles on pastoral counseling, some of them on the family.

Social Casework. Monthly. 44 E. 23rd St., New York, NY 10010. Published by The Family Service Association of America, this old-line journal publishes informative articles for social workers, et al.

FILMS AND TAPES (VIDEO AND AUDIO)

An ever-changing and growing supply of training films and tapes can be found among the catalogues of suppliers in universities, libraries, and publishers. Many (but not all) are splendid educational assets for students of family therapy. The following is a selected list of suppliers, and is not meant to be complete.

American Association for Marriage and Family Therapy, 924 W. 9th St., Upland, CA 91786.

American Personnel and Guidance Association, 1607 New Hampshire Ave., N.W., Washington, D.C. 20009.

Association Instruction Materials, 600 Madison Ave., New York, NY 10022.

The Boston Family Institute, 251 Harvard St., Brookline, MA 02146

The Center for Family Learning, 10 Hanford Ave., New Rochelle, NY 10805.

EDCOA Productions, Inc., 310 Cedar Lane, Teaneck, NJ 07666.
Focus International, 505 West End Ave., New York, NY 10024.
Guidance Associates, Pleasantville, NY 10570.
Human Relations Media, 175 Tompkins Ave., Pleasantville, NY 10570.
The Kempler Institute, P.O. Box 1692, Costa Mesa, CA 92626.
Marlin Motion Pictures, 47 Lakeshore Rd. E., Port Credit, ONT L5G1C9.
McGraw-Hill Co., 330 W. 42nd St., New York, NY 10036.
Mass Media Ministries, 2116 N. Charles St., Baltimore, MD 21218.
Nathan W. Ackerman Institute, Inc., 149 E. 78th St., New York, NY 10021.
New Day Films, P.O. Box 315, Franklin Lakes, NJ 07417.
Philadelphia Child Guidance Clinic, 2 Children's Center, 34th St. and Civic Center Blvd., Philadelphia, PA 19104.
Research Press, Box 3177R, Champaign, IL 61820.

LOCAL AGENCIES

The local community will have a variety of agencies whose facilities offer aid to families in crisis. Among these, but only illustrative of the many that exist, are:

- Family service agencies
- Community neighborhood agencies
- The Salvation Army
- Pastoral counseling centers
- Youth serving agencies
- Visiting nurse associations
- Meals on Wheels
- Alcoholism treatment centers
- Alternatives for Battered Women
- American Red Cross
- Association for the Blind
- Retarded citizens groups
- Mental health centers
- Rehabilitation services
- Services for the aged
- Child abuse services
- Planned Parenthood
- Prisoners and families services
- Health and hospital services
- Children's services

Index